Holistic Theology

Holistic Theology

Published in Korea
by Presbyterian University and Theological Seminary Press, Seoul

© Presbyterian University and Theological Seminary Press 2015
25-1, Gwangjang Ro 5 Gil, Gwanjin Gu, Seoul, 143-756, Korea
Tel. +82 (0)2 450 0794
Fax. +82 (0)2 450 0797
e-Mail. ptpress@puts.ac.kr
http://puts.ac.kr

This book was originally published in Sep. 2004
in Korean: 통전적신학 [by Jong Sung Rhee, Myung Yong Kim, Chulho Youn,
Yo-Han Hyun and Do-Hoon Kim] and translated in English by Junghyung Kim

ISBN 978-89-7369-361-0 93230
USD 24.50 | KRW 27,000

The National Library of Korea Cataloging in Publication Data

Kim, Myung Yong

Holistic theology / [written by] Myung Yong Kim... [et al.] ; translated
by Junghyung Kim. -- Seoul : Presbyterian University and Theological
Seminary Press, 2015
  p. ; cm

원표제: 통전적 신학
Translated from the korean
ISBN 978-89-7369-361-0 93230 : ₩27000

231-KDC6
230-DDC23   CIP2015002336

Holistic Theology

통전적 신학

by

Myung Yong Kim

Chulho Youn

Yo-Han Hyun

Do-Hoon Kim

Translated by Junghyung Kim

Presbyterian University and Theological Seminary Press
©2015

Preface

✝

Holistic theology came about when Dr. Jong Sung Rhee described holistic Christology in his book, *Christology* in 1984. It is the most fitting expression that describes the theology of the seven theological seminaries of the Presbyterian Church of Korea, including Presbyterian University and Theological Seminary (PUTS), which could be said to be the center of the Korean Presbyterian Church. It is the distillation of PUTS's 1985 Statement of Theology and 2001 Philosophy of Theological Education. Rhee's holistic theology has also been recently developing under a name, Ohn theology. 'Ohn' in Ohn Theology is a pure Korean description of the holistic theology that derives its meaning from Chinese characters.

Minjung theology, although a Korean theology developed in Korea, is not the representative theology of the Korean Church. The numbers of Korean churches that embrace minjung theology as their own are in the extreme minority. However, holistic theology is different from minjung theology in many ways. It is a representative theology that speaks for the Korean Church, because the numbers of Korean churches that embrace it as their own are by far the majority.

This is not only true for Presbyterian Church of Korea, but the theologies of many theologians of other denominations bear a close resemblance to Rhee's holistic theology.

The original texts of this English translation were first published in Korean in 2004. It lays out well the core contents of the holistic theology developed by its representative scholars at Presbyterian University Theological Seminary.

In the first four chapters Myung Yong Kim discusses "What is Holistic Theology," "Jong Sung Rhee's Holistic Theology," "Holistic Ecclesiology," and "Holistic Spiritual Theology." Then in Chapter 5 Chulho Youn deals with the historical Jesus and Christ of faith as well as doctrines of incarnation and atonement under the title of "Holistic Christology." In Chapters 6 and 7 Yo-Han Hyun discusses "God's Peaceful Life" and "The Spirit of Life as the Source of Life." In the final chapter, which was missing in the earlier Korean edition and is now added, Do-Hoon Kim describes "The Life and Theology of Chungye Jong Sung Rhee."

Rhee's holistic theology continues to be developed and inherited. It is my sincerest hope that the understanding of Rhee's holistic theology, today's Ohn theology, will spread worldwide.

January 2015
Myung Yong Kim
President
Presbyterian University and Theological Seminary

Preface to the Korean Edition

✝

Since 2002 the Presbyterian University and Theological Seminary (PUTS) holds the annual Chungye Theology Symposium. The symposium has two goals: first, to commemorate Chungye Jong Sung Rhee's theological achievements, and, second, to develop a theology that will guide the Korean Church in the 21st century.

The first Chungye Theology Symposium was held in the Luce Center for the Global Church at PUTS, Saemunan Church, and Myungsung Church in April 2002 in honor of Dr. Rhee's 80th birthday. The theme of the first symposium was 'holistic theology,' which Dr. Jong Sung Rhee had pursued throughout his entire life. The main speaker was Dr. Myung Yong Kim , professor of systematic theology at PUTS and one of Dr. Rhee's direct students. Dr. Kim gave four lectures: (1) what is holistic theology; (2) Jong Sung Rhee's holistic theology; (3) holistic ecclesiology; (4) holistic spiritual theology.

The second Chungye Theology Symposium was held in April 2003. There were four lectures on the theme of Christology and pneumatology in light of holistic theology. Dr. Chulho Youn and Dr. Yo-Han Hyun, professors of systematic theology at PUTS, were invited to give lectures. Dr. Youn discussed (1) the historical Jesus and Christ of faith and (2) doctrines of incarnation and atonement in his two lectures on holistic Christology. Meanwhile, Dr. Hyun gave two lectures on holistic pneumatology under to the titles of (1) "God's Peaceful Life," and (2) "The Spirit of Life as the Source of Life."

This book develops out of those lectures at the first two Chungye Theology Symposiums. In addition, Dr. Jong Sung Rhee's own summary of holistic theology is included at the beginning of the book. I am convinced that this book will provide Korean theologians with helpful resources for a holistic understanding of theology and readers will find great help from its academic stimuli and new theological insights.

I deeply appreciate Dr. Rhee and three professors of systematic theology for their contributions to this book. Also, I would like to give special thanks to Dr. Rhee's family who gave financial support for the publication of this book as well as for the events of the first two Chungye Theology Symposiums.

March 11, 2004
Yong Su Koh
President of PUTS

Contents

Chapter 1

What Is Holistic Theology?

Myung Yong Kim

T oday global theology is oriented toward holistic theology. Since the phrase "the whole gospel" was first introduced to the World Council of Churches (WCC) in its fifth assembly in Nairobi in 1975, the WCC has been moving toward holistic theology by rejecting both a narrow theological spirit and a narrow understanding of the gospel. In the Second International Congress on World Evangelization held in Manila in 1989, often called "Lausanne II," global evangelicals also began to use the phrase "the whole gospel," the same phrase adopted in the 1975 Nairobi Assembly, though with a difference in emphasis and inclination. From then on evangelicals have been moving toward holistic theology with a great emphasis on the whole gospel. Jürgen Moltmann called his discussion of the Holy Spirit a holistic pneumatology, and Jong Sung Rhee described his theology as a holistic theology. Then, what is holistic theology?

I

Definition of Holistic Theology

Holistic theology has two important aspects: methodological and substantial. From the methodological perspective holistic theology integrates everything. Holistic theology is translated into Korean as "통전적 신학" [tongjeonjeok sinhak]. Here "통(統, tong)" refers to integrating everything. But holistic theology does not end up with simply integrating, since in its worst case simply integrating may fall into the danger of syncretism. Instead, holistic theology aims to attain wholeness by integrating everything; holistic theology pursues wholeness. The term "holistic" in holistic theology has much to do with wholeness. In short, holistic theology may be defined as a theology that aims to overcome narrowness and to construct a whole theology by integrating every possible truth, while neither neglecting nor ignoring any essential idea or perspective.

In addition to the above-mentioned methodological definition, one can also think of the substantial definition of holistic theology. From the substantial perspective, holistic theology attempts to overcome narrow soul-centered theology. It recognizes the comprehensive horizon of God's creative, providential, and saving works. It affirms that God creates, rules, wills to save, and will make anew all things. In this vein, holistic theology intends to represent the whole gospel and the entire work of God within humanity, church, society, history, and the created world.

II
Current Movement Toward Holistic Theology

1. Pentecostal Theology and Holistic Theology

The Pentecostal spiritual movement, which appeared in the early twentieth century and had an enormous impact on the global church of that century, was a spiritual movement that pursued "the full gospel." The Pentecostal spiritual movement posed a challenge to the so-called "Christianity of souls" by emphasizing the corporeal and worldly aspects of the gospel. It understood the atoning death of Jesus not just as an event that redeems souls from sins, but also as an event in which Jesus takes away our disease and poverty. In this vein, the gospel of God's kingdom was reinterpreted in terms of liberation from disease and poverty.

The fact that Pentecostal theology, with its emphasis on the full gospel, applies the gospel of the kingdom of God not simply to souls but also to bodies, and even to liberation from poverty, should be appreciated as a significant development from the earlier "Christianity of souls," i.e., as an important step forward to holistic theology. Despite its emphasis on the full gospel, however, Pentecostal theology failed to embody it fully. One important reason for that failure is that it did not recognize the comprehensive horizon of the gospel of God's kingdom covering society, history, and the cosmos, and it thereby degenerated into a theology of blessing in the private realm only. Recently Pentecostal theologians have acknowledged the weak points of their theology and have begun to move toward the full gospel once again.

2. Evangelical Theology and Holistic Theology

In July 1989 about three thousand evangelicals gathered together in the Second International Congress on World Evangelization in Manila (often called "Lausanne II"). This assembly approved an important document, "the Manila Manifesto," which contains the core spirit of contemporary evangelical theology. From the perspective of holistic theology it is noteworthy that the first section of the second Part of the Manifesto is entitled "The Whole Gospel." This demonstrates that the theology of today's evangelical movement is oriented toward the whole gospel. What, then, does it mean by "the whole gospel"?

In 1970 Peter Beyerhaus and others announced the Frankfurt Declaration, a theological declaration objecting to the 1968 WCC Uppsala Assembly's adoption of the *missio dei* theology as well as to Karl Rahner's theory of the anonymous Christians. This declaration almost ignored the church's social and historical responsibilities and focused solely on evangelism and church growth instead. As a result, the 1970 Frankfurt Declaration lost theological integrity due to its one-sided emphasis on evangelism, salvation of souls, and church growth. This one-sided narrowness of evangelical Christians was overcome to a considerable extent in the 1974 Lausanne Covenant, which affirmed that "evangelism and socio-political involvement are both part of our Christian duty" (section 5).

The 1989 Manila Congress inherited the spirit of the Lausanne Covenant and developed it even further in the direction of holistic theology. One of the most important developments was the increasing awareness of Christian social responsibility. Section 8 of the first Part of the Manila Manifesto declares the importance of "caring for those who are deprived of justice, dignity, food and shelter." In the next section the Manifesto declares that "We affirm that the proclamation of God's kingdom of justice and peace demands the denunciation of all injustice and oppression, both personal and structural; we will not shrink from this prophetic witness." This declaration is quite significant in the sense of making explicit Christian responsibility for justice and peace of God's kingdom. Also, in section 4 of the second Part, one reads, "The proclamation of God's kingdom necessarily demands the prophetic denunciation of all that is incompatible with it." The evils to be denounced are specifically mentioned: "institutionalized violence, political corruption, all forms of exploitation of people and of the earth, the undermining of the family, abortion on demand, drug trafficking, and the abuse of human rights."

The 1989 Manila Manifesto still adheres to the earlier evangelical commitment to the uniqueness of Jesus Christ. "There is only one gospel because there is only one Christ, who because of his death and resurrection is himself the only way of salvation" (Part II section 3). The Manifesto finds the essence of the whole gospel in the commitment to the uniqueness of Jesus Christ. But proclamation of the whole gospel must be followed by the corresponding action, an essential part of which is social responsibility. In other words, elimination of social evils necessarily belongs to proclamation of the gospel of God's kingdom.

Another noteworthy point in the Manila Manifesto is explicit reference to the idea of the kingdom of God. The Manifesto explicitly mentions the task of establishing the kingdom of God and the need of fighting against the evil power that interrupts it. In this vein the Manifesto defines the whole gospel as "the good news of God's salvation from the power of evil, the establishment of his eternal kingdom and his final victory over everything which defies his purpose" (preface to Part II). This definition seems to have come close to the holistic understanding of the gospel.

However, it is not right to say that evangelical theology has finally completed holistic theology, for Christian responsibility for society, history, and creation is still much less emphasized than evangelism and the idea of individual salvation still claims precedence over other works. Even though some evangelical Christians began to argue that they claim only a logical precedence rather than a temporal one, the idea of individual salvation seems so overwhelming as to dominate the entire theology. In short, today's evangelical theology still gives precedence to the idea of individual salvation over the idea of holistic salvation that covers society, history, and the cosmos.

3. Ecumenical Theology and Holistic Theology

In objection to the *missio dei* theology of the 1968 WCC Uppsala Assembly some evangelical Christians in Europe, led by Peter Beyerhaus, announced the Frankfurt Declaration in 1970. Then, in response to the 1973 WCC Bangkok Assembly's emphasis on political-economic salvation, evangelical Christians declared the Lausanne Covenant in the First International Congress on World Evangelization in Lausanne in 1974. In appearance the WCC and evangelicals were walking along different trajectories, and mutually incompatible theologies were dividing the global church.

In the late twentieth century theological discussions in the WCC moved toward holistic theology, with an increasingly broadened horizon of the world and the cosmos. The 1954 WCC Assembly in Evanston witnessed a paradigm shift from the church-centered mission to the mission of God (*missio dei*), according to which the world is understood as a field of mission. Johannes Christiaan Hoekendijk insisted that the church is an instrument of God's saving work in the world and a measure at the hands of God for the purpose of establishing peace in the world. In the 1961 WCC Assembly in New Delhi the church's social responsibility and social involvement were more explicitly emphasized.

The 1975 WCC Assembly in Nairobi, according to Roger Bassham, is so explicit in its orientation toward holistic theology as to be called one of "holistic mission." On the one hand, it accepted the claim of evangelical Christians and emphasized the identity of the gospel. On the other hand, with a focus on God's activity in society and history, it emphasized the church's comprehensive responsibility for humanity and the world. From the 1975 Nairobi Assembly the WCC began to use the phase "the whole gospel," by which it meant:

> To proclaim God's kingdom and love through Jesus Christ, grace and forgiveness of sins as a gift, invitation to believe in Jesus and repent from sins, call to fellowship in the church of God, command to witness to the word and action that bring about God's salvation, duty to participate in the struggle for justice and human dignity, responsibility to denounce everything that interferes the whole being of humanity, and responsible devotion even unto the sacrifice of one's life.

In the 1983 Assembly in Vancouver the WCC began to pay serious attention to the issues of justice, peace, and integrity of creation (JPIC). One of the important developments is that integrity of creation was adopted as a task of the global church. It seems that the WCC's decision was directly influenced by the 1982 Assembly of the World Alliance of Reformed Churches (WARC) in Ottawa, where the agenda of justice, peace, and integrity of creation was first proposed and discussed. The fact that both the WARC and the WCC adopted integrity of creation as one of the essential tasks of the church suggests that both are developing a cosmic theology. In other words, holistic theology, covering humanity, the world, and the cosmos, began to develop in the WCC and the WARC. The WCC delved further into issues of justice, peace, and integrity of creation in the 1989

Convocation in Seoul.

Today's ecumenical theology overall represents a form of holistic theology. It is a holistic theology in the sense of understanding humanity from a holistic perspective, thinking highly of manifesting the kingdom of God in the world, and developing a cosmic theology that covers the created world. Even though ecumenical theology is weaker than evangelical theology in its emphasis on evangelism, the former has a much broader and deeper horizon than the latter. In conclusion, the WCC movement of the twentieth century should be highly regarded as embodying and developing the integrity of Christian theology.

4. Representative Theologians of Holistic Theology

1) Jong Sung Rhee

Jong Sung Rhee accuses the ecumenical movement of degenerating into a humanistic, worldly movement. According to Rhee, the ecumenical movement has stopped being a purely church movement and entered too deeply into the realm of world politics.[1] Rhee continues to say, "Recently the programs of the WCC have become so oriented toward socio-political revolution as to neglect the growth and development of the church herself." As a result, and to his regret, the WCC became a maverick that went out of the nest of the church. It is a criticism that the WCC has no interest in issues of the church herself. "Now programs related to evangelism have almost disap-

---

[1] Jong Sung Rhee, *Hankukgohoeui hyeonsilgwa isang* 『한국교회의 현실과 이상』 [The Reality and Ideal of Korean Church] (Seoul: Academia Christiana Korea, 2001), 163.

peared, while a much greater amount of budget is assigned to issues of society, culture, education, medical care, and human rights."[2]

Rhee worried that the ecumenical movement is too much inclined toward politics. For the church to take social and political responsibility is one thing, but for her to enter too deeply into the socio-political realm with little concern for the church and evangelism is another. Meanwhile, he also accused evangelical theology of putting too much emphasis on individual salvation. Instead, he pursued a holistic theology that is not only evangelical, but also responsible for the world, history, and the entire cosmos. With this purpose in mind he wrote the fourteen volumes of *Jojiksinhak daegye* 『조직신학 대계』 [Outline of Systematic Theology] and described his theology as holistic theology.

In his book *Geurisdoron* 『그리스도론』 [Christology] (1984) Rhee first describes his theology as "tongjeonjeok" (통전적) [holistic] and develops his theology explicitly in this direction. Here he summarizes and evaluates many different Christologies, from ancient times to recent years, and then concludes that to his regret none of them succeeded in disclosing a picture of the total Christ (*totus Christus*).[3]

In the ancient church Ebionists denied the divinity of Christ, while Marcionists, Apollinarianists, and Docetists denied Christ's full humanity. Rhee was also critical of the Chalcedon Creed (451), generally regarded as representing orthodox Christology resulting from

---

[2] Ibid.

[3] Jong Sung Rhee, *Geurisdoron* 『그리스도론』 [Christology] (Seoul: The Christian Literature Society of Korea, 1984), 501.

the fierce theological debates in the ancient church. For Rhee it is "too speculative" and does not suggest any positive interpretation but only four negative statements of the relation between the humanity and divinity of Jesus Christ.[4]

Rhee believed that the satisfaction theory and the moral influence theory in the medieval church both failed to represent total Christology due to their narrow perspective. Moreover, he accused both the recent Christology of "Jesus the liberator" and John Hick's proposal of the Copernican Revolution for the sake of religious pluralism of deviating from the right Christology.[5]

According to Rhee, the right Christology should be holistic Christology. He describes the five features of holistic Christology as follows:[6]

(1) Holistic Christology affirms all of the creeds that every church accepts and confesses regarding Christology—in particular, those creeds approved in ecumenical councils from the second to the seventh century, i.e., during the most determinative period in the formative years of the Christian church and theology.

(2) Every creed is limited by time and space; therefore, no creed should be regarded as an absolute one. Since each creed is produced and confessed by certain persons in certain regions in certain times, it should be reinterpreted and supplemented

---

[4] Ibid., 499.

[5] Ibid., 466-468.

[6] Ibid., 503-506.

by each subsequent generation's new interpretation and understanding of the Bible.

(3) Christology should be indigenized and contextualized in the soil of our church.

(4) Holistic Christology should not give precedence to any one aspect of Christ over the others. In the past Christology sometimes emphasized the divinity of Jesus Christ more than his humanity, and sometimes the other way around. And recent Christological discussions completely deny Christ's divinity and claim to reconstruct a new Christology solely based upon Christ's humanity. Holistic Christology needs to revise these narrow pictures of Christ and draw a total picture of Christ.

(5) Holistic Christology extends the lordship of Christ as far as the Bible tells. Up to now Christology confined Christ's lordship only to individuals and church history. But the Bible tells that all things are under the lordship of Christ.

Rhee's holistic theology rejects an exclusive emphasis on either one of the two natures of Christ, i.e., his humanity or divinity. Also, he respects not only Western Christologies but also indigenous Christologies that have developed in Korean and other Asian soil. Of the above-mentioned five features of holistic Christology, emphasis on the cosmic Christ in the last section is most remarkable. Already in 1984 Rhee was a pioneer who had introduced cosmic Christology to Korean theology. He was deeply interested in Dietrich Bonhoeffer's understanding of Christ as the mediator between God and nature, as found in his posthumous *Christology.* In this vein he stressed the cosmic dimension of Christ's works of reconciliation and salvation, which is now one of the most important pillars of holistic theology. He says, "Christ is the center of human existence, of history, and of nature... One should not divide them into three separate concepts in the abstract level. Human existence is all the time history and is nature. Christ is the liberator and mediator of the created world."[7] In other words, Rhee argues, Christ is the life not only of humanity, but also of the whole world.

2) Jürgen Moltmann

The theology of Jürgen Moltmann focuses on the kingdom of God. Moltmann played an important role in bringing about the paradigm shift from soul-centered theology to God's-kingdom-centered theology. This is regarded as his significant contribution to the development of holistic theology. At the beginning of this paradigm shift is Moltmann's publication of *Theology of Hope* in 1964.

In his later work, *God in Creation* (1985), moreover, Moltmann develops the cosmic framework of Christian theology with regard to the salvation of creation, which is an important pillar of holistic theology. He claims that the Christian church and theology should have interest in, and take responsibility for, not just society and human life but also the entire created world. In this way he develops a system of holistic theology.

In 1991 Moltmann published *The Spirit of Life,* in which he

---

[7] Ibid., 506.

calls his pneumatology a holistic pneumatology (*ganzheitliche Pneumatologie*). Here he made explicit his commitment to the integrity of all his theological works. In *The Coming of God* (1995) he sought to develop an all-encompassing eschatology (*alles integrierende Eschatologie*).

Moltmann influenced ecumenical movement to accept holistic theology that takes responsibility for society, the world, and the entire creation. His influence on theology and theological education is worldwide. He helped orient global theology and theological education toward the kingdom of God. In this sense, Moltmann is one of the major figures who represent today's holistic theology.

3) Howard Clinebell

Howard Clinebell's pastoral counseling is a holistic practical theology. Clinebell has a holistic view of humanity. First of all, the soul is not separate from the body. Humanity is understood as a psycho-somatic unity. Also, he brings a sociological perspective to his understanding of humanity. Furthermore, he takes into account both the feminist perspective and ecological spirituality.

Clinebell's pastoral counseling aims at wholeness. He distinguishes six important dimensions of wholeness:[8]

(1) physical: "glorifying God in your body"
(2) mental: love God "with all your mind"
(3) relational: nurtured in relationships

---

[8] Howard Clinebell, *Basic Types of Pastoral Care and Counseling* (Nashville: Abingdon, 1984).

(4) ecological: respect for and stewardship toward all of creation

(5) institutional: growth in the relationship with institutions

(6) spiritual: gifts of the Holy Spirit as the creator of the universe

Clinebell's discussion of these six dimensions can be understood as an extension of holistic theology to the discipline of pastoral counseling. In consonance with holistic theology, he stresses the psychosomatic unity of the whole person. In addition, he overcomes the past individualistic pastoral counseling with careful attention to the evil working in the society, such as racism, sexism, generational conflict, classism, nationalism, militarism, economic exploitation, and political oppression. Furthermore, he discusses human healing and health in terms of wholeness—that is, not only in human relationship, but also in the relationship with the natural or ecological world. In short, I think, Clinebell is an important contemporary theologian who has transformed the private, soul-centered pastoral counseling to a holistic one.

III
Method of Holistic Theology

Holistic theology aims to investigate every possible truth in order to attain to the Truth. Its theological method is summarized as follows.

1. Holistic theology seeks to integrate ecumenical and evangelical theology.

Holistic theology aims to overcome the narrow perspective of evangelical missionary movement. The latter takes a critical stance against the idea of *missio dei*, while insisting on Christ-centered mission. According to holistic theology, however, they are not an either-or issue but need integration. Jong Sung Rhee once said:

> The accusation that the *missio dei* theology is 'liberal' and thus false theology derives from a misunderstanding of it. God rules over the universe as well as over human history. Even in the areas, realms, and dimensions that lie beyond the reach of humanity or the church God is at work preventing them from running contrary to divine will. God works independently from missionary works of the church. No one can deny it.[9]

Holistic theology recognizes the importance of both Christ-centered mission and the mission of God. Thus, holistic theology takes seriously not only evangelism but also establishment of God's reign. In this vein, it stresses Christian social and historical responsibility. In short, holistic theology seeks to integrate ecumenical and evangelical theology.

---

[9] Jong Sung Rhee, *Jongmalgwa hananimui nara*『종말과 하나님의 나라』[Eschaton and the Kingdom of God] (Seoul: Academia Christiana Korea, 2001), 365.

2. Holistic theology seeks a comprehensive review and evaluation of Protestant, Catholic, and Eastern Orthodox theology.

Moltmann's doctrine of the Trinity, which made a significant contribution to the trinitarian discussions in the late twentieth century, was in fact an outcome of his engagement with Eastern Orthodox theology. When he developed his own doctrine of the Trinity, Moltmann gleaned great insights from Gregory of Nazianzus and other Orthodox theologians' discussion of the social Trinity. Also, Moltmann's objection to inserting "filioque" to the creed resulted from his dialogue with Eastern Orthodox theologians. According to holistic theology, one should avoid absolutizing any particular theological tradition. This is the reason why holistic theology attempts a comprehensive review of every theological tradition—not just Protestant, but also Catholic and Orthodox. Holistic theology, according to Jong Sung Rhee, "seeks to integrate Catholic, Orthodox, and Protestant theologies and pursues the possibility of harmony between their doctrines. It is a theology that seeks a convergence between the three theological traditions."[10] In short, holistic theology is ecumenical theology in its genuine sense, oriented toward the integration of Catholic, Eastern Orthodox, and Protestant theologies.

---

[10] Quoted from Jong Sung Rhee's note on the outline of his holistic theology, which he sent to me when I prepared for the first Chungye Theological Symposium.

3. Holistic theology reviews and evaluates not only Christian theology but also all other religions and cultures from a theological perspective.

According to Jong Sung Rhee, holistic theology stresses the absoluteness of God as well as the universal providence of God who works in every human society. Hence, other religions and other cultures are not removed from the reign and providence of God. For this reason it would bring great benefits to study their core teachings and characteristic features from a theological perspective. "Holistic theology," Rhee says, "is ready to accept teachings of other religions that are consonant with, or have the same purpose with, those of Christianity."[11]

4. Holistic theology emphasizes dialogue between theology and other scientific disciplines, while offering theological evaluation and guidelines to the latter.

One of the major premises of holistic theology is that all realms of the world—e.g., politics, economics, society, culture, and so forth—are under the rule of God. Jong Sung Rhee argues that the reign of God reaches "not only human history but also the entire world and the whole cosmos."[12] Therefore, theology can and must engage in dialogue with all other scientific disciplines.

---

[11] Quoted from Jong Sung Rhee's note on the outline of his holistic theology.
[12] Quoted from Jong Sung Rhee's note on the outline of his holistic theology.

In this dialogue theology gets help from other disciplines, whereas the former plays a guiding role for the latter. Since God is the One who rules the whole cosmos, according to Jong Sung Rhee, cosmic theology is an essential part of holistic theology. Rhee believes that, while conflict between creation and evolution needs more careful investigation, holistic theology may accept some parts of evolutionary theology which does not contradict the doctrine of creation. In a similar vein Moltmann understands evolution in terms of continuous creation and incorporates Carl Friedrich von Weizsäcker's idea of the history of nature into his doctrine of creation.

5. Holistic theology takes as its major premises the ultimate divine revelation in Jesus Christ and the normative Scriptures.

Holistic theology seeks to integrate ecumenical and evangelical theology, attempts a comprehensive review of Protestant, Catholic, and Eastern Orthodox tradition, and engages in dialogue with other religions, other cultures, and all other disciplines, including the natural sciences. However, it does not lead to syncretism which mixes everything without any criterion. The primary presupposition of holistic theology is, Jong Sung Rhee says, "the recognition of the absolute Yahweh-God."[13] Moltmann and Wolfhart Pannenberg assert that the resurrection of Jesus Christ is an anticipation of the eschatological kingdom of God that will determine the ultimate meaning of every

---

13 Quoted from Jong Sung Rhee's note on the outline of his holistic theology.

history.

Holistic theology is willing to accept part of other religions and cultures, yet only in light of the gospel revealed in Jesus Christ. And the light of the gospel in turn corrects and sanctifies other religions and cultures. Holistic theology develops against the broad horizon but rejects syncretism that merges different religions.

IV
Characteristics of Holistic Theology

1. Trinitarian Theology

Holistic theology is rooted in the trinitarian conviction. Jong Sung Rhee devoted two of his fourteen-volumes of *Outline of Systematic Theology* to the doctrine of the Trinity, and even designed his entire systematic theology from a trinitarian perspective. At the very beginning of his systematic contributions to theology Jürgen Moltmann also wrote a book on the doctrine of the Trinity, *Trinity and the Kingdom of God*, and then discussed Christology, pneumatology, the doctrine of creation, and eschatology from the perspective of trinitarian theology.

Rhee says, "Holistic understanding of God leads to the trinitarian understanding of God. The idea of the triune God is the most Christian aspect in Christianity."[14] Korean minjung theology, lacking the idea of the triune God, is not a holistic theology. It is praiseworthy that minjung theology contributed to the democratization of Korean society, human rights of the oppressed, and the establishment of social justice. However, one should not overlook its theological weakness in Christology and pneumatology and the resulting problems in the church and mission. Jesus Christ is not merely one of minjung, but the Son of God. He is the second Person of the triune God. The idea that minjung are Jesus and save themselves falls far short of theological integrity. The claim that Tae-Il Jeon is a Korean Jesus and one can pray in the name of Tae-Il Jeon is an extremely distorted idea that may tear the right theology from its very root. Salvation of humanity and all things is grounded upon the suffering and death of Jesus Christ, not upon the death of Tae-Il Jeon or any other social activist.

The pneumatology of minjung theology is as distorted as its Christology. Minjung theologians' claim that *Ki* (氣, the life force) is the Holy Spirit contradicts trinitarian pneumatology. To say that the Holy Spirit, as the source of all life, is at work in all things is one thing, but to say that *Ki* is the Holy Spirit is another. The latter claim makes a serious theological mistake in ignoring the personality of the Holy Spirit and it blurs the distinction between God and creatures.

The Nicene-Constantinopolitan Creed (381) is the theological foundation of both trinitarian theology and holistic theology. Holistic theology respects the creeds approved in the ancient ecumenical councils—particularly, their trinitarian formulation. Hence, it objects to false monotheistic ideas, such as modalism, adoptionism, and subordinationism.

---

[14] Jong Sung Rhee, *Sinhakseoron* 『신학서론』 [Introduction to Theology] (Seoul: The Christian Literature Society of Korea, 1993), 70.

Today's holistic theology pursues the community of love and *koinonia* based upon the perichoretic relationship between the three Persons of the Trinity. Today's trinitarian theology understands the doctrine of the Trinity as a social program and attempts to embody the loving *koinonia* between God the Father, the Son, and the Spirit within human society. Leonard Boff represents contemporary theologians who understand the doctrine of the Trinity as a social program. And Moltmann appeals to the perichoretic understanding of the triune God and resists every form of monotheistic hierarchy. Trinitarian theology, Moltmann believes, contradicts every form of top-down hierarchy—whether ecclesiastical, political, patriarchal (males above females), or anthropocentric (humanity above nature).

When we assert that holistic theology is rooted in the trinitarian understanding of God, it does not imply that holistic theology takes tradition too seriously to have anything to do with today's issues in our life, the world, and the cosmos. Rather, holistic theology follows the trajectory of contemporary trinitarian theology that seeks more actively than any other to solve today's urgent problems. In addition, according to holistic theology the ultimate solution to problems of humanity, the world, and the cosmos today is found only in the saving work of the triune God.

2. The Whole Gospel

Holistic theology presupposes the holistic understanding of the gospel with regard to the following five dimensions.

1) Each individual person attains to salvation and eternal life through Jesus Christ. To know and believe in Jesus Christ is essential to one's personal salvation. It is an indispensible part of the gospel that through Jesus Christ human beings enter a new relationship with the triune God and become the children of God who call God Abba, our Father.

2) The gospel is not simply good news about the salvation of human souls. It also refers to liberation of human bodies from the power of death. The resurrection of the dead, which is the core of the gospel, necessarily presupposes corporeality.

3) The gospel also refers to liberation from the power of darkness and death—for instance, injustice, war, murder, racism, drugs, and atheism. In order words, the whole gospel covers liberation from structural evils in political, economic, social, and cultural dimensions.

4) Christ did not die for humanity alone. The event of reconciliation in Christ also applies to salvation of the entire creation from lamentation and deadly power. The anthropocentric interpretation of the gospel falls short of the whole gospel.

5) Jesus proclaimed the gospel of the kingdom of God. In other words, the gospel is oriented toward the kingdom of God and concerned with its establishment on earth. The evangelical church, therefore, seeks to embody God's kingdom. The kingdom of God is the place where God's glory shines forth and the eternal life, peace, and joy penetrates the entire creation, including humanity.

3. Theology of the Whole Person

Holistic theology understands humanity as the whole person. In this sense, it contradicts soul-centered theology, which was first articulated by Augustine and then developed in the Western church. According to Augustine, the image of God in humanity refers to the spiritual dimension of humanity. Thus, the human body has nothing to do with the image of God. Within the Augustinian tradition, Thomas Aquinas understands the image of God in terms of human rationality. Such an idea of the image of God tends to exclude or underestimate human body. This is incompatible with the spirit of holistic theology.

The Western tradition after Augustine continued to develop soul-centered theology, which was also male-centered theology. According to Augustine, the female is not herself an image of God. She becomes an image of God only under the rule of her husband, who is her head. This male-centered ideology belongs to the same logic as soul-centered theology, for the male is regarded as the female's soul and the female as the male's body. Holistic theology objects to this ideology that makes males representative of humanity.

Holistic theology takes seriously the human body as well as the human soul. As far as humanity is concerned, holistic theology understands the image of God as the whole person. Furthermore, it finds the authentic image of God in the fellowship between male and female and between parents and children. Moltmann says that the image of God is found in intersexual and intergenerational fellowships. The loving *koinonia* of the triune God is found in the love between male and female, in the love between parents and children, and in the friendly fellowship between human beings. Holistic theology does not exclude the human body from its anthropology nor despise females within human community.

Modern medical science in the late twentieth century made a significant contribution to the development of the idea of humanity as a whole person, for in the process of treatment it recognized the close connection between human body and mind. One can find the influence of modern medical insights even in Christian counseling. A leading American pastoral counselor, Howard Clinebell, in his book *Well Being*, develops a holistic pastoral counseling whose ultimate goal is well being or wholeness. Clinebell's holistic pastoral counseling is a pastoral counseling version of holistic theology. It assumes a holistic view of humanity and the world, as well as a holistic theory of healing.

Indeed, the theological idea of humanity as the whole person has a close connection with the development of modern medical science in the late twentieth century. However, the decisive momentum for the development of such a theological idea was given by biblical theologians of the twentieth century, for they discovered that, in contrast with Hellenistic dualism, the Bible understands humanity as the whole person. The discovery that Hebrew anthropology was fundamentally different from Hellenistic anthropology had an enormous potential to shake to its very foundations the post-Augustinian Western tradition that formulated and organized doctrines into a systematic whole on the basis of the Hellenistic dualistic understanding of humanity. In his book, *Anthropology of the Old Testament*, Hans Walter Wolff demonstrates that the Hebrew people understood humanity as the whole person, in clear contrast with the Greek people. Rudolf Bultmann, Werner Kummel, and other New Testament theologians also disclosed that the Bible does not suggest the dualistic anthropology of Hellenism but a holistic view of humanity as the whole person.

Holistic theology accepts the biblical understanding of humanity as the whole person, as discovered by biblical theologians of the twentieth century. Developing this idea further, Moltmann maintains that the completion of the human body corresponds to the ultimate fulfillment of God's saving works. According to Moltmann, Christian hope is not oriented toward the immortality of souls but towards the resurrection of the dead, which implies the completion of the body. In this sense, there is a fundamental difference between the Christian hope for resurrection and the Hellenistic hope for immortality. In the same vein Moltmann believed that the human body lies at the center of God's saving works, and he interpreted Jesus' healing as the prolepsis (*Prolepse*) of the resurrection of the body. In other words, the miracles of Jesus' healing were anticipations (*Verwegnahme*) of the kingdom of God.

Jong Sung Rhee further advanced holistic anthropology from a different point of view. His holistic theology rejects a purely negative understanding of humanity and stresses the positive aspect, as found in the biblical idea of humanity. Thus, he quotes from the Bible: "You made him a little lower than the heavenly beings and crowned him with glory and honor" (Ps. 8:5), and "There is no one righteous, not even one" (Ps. 14:1-3; Rom. 3:11). Rhee says, "Therefore, holistic theology pursues a total understanding of humanity. It does not focus either on the negative or on the positive aspect of humanity but deals with the total humanity as a concrete being in relationship with God, neighbors, and history."[15] In other words, holistic theology takes seriously both the positive and negative aspects of human beings and seeks to understand the total humanity as a concrete existence.

4. Theology for the Church and the World

Holistic theology is distinguished from other theologies that think of the church as an ark of salvation and, with a focus on saving souls, seek first of all church growth. The latter are narrow in scope and thus lack wholeness. Holistic theology recognizes the importance of salvation of human souls and church growth, but it also pays careful attention to divine actions for the world. It is Catholic theologian Johannes Baptist Metz who first brought to our attention the phrase "theology for the world" by publishing a book entitled *Theology of the World* (*Theologie zur Welt*) in 1968. But his theological ideas are indebted to Moltmann's *Theology of Hope* (1964). To put it another way, in the late twentieth century the idea of theology for the world was first provoked by Moltmann's work. Through *Theology of Hope* many Christians were convinced that both the church and theology have responsibility for the world. In this way Moltmann supported global democracy movements, struggles against dictatorships, move-

---

[15] Jong Sung Rhee, *Sinhakseoron* [Introduction to Theology], 71.

ments for human rights, anti-racist movements, various forms of efforts for justice, and church movements for the poor.

Holistic theology fully affirms Moltmann and Metz's proposal of theology for the world. It also makes positive evaluations of the WCC's theology for justice and peace, as well as the post-Vatican II Roman Catholic Church's efforts to promote justice and peace in the world. Holistic theology is open to dialogue with black theology, minjung theology, theology of peace, feminist theology, and any other theologies that seek to solve problems of the world. Holistic theology aims to serve both the church and the world and to embody the reign of God in both realms.

Furthermore, holistic theology is open to other religions and other cultures as well. How to deal with other religions and cultures is one of the most important theological issues in the twenty-first century. Holistic theology encourages careful studies of all religious cultures in the West and East. In his holistic theology Jong Sung Rhee engages in dialogue with other world religions—such as Confucianism, Buddhism, Taoism, Islam, and Hinduism—concerning their views of salvation, humanity, and ethics. His dialogue partners also include various philosophies of the East and West. He was convinced that holistic theology should be constructed in dialogue with other religions and cultures, without abandoning its commitment to the absoluteness of the divine revelation in Jesus Christ. Holistic theology attempts to grasp both positive and negative aspects of other religions and other cultures in light of the whole revelation of God in Jesus Christ.

5. Cosmic Theology

Holistic theology is not anthropocentric. For the past several decades there has been an increasing awareness that anthropocentric theology, which confines God's saving work only to humanity, should be overcome. Holistic theology agrees with this contemporary theological current. Holistic theology takes into account not just cries of human beings but also the groaning of creation. In the reconciling death of Jesus Christ it witnesses to the divine plan to save the entire creation, not just humanity (Rom. 8:19-21; Eph. 1:20; Col. 1:20).

Today, all living things on the Earth are groaning in crisis. The current environmental crisis is developing into a crisis affecting every living creature on the Earth. People today are recognizing that the destiny of humanity is inseparable from our ecological crisis. Holistic theology seeks to help save living creatures on the Earth from this crisis.

Howard Clinebell refers to ecological spirituality as an important part of Christian spirituality and contributes to its development. His effort is noteworthy for the holistic theological approach to spirituality. Christian spirituality in its genuine sense preserves the Earth, regards air and water pollution as a sin of rebellion against God the Lord of the Earth, seeks solidarity with the groaning creation, and makes efforts to love and save every life in the cosmos.

Hildegard of Bingen was a remarkable female theologian who taught ecological spirituality in the Medieval Age. She resisted the Cathari School's disregard of the material world and instead taught a creation-centered spirituality. As a Gnostic and Manichean school, the Cathari regarded the spiritual mind as superior, and they exalted it to the status of divinity, while disregarding the material body as inferior and demonic. In contrast, Hildegard denied such a dualistic view of mind and body; rather, she emphasized the love and power of God who is immanent in humanity, nature, the world, and the cosmos. Thus, Mi-Hyeon Jeong describes Hildegard as a female theologian who envisioned "a holistic cosmology."[16] Hildegard says, "The divine love is the most fundamental power in the cosmos; it is a green power that sustains the entire creation."[17]

In 1985 Jürgen Moltmann published *God in Creation*, in which he developed a holistic theology in the cosmic dimension. While in *Theology of Hope* (1964) he articulated a theology that is responsible for the world and history, in *God in Creation* (1985) he expanded the horizon and stressed the cosmic dimension of theological responsibility.

Holistic theology recognizes the history of nature. In the theological tradition nature has long been regarded only as a stage for human history, and the category of history did not apply to nature but only to humanity. But holistic theology overcomes such an idea of history. According to holistic theology, not only humanity but also nature as well has a history and, furthermore, human history appeared within the history of nature. Holistic theology does not contrast humanity with nature, nor creation with evolution. Today's physics tells us of the history and evolution of the universe, and holistic theology

---

16 Mi-Hyeon Jeong, "Changjojungsimjeok yeongseong—Hildegard of Bingeneul jungsimeuro" [Creation-Centered spirituality: With Focus on Hildegard of Bingen], *Korean Journal of Christian Studies* 15 (1998), 254.

17 Ibid., 354.

engages in dialogue with today's physical cosmology. Holistic theology tries to detect and take into theological consideration concrete actions of God the Creator and the Ruler of the entire universe that are now under scientific investigation. Also, it helps orient all of the natural sciences toward the kingdom of God. As a cosmic theology, holistic theology is open to dialogue between theology and the natural sciences and asserts that the cosmic dimension of God's saving works is concerned with the entire realm of the natural sciences and, thus, God calls some of us to be scientists.

6. Theology for the Kingdom of God

Holistic theology is oriented toward the kingdom of God. Holistic theology aims to manifest the reign of God in the world—not just in individual souls but also in the whole person, consisting of soul and body, not just within the church but also within the whole world, and not just in human life and history but also in the entire creation. Holistic theology is distinct from both theology focusing on the saving of souls and theology that is irresponsible toward the world and history.

Hyung Ryong Park's theology was thoroughly evangelism-centered, as if "only evangelism" were its catch phrase. Such an evangelism-centered theology has its own value; it evoked enthusiasm for evangelism within the church and made a significant contribution to church growth. Be that as it may, it is not a holistic theology. Park's theology lacks historical responsibility. He accused the liberal theology of the kingdom of God in the nineteenth century as having nothing to do with the gospel, and he denounced efforts to establish the kingdom of God in history as demonic. With a pessimistic view of history, Park believed that human efforts to transform history and realize the kingdom of God in history conflict with the divine plan. His commitment to historical premillenarianism convinced him that the history becomes darker and darker until it ends up in catastrophe.

Park's theological legacy, in its positive and negative aspects, was inherited by his followers. Its emphasis on evangelism led to church growth, while its lack of historical responsibility produced impotent churches in the face of social and historical issues. As a consequence, during the period of military dictatorship, churches under Park's theological influence turned out irresponsible and helpless.

Holistic theology is a historically responsible theology. It underlines historical responsibility of the church as much as evangelism. Thus, Jong Sung Rhee stressed both evangelism and historical responsibility and emphasized Christ's victory over the evil powers working in history. This is a distinctively strong point of Rhee's holistic theology, when compared with Park's theology. In his book *Ecclesiology* Rhee was emphatic about the importance of the church's task to establish the kingdom of God.

Here some may ask whether the idea of God's kingdom, which holistic theology is oriented toward, has the same reference as one that liberal theologians of the nineteenth century pursued. If holistic theology adheres to the same concept of God's kingdom as liberal theologians, then does it not imply that holistic theology is a descendant of the nineteenth century liberal theology and thus Park's criticism is also true of holistic theology?

There is a fundamental difference in the concept of God's kingdom between liberal theology and holistic theology. In this regard Karl Barth may help us. In the first edition of his commentary on the Epistle to the Romans Barth explained in detail why he departed from liberal theology. Before he wrote the book Barth met Christoph Blumhardt at Bad Ball in the southwestern region of Germany. From this encounter Barth learned an important lesson that the kingdom of God should be built by God. This insight liberated him from liberal theology. In other words, Blumhardt convinced Barth that sinful human beings cannot establish the kingdom of God, but only God can do so.

In contrast with liberal theology, holistic theology does not say "Hurray!" to humankind, nor believe in the utopian world to be built by human reason and morality. Holistic theology sees through the demonic power that is at work in the history of sinful humans. In the late twentieth century Jürgen Moltmann not only contributed to the theology of God's kingdom, but also urged theologians to remember that the cross of Christ is standing at the very center of the world. It is still possible that world history may come to a catastrophic end by a demonic power. The nineteenth century liberal theology failed to take seriously the demonic power working within sinful human nature and the history of humankind.

However, the recognition of such a demonic power working in human nature and history should not lead us to a pessimistic view of history. Hyung Ryong Park's historical pessimism emphasized only the dark side of human history. According to Barth, the No to humanity is enclosed by the Yes to humanity, and the tragedy of the world is enclosed by the light and joy deriving from the gospel. In a similar vein, Jong Sung Rhee insisted that in order to attain to a holistic understanding of human beings one should take note of both the negative and positive aspects. Even if evil is raging, he argued, it is essential to a true evangelical understanding of history to believe in the final victory of the incarnation.

In short, holistic theology takes into account both the positive and negative aspects of humanity and human history. Nonetheless, holistic theology continues to hope for history, because Christ is even more powerful than evil, however strong the latter may be. In *Theology of Hope*, a standard textbook about the kingdom of God, Moltmann speaks of Christ's victory and God's reign over the evil powers. The idea of God's kingdom, according to holistic theology, appears similar to, but is in fact fundamentally different from, that of liberal theology in the nineteenth theology. According to holistic theology, the kingdom of God is built by God. Jong Sung Rhee says that it is God the Lord of history who establishes the kingdom of God. Hence, there is a great difference between the idea of God's kingdom and the secular idea of the utopia.

Chapter 2

Jong Sung Rhee's Holistic Theology

Myung Yong Kim

J ong Sung Rhee is a very important Korean theologian. In 2001 he published his completed works, consisting of forty theological books, fourteen of which were devoted to *Outline of Systematic Theology*. He is the father and one of the representative theologians of holistic theology in Korea. Thus, in order to know Korean holistic theology it is essential to study Rhee's theological works. Now I discuss the main characteristics of Jong Sung Rhee's holistic theology.

I
Theological Method of Jong Sung Rhee's Holistic Theology

1. Various Theological Methods and Holistic Method

In order to understand Rhee's holistic theology it is important to know his holistic method. In the theological tradition Rhee discerns four distinct theological methods: namely, deductive, inductive, revelatory, and correlational. He then proposes the holistic method as superior to all of them.

The holistic method integrates both the deductive and inductive methods, and acknowledges both the unity and diversity of revelation. Rhee regards the inductive method based upon historical and religious experience as one of the important theological methods. Contrary to a prejudice against the value of historical and religious experience that one might expect from an Orthodox theologian who stresses the authority and standard of the Bible, Rhee thinks that the revelatory and deductive methods in themselves are limited—that is, fall short of integrity. Appealing to the Calvinist teaching of common and special grace and Emil Brunner's idea of general and special revelation, Rhee argues that according to the Bible there is general revelation as well as special revelation.

"For since the creation of the world God's invisible qualities—his eternal power and divine nature—have been clearly seen, being understood from what has been made, so that people are without excuse" (Rom. 1:20). Rhee says, "An indirect knowledge of God, whether it is called *imago dei* or religiosity or conscience or *nouminose* (Rudolf Otto), is possible."[1] Rhee's holistic theological method reviews and affirms the value of even John Locke and David Hume's empiricist philosophy and Friedrich Schleiermacher's liberal theology based upon human religiosity. Taking seriously the actuality of natural revelation, the holistic theological method recognizes the limitation of either the deductive or revelatory method alone, and thus employs the inductive and relational methods as well. According to Rhee, "In order to attain the most comprehensive, holistic, and foundational knowledge of God, we need both the knowledge of God through Jesus Christ and that through general revelation—in short, the whole knowledge of God."[2]

2. The Wide Range of Sources of Holistic Theology

Since Jong Sung Rhee affirms common grace and natural revelation, sources of his theology are not confined to Jesus Christ and the Bible alone. As for theological sources, Rhee is willing to make use of everything in the world. According to him, the Bible is the most important source for theology. In addition to the Bible, not only church history but also secular history is a source for theology. Furthermore, philosophy, religious studies, psychology, literature, social sciences, and natural sciences are also theological sources.

Rhee includes secular history beside the Bible and church history

---

[1] Jong Sung Rhee, *Sinhakseoron* 『신학서론』 [Introduction to Theology], 68.
[2] Ibid.

as important sources for theology. It is not just because he affirms common grace and natural theology, but also because he believes that God is omnipresent and that even secular history is not excluded from God's governing providence. Since God is the one and only Lord of history, every event in world history is, either directly or indirectly, related to God. It is also true of the events in the natural world. Therefore, observations and knowledge in the natural sciences may have something to do with God. In that sense they are useful sources for theology.

In the fourteen-volumes of his *Outline of Systematic Theology* Rhee deals with all of the theologies and thoughts of both the East and West and incorporates every good idea into his theology while criticizing problems. Thus, his works look like an encyclopedia. He is a Reformed theologian, but he discusses not only Reformed theologies, but also the theologies of other Protestant traditions and even Eastern Orthodox theologies. In addition, he enters dialogue with world religions, including Confucianism, Buddhism, Taoism, Hinduism, and Judaism, as well as with great thinkers of the world such as Karl Marx, Ernst Bloch, Arnold Toynbee, and Karl Jaspers. While struggling with their thoughts Rhee develops a very broad spectrum of theological thought. Rhee's holistic theology is noteworthy for its great width and breadth.

3. The Authority and Standard of the Bible

Even though Jong Sung Rhee affirms common grace and natural revelation and thus draws from a wide range of theological sources, his holistic theology should not be confused with syncretism. It is true that in his holistic method Rhee integrates the deductive and inductive methods, as well as the revelatory and correlational methods, but he does not simply mix them without any standard. Rather, he hates and objects to syncretism and views it as an enemy of the right theology.

Jong Sung Rhee's theology is grounded upon the authority and standard of the Bible. He is deeply aware of the imperfection of the knowledge of God through natural revelation. The knowledge of God through natural revelation falls far short of the whole knowledge of God; it is no more than "an indirect knowledge of God."[3] Hence, philosophy, religious studies, psychology, literature, social sciences, and natural sciences are simply subsidiary disciplines for theology.[4] According to Rhee, it is only through Jesus Christ and the Bible that one can attain the right knowledge of God.

The Bible, Rhee says, "is the standard of Christian life and the only authority for theology."[5] With this statement he is not advocating the biblicist idea of the literal inerrancy of the Bible. In fact, he is critical of biblicists who do not take seriously inconsistencies in the biblical writings.[6]

According to Rhee, the revelation in Jesus Christ is the special and final revelation.[7] One can attain the correct knowledge of God only through Jesus Christ. He does not accept Barth's idea that Christ

---

[3] Ibid.
[4] Ibid., 139-197.
[5] Ibid., 220.
[6] Ibid., 43.
[7] Ibid., 252-253.

is the only revelation, because he affirms the possibility of natural revelation.[8] But he believes that Barth was right for emphasizing the finality of revelation in Jesus Christ. The Bible that witnesses to the revelation of Jesus Christ is the one and only authority and standard for Christian theology. After enumerating a number of challenges posed by liberal theologians to the authority of the Bible, Rhee concludes:

> Contemporary theologians, especially those in the Reformed tradition, emphasize anew that the Bible is the standard of doctrinal judgment in Protestant theology. For instance, Horst Georg Pöhlmann argues that the Creeds are the normed norm (*norma normata*), while the Bible is the norming norm (*norma normans*). G. C. Berkouwer accepts Martin Luther's idea of "canon within canon" and argues for the standard status of the Bible. H. Berkhof asserts that the Bible is both the source and the standard of our knowledge of God. Donald G. Bloesch maintains that the Bible is the transcendent norm, even though the Bible has many human problems and is open to different interpretations. In contrast with liberal theologians who make effort to relativize the authority of the Bible, all these contemporary theologians stress the authority and normativity of the Bible for theology.[9]

---

[8] Ibid., 253.
[9] Ibid., 220.

According to Jong Sung Rhee, although there are some human limitations in the Bible, the Bible is the Word of God and the only authority and standard for theology. For this reason every natural knowledge of God should be corrected and supplemented by the authority and standard of the Bible. It is untrue that any natural knowledge of God combined with the biblical spirit may create something new.

4. God and God's Plan as the Answer to the Question of Humanity and the World

According to Jong Sung Rhee's holistic theology, all ultimate questions of humanity and the world find their answer in the triune God, and the answer is the church and the kingdom of God. For instance, the answer to the question of being is God; the answer to the question of human existence is Jesus Christ; the answer to the question of life is the Holy Spirit; the answer to the question of community is the church; the answer to the question of society is Christian ethics; and the answer to the question of history is Christian eschatology. This question-answer scheme was first proposed by Paul Tillich. Rhee further develops Tillich's method of correlation. This scheme is very important when one tries to understand the relationship between biblical truth and worldly truth in Rhee's holistic theology. In order to make explicit the relationship I will discuss how Rhee perceives Christ as the answer to the question of human existence.

According to Rhee, the proper answer to the question raised by human existence is found in Christ. It is true that world religions and philosophy grasped partial truths concerning human existence. But they failed to perceive the true problem of human existence and thus could not solve it. According to Rhee, existentialist philosophy, one of the representative philosophical movements that took seriously the problem of human existence and attempted to grasp the situation of human existence, neither understood the true problem of human existence nor solved it. Martin Heidegger, one of the major existentialist philosophers, described the situation of human existence in terms of death, anxiety, and relativity. Then, can humans overcome death, anxiety, and relativity in the condition of human existence? According to Rhee, Heidegger's understanding of humanity is basically humanistic, just like many atheistic existentialists'. Rhee says that Heidegger

> understands humanity as a living being who starts from the given reality and tries to solve one's own problem all by oneself—that is, only with what she or he possesses. But what she or he finds is not hope or something positive and encouraging, but rather a being who is anxious and fearful in the face of approaching death and the danger of nothingness. In order to overcome the fear of death people speak of "the freedom toward death," which is no more than a psychological manipulation and self-deception. "The freedom toward death" is nothing but a self-resignation. Heidegger came to this awkward conclusion because he looked only into the inside of human existence and tried to find an exit within it. Human beings cannot solve their

existential problem by themselves.[10]

According to Rhee, although existentialists made an effort to an-
alyze and understand human existence as it is, they attained only a
partial and fragmentary truth. Also, their answer to the problem of
human existence is not sufficient but remains a human being's psychological self-manipulation.

> Every contemporary problem derives from the misunder-
> standing that humanity is an isolated and lonely being, or
> from a lack of understanding that humanity has been rec-
> onciled with God. People misunderstand the God-given
> possibility as one's own possibility and do not understand
> their current state in terms of the new creation but in terms
> of perishable flesh. This brings about many complicated
> problems. Existentialists made an effort to analyze and un-
> derstand humanity as it is, only to find the 'I' who is in
> isolation and despair. Therefore, they do not know tomor-
> row but only today. In reaction to such anxiety and despair,
> people cause many immoral anti-social problems.[11]

According to Rhee, the primary reason for human despair, anxiety, and death is disconnection from God. Not until humans truly
find God do they truly know themselves. Furthermore, the discon-

---

10 Jong Sung Rhee, *Sinhakjeok inganhak* 『신학적 인간학』 [Theological Anthropology] (Seoul: The
Christian Literature Society of Korea, 1979), 103-104.

11 Jong Sung Rhee, *Jojiksinhak gaeron* 『조직신학 개론』 [Introduction to Systematic Theology], 72-
73.

nection of humanity from God has been overcome in Jesus Christ. Rhee claims that all the unsolved problems of human existence have been solved and overcome in Jesus Christ.

> When from the cross Jesus cried out in a loud voice, "*Eloi, Eloi, lama sabachthani?*" the curtain of the temple between the holy place and the holy of holies was torn in two from top to bottom. That is, the obstacle that had blocked the relationship between God and humanity was eliminated and, as a consequence, the relationship between God and humanity was restored. Theologically speaking, the once disconnected relationship of humanity from God was fully recovered through the event of the cross of Christ. For believers this is a firm reality and implies infinite possibility. In other words, in Christ the relationship between God and humanity was restored and the problem of sin was solved. This is the reason why we call Christianity a religion of hope.[12]

Rhee's holistic theology integrates both the Eastern and Western ideas in order to reach the right understanding of humanity. Without Christ, however, neither a right understanding of human predicament nor a right answer to it is possible. All explanations of humanity in the East and West provide us with comprehensive perspectives, but what we find through them is only a human being who is in isolation

---

12 Ibid, 72.

and despair and in search of a vain hope. According to Rhee, the true solution to the predicament of human existence is found in Christ.

II
Outline of Jong Sung Rhee's Holistic Theology

1. Holistic Christology and Doctrine of the Trinity

Jong Sung Rhee's Christology is a holistic Christology. It is in his *Geurisdoron* 『그리스도론』 [Christology] (1984) that Rhee first used the expression "tongjeonjeok" (통전적, holistic) and began to develop his holistic theology. In this book the confession that Jesus Christ is the true God (*vere Deus*) and the true humanity (*vere Homo*) is regarded as confirmed in the Creed of Nicene (325) and the Creed of Chalcedon (451), and as the essence of holistic Christology. According to him, "when any one aspect of Christ is overly emphasized at the expense of others" it falls short of holistic Christology.[13] Thus far Christology focused on either the divinity or the humanity of Christ. This is not a holistic Christology. In particular, the nineteenth century theology focused too much on the humanity of Christ and almost ignored the divinity of Christ. In this way it looked like a revival of the ancient Ebionite heresy. Rhee finds this wrong.

According to Rhee, the confession that Jesus Christ is the true

---

13 Jong Sung Rhee, *Geurisdoron* 『그리스도론』 [Christology], 504.

God and the true humanity contains a mysterious aspect that cannot be completely understood by human reason. However, it reflects the first disciples' experience and the biblical writings. Rhee says that the Son of God pre-existed with God before he came to the world and was born into the world through the body of a virgin. This is very difficult to understand by human reason. But Jesus' disciples believed his virgin birth "without any doubt."[14] And Jesus was raised from the dead; the empty tomb is an undeniable fact.[15] And Jesus "ascended into heaven before the eyes of his disciples."[16] This Jesus is the mediator between God and humanity and the savior of all humanity and the world. According to Rhee, the truth that Jesus is the true God and the true humanity is demonstrated by the following facts: Jesus died on the cross as a human being, his disciples scattered in great disappointment, a new community formed after Jesus' resurrection, and his disciples confessed without fear that Jesus is the Lord.

Rhee agrees with Emil Brunner that the idea that Jesus Christ is the true God and the true humanity is a mystery that transcends limitations of human reason.[17] However, he criticizes Brunner for denying the virgin birth of Jesus Christ and thereby discarding the mysterious dimension of faith and degenerating into rationalism. In this regard Rhee thinks of Barth as more reliable than Brunner because Barth accepted Jesus' virgin birth as a mysterious event.[18]

The holistic orientation of Rhee's theology is evident not only

---

14 Ibid., 486.
15 Ibid., 487.
16 Ibid., 488.
17 Ibid., 439.
18 Ibid., 440-445.

in his Christology but also in his trinitarian theology. According to Rhee, trinitarian theology corresponds to the holistic understanding of God. He insists that we ought to understand God "holistically— that is, in trinitarian terms."[19] In his *Samwiilcheron* [Doctrine of the Trinity] Rhee discusses the broad spectrum of trinitarian theology in the East and West. He makes the doctrine of the Trinity as formulated in the Athanasian Creed into the foundation of his own holistic doctrine of the Trinity, regarding it as one that has been confirmed.[20] According to Rhee, just like the doctrine of Christ's two natures, the doctrine of the Trinity contains a mysterious aspect that transcends limitations of human reason. For this reason he believes that many anti-trinitarian theologies have thus far failed to reach the holistic understanding of God. Rhee asserts that one can reach the holistic understanding of God by developing holistic trinitarian theology with the conviction that the Father, the Son, the Holy Spirit are one God.

From the dogmatic perspective, Rhee's holistic theology has two fundamental foundations: the doctrine of Christ's two natures as formulated in the Creed of Chalcedon and the doctrine of the Trinity as developed in the Athanasian Creed. However, Rhee's theology does not simply remain within these classical doctrines. While reviewing both ancient and modern discussions, he tries to develop a truly holistic trinitarian theology as well as a truly holistic Christology. It is noteworthy that Rhee incorporates contemporary discussion of the social Trinity into his holistic doctrine of the Trinity, and contempo-

---

[19] Jong Sung Rhee, *Sinhakseoron* [Introduction to Theology], 70.
[20] Jong Sung Rhee, *Samwiilcheron* 『삼위일체론』 [Doctrine of Trinity] (Seoul: The Christian Literature Society of Korea, 1991), 275-278.

rary cosmic Christology into his holistic Christology. Rhee thinks that the doctrine of the social Trinity as developed by Jürgen Moltmann and Leonardo Boff has a strong point in terms of social praxis. Thus, he supplements the past—primarily metaphysical—doctrine of the Trinity with the doctrine of the social Trinity. He emphasizes the practical doctrine of the Trinity that suggests a model of the true *koinonia*.

Moreover, Rhee incorporates into his holistic Christology contemporary discussion of cosmic Christology, a very important aspect of holistic theology. The Bible speaks of "the relation between Christ and all things."[21] For instance, Colossians 3:11 says, "Christ is all and is in all." Rhee asserts that "all" in this passage refers to all creatures and thus implies a cosmic dimension. He also notes that the natural world desires not only reconciliation but also redemption and liberation. "In Christ, nature finds redemption. In other words, Christ is the center of human existence, history, and nature."[22] Rhee says that Dietrich Bonhoeffer's posthumous publication, *Christology*, shows that Bonhoeffer recognized this issue. Also, Rhee speaks highly of the sixth Assembly of the WCC where the cosmic dimension was first mentioned under the theme of "Jesus Christ—The World's Life."[23] "The fact that Christian theology began to realize the theological significance of the entire cosmos, including the natural world, and understood the cosmos in connection with Christology, should be appreciated, though somewhat late."[24] Rhee believes that the idea of

---

[21] Jong Sung Rhee, *Geurisdoron* [Christology], 494.
[22] Ibid., 505-506.
[23] Ibid., 506.
[24] Ibid.,

Christ as Lord of the cosmos belongs to the biblical teaching and, therefore, holistic Christology should develop in this direction.

2. Holistic Pneumatology

Pneumatology of the twentieth century was inclined to Pentecostal emphasis on speaking in tongues, prophecy, and divine healing. Also, many Korean churches, influenced by the Pentecostal spiritual movement, have, until recently, emphasized mysticism or fanaticism.

Jong Sung Rhee's pneumatology does not dismiss Pentecostal pneumatology that stresses speaking in tongues, prophecy, and divine healing. He distinguishes between general and special works of the Holy Spirit. Calling, repentance, regeneration, justification and faith, sanctification, love, and hope belong to the former, while speaking in tongues, prophecy, and divine healing belong to the latter. In this way he incorporates into his pneumatology such works of the Holy Spirit as are highlighted in the Pentecostal spiritual movement. In short, Rhee develops a holistic pneumatology by integrating both traditional and Pentecostal pneumatology.

However, Rhee repudiates the one-sided emphasis of Pentecostal pneumatology. He points out the narrowness and errors of Pentecostal pneumatology from exegetical and theological perspectives. Instead, he aims to develop his holistic pneumatology on the firm ground of traditional pneumatology. Rhee says:

The essence of the Pentecostal event is not the disciples' speaking in tongues but their commission to proclaim the gospel. Speaking in tongues was one of many ways to proclaim that Jesus Christ is the savior. But the Pentecostal movement ignored the original purpose and focused only on the means. Thus, its theology lacks the message. It simply says that faith is not enough. This contradicts the major premise of the Reformation.[25]

In addition, according to Rhee's critique, the Pentecostal spiritual movement is a kind of subjective mysticism and presupposes a humanistic understanding of the Holy Spirit that exaggerates human agency and limits the freedom of the Holy Spirit.

Only on the right foundation does Rhee affirm Pentecostalism's emphasis on speaking in tongues, prophecy, and divine healing. He believes that the errors and narrowness of Pentecostal pneumatology should be corrected. In his discussion of the relation between the Holy Spirit and culture he further argues that the Holy Spirit "is at work in society, history, and even the entire cosmos."[26] Rhee says, "Thus far Christian theology has neglected the cosmic dimension of the Holy Spirit's work. In its discussion of the *missio dei* the role of the Holy Spirit was not mentioned. Without the Holy Spirit's participation the mission of God is impossible; it is no more than propaganda."[27] Hence, all events in politics, economy, society, culture, and the cosmos, which are all related to the *missio dei*, have a pneumatological

---

[25] Jong Sung Rhee, *Seongryeongron* 『성령론』 [Pneumatology] (Seoul: Academia Christiana Korea, 2001), 399-400.

[26] Ibid., 508.

[27] Ibid.

dimension.

Furthermore, Rhee understands the development of the natural sciences in terms of their pneumatological dimension. He says, "The idea that the natural sciences are simply products of human reason may result in constraining the role of the Holy Spirit to the so-called spiritual dimension. This is an imperfect peumatology, falling far short of the biblical, trinitarian pneumatology."[28] "The pneumatology that we advocate to retrieve and further develop," he continues to argue, is one that makes clear "that the Holy Spirit is engaged, whether directly or indirectly, in all human history and civilization, including the natural sciences."[29]

In the final analysis, Rhee's pneumatology is comparable in its breadth and width to Moltmann's holistic pneumatology as developed in *The Spirit of Life* (1991). When one compares Rhee and Moltmann, one can grasp the characteristics, value, breadth, and width of holistic pneumatology. Both of them point out the errors and narrowness of Pentecostal pneumatology and insist that all human history and the entire network of life in the cosmos are connected with the pneumatological dimension. While Moltmann emphasizes that the Holy Spirit is the source of all life in the world and the cosmos, Rhee is more balanced in his emphasis on the works of the Holy Spirit in the church, the history of human salvation, world civilizations, world history, and the cosmos.

---

[28] Ibid., 501.
[29] Ibid.

3. Holistic Ecclesiology

The holistic nature of Jong Sung Rhee's ecclesiology is well demonstrated by his theological inclination to integrate both the ecumenical and evangelical movements. According to Rhee, these two movements have their respective strong points and have contributed to the development of the global church in their respective ways. First, Rhee says that the ecumenical movement "has made great efforts to become a faithful servant for God and Christ in a rapidly changing world."[30] Rhee mentions many positive aspects of the movement:

> While defining politics, the economy, and the military system as the major powers that obstruct the life of human beings, it [ecumenical movement] has made great efforts to prevent them from doing injustice. It has established strategic plans and worked systematically and actively for social justice, human rights, women's liberation, and peace. In this way, it has brought about remarkable changes that the established church could not make. In short, the contemporary ecumenical movement is not a movement simply for evangelism and the unity and renewal of the church. It is now a powerful agent of the global church that reviews, theologically interprets, and seeks to give a theological answer to every issue in contemporary human society.[31]

[30] Jong Sung Rhee, *Gyohoeron* 『교회론』 [Ecclesiology], vol. 1 (Seoul: The Christian Literature Society of Korea, 1989), 257.

[31] Ibid., 256.

Despite the fact that the ecumenical movement has made considerable contributions to the church's unity and social-historical responsibility, Rhee argues that it also has the following problems.[32]

First, the World Council of Churches (WCC) discarded the promise that it humbly confessed and announced in its first Assembly, i.e., the promise that it will humbly serve its member churches. On the contrary, now it has become a super church that rules over its member churches.

Second, it appears that the WCC-centered ecumenical movement has more interest in social issues than in the reformation, growth, and development of the church.

Third, it is problematic that the WCC stresses institutional integration rather than the integration of churches. The integration of churches should be preceded by mental integration, spiritual integration, and confessional integration. The emphasis on the priority of institutional integration may produce side effects. Another problem related to this is that the WCC's pursuit of the integration of churches shows eclectic and syncretic tendencies.

Fourth, another frequent criticism is that the WCC-centered ecumenical movement lost enthusiasm for evangelism.

Fifth, people often criticize the WCC for breaking away from biblical ecclesiology and coming close to a cultural-historical understanding of the church. It is regretful that the WCC goes beyond the unity of different denominations within Christianity and pursues the

---

[32] Ibid., 247-268.

integration of all religions.

In short, Rhee accuses the ecumenical movement of the weakened interest in evangelism, radical politicization, and the syncretic tendency toward the fusion of religions. With this regard evangelical churches are doing quite well in some points. For this reason Rhee pursues a holistic church movement that integrates both ecumenical and evangelical movements.

The holistic nature of Rhee's ecclesiology is also explicitly disclosed in his effort to integrate both the mission of the church and the mission of God.[33] He distinguishes between the two types of mission: "the mission led by the church, and the mission led by God." For the mission led by today's church he emphasizes the following nine points.[34]

First, the life, cross, resurrection, and parousia of Jesus Christ should be the subject matter of mission.

Second, the mission of the church should always be kerygmatic and evangelical. It is not allowed to negotiate with the listener. Even in evangelism through dialogue, dialogue plays only the role of midwife until the listener accepts the communicated truth.

Third, evangelism is one thing, and social service is another. Church reform movement is not identical with social movements for human rights or democracy.

Fourth, the Bible is the best instrument for preaching and mission. It is only in the Bible, not in any other literature, philosophy, or ideology, that people can realistically listen to the Word of God.

---

[33] Ibid., 475-545.
[34] Ibid., 489-492.

Fifth, as people who have received salvation, we do not aim to make a socialist or a democratic country in which humans become lord and governor; rather, we work for the establishment of God's kingdom, which has already begun. It is the kingdom of God, rather than a socialist or democratic country, that the church should pursue.

Sixth, salvation does not consist in the equal relationship between human beings or the humanization of humanity but in the restoration of the original relationship with God by the forgiveness of sins through the mediation of Christ.

Seventh, the Holy Spirit informs and ensures the certainty of salvation. Some evangelists ask whether one knows the certainty of one's salvation, but this is a wrong question.

Eighth, through evangelism we encourage the listener to repent and enter the community of Christ.

Ninth, the mission of the church should give a theological answer to issues of the times.

After discussing the desirable direction of the mission of the church Rhee then emphasizes the importance of the mission of God. According to him, God works for salvation in many different ways, even if the church and Christians have no idea of them.[35] Fundamentally, the church and the world are not two separate entities. The mission led by the church and the mission led by God are not two separate projects but will finally be united. He maintains that church and world are distinct from each other, but integration of the two is

---

35 Ibid., 494.

possible in terms of the kingdom of God.[36] "The unity of the two is affirmed and accomplished in the dialectical hope for the kingdom of God."[37] He affirmatively quotes from J. M. Lochman: "The kingdom of God is not only the future of the church, but also the future of the world. Therefore, according to the protological and eschatological plan of God's salvation, the church and the world are inseparable."[38]

With regard to the importance of the mission of God, Rhee asserts that the theology of the mission of God should be incorporated into today's ecclesiology and "take the central place" in it.[39] At the same time, Rhee emphasizes human rights as an important issue in the mission of God. Meanwhile, though in his holistic theology Rhee stresses both the mission of God and human rights, he also hopes to make clear that our understanding of human rights should always be grounded upon the theology of Christ's cross. For such a cross-based and kingdom-oriented understanding of human rights is more legitimate than the secular understanding of human rights.[40] Rhee says, "The church should develop this fully theological understanding of human rights and make efforts to protect our human rights ensured by Christ, rather than human rights in the secular sense, whose concept changes from time to time."[41]

Rhee takes a similar approach to the issue of social justice. He

---

[36] Ibid., 495.
[37] Ibid.
[38] Ibid.
[39] Ibid., 496.
[40] Ibid., 500.
[41] Ibid.

believes that the church that neglects the importance of social justice is not a right church. Since the church has the duty to make society into the society of God and the place where divine righteousness, faith and love, and divine will are realized, the church should participate in efforts for social justice.[42] However, according to him, the church should pursue social reform on the basis of the Word of God, rather than philosophical ideology.[43] Rhee says, "The gospel is an absolute justice. Social justice is a relative justice."[44] Social reform on the basis of the Word of God is the genuine reform for the kingdom of God.

Rhee's holistic ecclesiology seeks a harmony between two aspects of the church's task: the vertical aspect related to God and the horizontal aspect related to the world and history. He warns that without the transcendental aspect every effort to establish a welfare society for God's kingdom would necessarily fail. "In the three Scandinavian countries (Sweden, Norway, and Denmark), known as the most ideal social welfare countries in the world in the twentieth century, we hear so many news about suicide, alcohol addiction, and sexual immorality. This is because their social welfare system has focused too much on the material aspect."[45] From this fact he learns that the happiness of humankind does not consist in material richness but in the Word of God. According to him, "As Jesus taught, we ought to establish the true welfare society that provides everyone with both spiritual food and physical food."[46] Such a welfare society without spiritual food is

---

[42] Jong Sung Rhee, *Hangukgyohoeui isanggwa hyeonsil* 「한국교회의 이상과 현실」 [The Ideal and Reality of the Korean Church] (Seoul: Academia Christiana Korea, 2001), 228.

[43] Jong Sung Rhee, *Gyohoeron*, vol. 1., 525.

[44] Ibid.

[45] Ibid., 533.

not a true welfare society. "Every humanistic socialism necessarily fails, since it has no transcendental foundation."[47] Rhee's holistic ecclesiology pursues a welfare society that is firmly grounded upon the transcendental foundation. "We should establish a welfare society led by faithful Christians who have spiritual power under the guidance of the church."[48] According to Rhee's holistic theology, this welfare society is approximate to the kingdom of God. He says, "We should make efforts to build a welfare society until the moment when the kingdom of God will be consummated."[49]

4. Holistic View of History

The holistic orientation of Jong Sung Rhee's theology is also well demonstrated in his holistic view of history. He calls his view of history a holistic one.[50] In his book, *Jongmallon* [Eschatology], Rhee first discusses the strong and weak points of each of six major views of history: namely, metempsychosis, determinism, dualism, a linear view of history and eschatology, centralism, and duplication. According to him, all these views of history have fatal flaws and thus fall short of a right interpretation of history. For instance, the concept of metempsychosis does not suggest the purpose of history or the goal that guides human history; the dualistic view of history, which treats good and

---

[46] Ibid.

[47] Ibid.

[48] Ibid.

[49] Ibid.

[50] Jong Sung Rhee, *Gyohoeron* 『교회론』 [Ecclesiology], vol. 2 (Seoul: The Christian Literature Society of Korea, 1990), 492.

evil equally and assumes that the good god and the evil god are in conflict, does not do justice to the providence of God as the Lord of history; and the deterministic, fatalistic view of history makes humans totally passive beings dominated by others, and discourages them from walking along the way of life and overcoming tragedy for themselves.[51]

According to Rhee, the right view of history should be holistic. The holistic view of history "absorbs everything positive from the six views of history."[52] Rhee describes it as spiral. The spiral view of history is different from the linear view of history, for according to the former history does not develop in a linear way. Rhee says:

> History does not proceed in a linear way, as Cullmann conceived. Not only the history of Israel, but also the history of all humanity does not proceed to the goal of humanity in a linear way. It does not follow the way of metempsychosis, which repeats what is gone, nor the linear way. History from time to time advances and retreats, goes up and down, develops and degenerates. Therefore, one cannot speak of the linear development from creation to parousia with Israel at its center.[53]

According to Rhee, the right view of history is a spiral one. The spiral view of history is holistic because it eliminates the weak points, while absorbing the strong points, of the linear view of history. Ac-

---

[51] Ibid., 427.
[52] Ibid., 492.
[53] Ibid., 448.

cording to the spiral view of history, there is an axle that penetrates all of history, to which a number of spirals are connected. That is, every event in history is connected with divine providence as the axle of history. Rhee says:

> Is it really true that every event in history is connected with divine providence, the axle of history? Our ultimate answer to this question should be "Yes." In appearance God does not directly intervene or command. In some exceptional cases God directly intervenes, but even in those cases only through a third party. However, if one believes that divine providence is the original cause of all of them, then every event in history is ultimately connected with God. The doctrine of divine omniscience also supports this conclusion.[54]

Even if every event in history is ultimately connected with God, according to Rhee's spiral view of history, not every event is in equal distance from the axle of history, or divine providence. Some events are closer to divine providence, while others are farther from it. In other words, some circles are closer to divine providence as the axle of history, while other circles are farther from it. According to the spiral view of history, a number of circles connected with God are moving toward the goal of history. With regard to the distance from divine providence as the axle of history, Rhee says:

---

[54] Ibid., 486.

In substance, some events are closer to divine will, while others are farther from it. With this regard the standard of judgment is the distance from divine attributes. That is, God is righteous. Then, a righteous event is closer to divine providence, while an unrighteous event is farther from it. Therefore, if one describes each event in history as a circle, there are different sizes of circles. Whether they are small or large, all of them are connected with the axle of history and thus cannot deviate from the reign of God.[55]

According to Rhee's spiral view of history, which describes history as a number of spiral circles surrounding the axle of history, bigger circles refer to events that take place farther from divine will and smaller circles refer to events that take place closer to divine will. According to Rhee, every part of history, whether big or small, is connected with the ultimate and transcendental dimension—namely, God.

This spiral view of history is distinct from the concept of metempsychosis, for the former has a clear goal of history in view. With regard to the goal of history Rhee's holistic theology has the following characteristics.

1) There is One History

Rhee speaks of the unity of history. History has one origin and one purpose, and is guided by the providence of God.[56] "Every history has the one and same goal. In the history of some civilizations and

---

[55] Ibid., 487.

nations one sometimes finds such phenomena as atheism and indulgence, but the omnipotent God governs all of them toward the end of history through divine providence."[57] No nation or civilization or history can escape from the providence of this God.

2) God as the Only Lord of History

According to Rhee, the Lord of history is Yahweh. Marxists refer to the labor class as the primary subject of history. But this is not true. Activists in the minjung movement are also wrong when they think of minjung as the subject of history. According to Rhee, the only Lord of history is God, and Jesus Christ is "the original cause, the efficient cause, and the final cause."[58] History moves toward the parousia of Jesus Christ, and God will finally consummate history and make the new heaven and the new earth.

3) Kingdom of God as the Final Goal of History

Rhee's holistic theology aims at the kingdom of God. Thus, it is open to God's kingdom. According to his holistic view of history, the final goal of history is the kingdom of God. And this kingdom of God is not identical with the secular utopia. For the secular utopia as a human ideal is the world established by humans. As the story of the Tower of Babel tells us, such a project necessarily fails. The kingdom of God as the end of history is established by God, who is the only Lord of history.

---

[56] Ibid., 495.
[57] Ibid., 495-496.
[58] Ibid., 500.

Rhee's reference to the kingdom of God as the goal of history is related to his view of history that every event in the world is connected with the goal of history. Rhee objects to dualism of the sacred and the profane as well as dualism of secular history and salvation history, because everything is open and related to the kingdom of God.

4) History and Hope for God's Salvation

Since the providence of God who wills to save the world penetrates the center of history, Rhee believes that history is fundamentally grounded upon hope. Rhee objects to the dualistic view of history that this world is a battlefield between the good god and the evil god. It is true that there is confusion, war, and tragedy in the world; nonetheless, the pessimistic view of history is wrong because God governs and saves history. Rhee objects to the pessimistic view of history and instead stressed hope for history. He argued for Christ's ultimate victory in history.

III
Rhee's Holistic Theology and the Theology of PUTS

1. Hyung Ryong Park's Fundamentalist Theology and Jong Sung Rhee's Holistic Theology

For the past one hundred years what is now Presbyterian University and Theological Seminary (PUTS) brought forth two preeminent systematic theologians: Hyung Ryong Park and Jong Sung Rhee. They do not simply represent systematic theology but also the entire theology of the Korean Presbyterian Church. Though both of them espoused orthodox theology, there is a great gap between them, which corresponds to the theological gap between two major denominations of the Korean Presbyterian Church today: the Presbyterian Church of Korea (PCK, Tonghap) and the General Assembly of the Presbyterian Church in Korea (GAPCK, Hapdong).

1) Hyung Ryong Park's Conservative Fundamentalist Theology

Until Namsan Presbyterian Seminary was divided in two (currently PUTS and Chongsin University) in 1959, the theology of the Presbyterian Seminary had been dominated by Park's conservative fundamentalist theology. Even after the division in 1959 Park's conservative fundamentalist theology continued to influence the GAPCK, so that the theology of the GAPCK is still under the influence of Park's theology even in the twenty-first century.

Park's conservative fundamentalist theology emphasizes first of all the inerrancy of the Bible. In his teaching Park maintains that the Bible has no error, whether scientific, historical, or moral. Even in the quotations and reports of the Bible one cannot find any error. Around the time when Princeton Theological Seminary was divided in 1929, fundamentalist theologians such as Grasham Machen and Cornelius van Til, emphasized this doctrine of biblical inerrancy, which Park accepted and taught in Korea. Since Park was following Machen's theology, he was often called "Machen of Korea."

The second feature of Park's theology is that the task of the church is understood primarily as saving souls. Park denied that the kingdom of God will be established on earth. According to him, "the kingdom of God is an otherworldly concept."[59] The kingdom of God "does not refer to a new social order that will be realized by the penetration of the Spirit of Christ and through human, external means like good law, civilization, education, and social reform. It refers to the reign of God in which the mind of God's people is established and salvation is freely granted to them."[60] For this reason, he believed that all the political, economic, and cultural efforts to establish the kingdom of God on earth are meaningless. Thus, the duty of the church is "to proclaim and witness to the Word of God."[61] And the gospel is concerned primarily with individual salvation, rather than social salvation.

Park's theology, as discussed above, is quite contrasted with that of Jae-Jun Kim , the father of the theology of the Presbyterian Church in the Republic of Korea (PROK), whom Park managed to drive out of the Presbyterian Church of Korea (PCK) in 1953.[62] Jae-Jun Kim recognized errors and inconsistencies in the Bible and affirmed the value of biblical criticism. Also, Kim stressed the importance of the church's social and political responsibilities. Later Kim became the father of historically responsible theology in Korea. It was Kim's theol-

---

[59] Hyung Ryong Park, *Gyohoesinhak*『교회신학』[Church Theology], vol. 4 (Seoul: Korean Institute of Christian Education, 1977), 50.

[60] Ibid.

[61] Ibid., 192.

[62] Concerning the theological debates between Hyung Ryong Park and Jae-Jun Kim, cf. Bong-Rang Park, *Sinhagui haebang*『신학의 해방』[Liberation of Theology] (Seoul: The Christian Literature Society of Korea, 1991), 45-96.

ogy, not Park's, that undergirded the church's holy protest against the Yushin military dictatorship in the 1970s. For this reason the PROK, under the influence of Kim's theology, produced a number of church leaders who committed themselves to the democracy movement, but the GAPCK, under the influence of Park's theology, produced many people who accommodated themselves to the dictatorship.

Meanwhile, the GAPCK, under the influence of Park's theology, was very good at evangelism that aimed to increase the number of churches. In other words, the strong and weak points of Park's theology are clearly disclosed in churches that were under his theological influence. Park's evangelism-centered theology produced evangelism-centered churches and brought about church growth.

Another important aspect of Park's theology is his historical premillenarianism. Though distinct from dispensational premillenarianism, historical premillenarianism, due to its literal interpretation of the Book of Revelation, provided the Korean church with a theological basis for irrecoverable confusions related to eschatology. Also, it produced a pessimistic view of history as being under the power of the devil and headed toward a catastrophic end. This pessimistic view of history made people abandon any will to reform and prevented the church from becoming historically responsible.

2) Jong Sung Rhee's Holistic Theology

In the 1960s, what is now Presbyterian University and Theological Seminary (PUTS) constructed a new building in Gwangnaru and began the new era of Gwangnaru. Also, another preeminent systematic theologian, Jong Sung Rhee, joined the school, which brought about a great theological change within it. While working as an academic dean for four years and as a dean for twelve years, Rhee made a significant contribution to transform the theology of the school. Above all, he broadened the theological horizon of the school.

The fundamental difference between the theologies of Hyung Ryong Park and Jong Sung Rhee consists in their breadth and width. Rhee's theology was often compared to an encyclopedia. His theology was broad enough to know many different theologies with regard to their respective strong and weak points. For this reason he did not like Park's theology. He introduced theological students to various theologies in the world and opened their eyes to see better theologies than Park's conservative fundamentalism. He taught not only Augustine, John Calvin, Louis Berkhof, but also Karl Barth, Emil Brunner, Wolfhart Pannenberg, Jürgen Moltmann, Paul Tillich, Dietrich Bonhoeffer, and Richard Niebuhr.

Rhee defined his own theology as a biblical and evangelical theology. This description discloses a characteristic aspect of his theology, though the expression itself should be understood in relation to the complex reality of church politics and theological controversy within the PCK. Rhee's theology was a biblical theology based upon the Bible. Though he has a negative view concerning the doctrine of literal inerrancy of the Bible, he never doubted that the Bible is the Word of God. He insisted that "even if human errors are found in the Bible, no one can deny the Word of God contained in it."[63] Also, he argued, the Bible should be the standard and guide of Christian theology, be-

---

[63] Jong Sung Rhee, *Sinhakseoron* [Introduction to Theology], 208.

cause the authors wrote the Bible by the inspiration of God, not arbitrarily.[64]

In addition, Rhee's theology was an evangelical theology. He emphasized the importance of the gospel that the Reformers rediscovered. He never explicitly affirmed the possibility of salvation in other religions. Meanwhile, the biblical and evangelical theology he espoused was a Reformed theology rooted in the theology of John Calvin. He redefined the biblical and evangelical theology as the evangelical theology grounded in Calvin's theology. While developing a theology rooted in the Bible and the gospel, he positively appropriated theological ideas of Reformed theologians—including Calvin, Barth, Brunner, G. C. Berkouwer, and H. Berkhof—and made them into the foundation of his own theology. In this sense his theology reflects the broad spectrum of the Reformed theological tradition. In this way Rhee contributed to develop PUTS' Reformed theology into a comprehensive Reformed theology oriented toward holistic theology.

In addition to their views of the Bible and theological breadth, another significant difference between the theologies of Park and Rhee consists in their theological ideas. First of all, their views of history are quite different. Park has basically a pessimistic view of history, whereas Rhee has a hopeful view of history. In the discussion of eschatology Rhee mentioned different views of history and then advocated the hopeful view of history. However strong the power of evil and death is, Rhee believed, the incarnation would finally win the victory.[65] Rhee's hopeful view of history is almost in agreement with

---

[64] Ibid.

[65] Jong Sung Rhee, *Jongmallon* [Eschatology], vol. 2, 208-232.

those of H. Berkhof, G. C. Berkouwer, Jürgen Moltmann, and J. M. Lochman.

The final remarkable difference in the theologies of Park and Rhee lies in their understanding of the mission of the church. Rhee positively evaluates the concept of the mission of God, which is not found in Park's theology,[66] and stresses the church's social responsibility. "The church should contribute to make a just society by proclaiming righteousness."[67] "The church has the task to make a holy society, as John Wesley claimed."[68] Furthermore, Rhee argued that we are commanded to affirm the lordship of Christ not only in our private life but also in the public area—namely, in the realms of politics and economy.

In this way Rhee restated for the twenty-first century what Calvin taught about the sovereignty of God over all the realms of the world. According to Rhee, the reign of God should be explicitly manifested not only in politics and economy but also in culture. He spoke highly of the legacy of Calvinists who affirmed the value of culture and contributed to the development and promotion of Christian culture.[69]

2. Yi-Tae Kim's "Theology Standing at the Center"

On the eightieth anniversary of PUTS in May 1981 Yi-Tae Kim

---

[66] Jong Sung Rhee, *Jongmallon* [Eschatology], vol. 1, 493-545.
[67] Ibid., 519.
[68] Ibid., 524.
[69] Ibid., 537.

gave a lecture entitled "The Location and Features of the Theology of PUTS" in which Kim described PUTS' theology as "theology standing at the center."[70] The theology standing at the center that Kim advocates is, in its content, almost identical with Jong Sung Rhee's holistic theology, and thus can be regarded as another expression of holistic theology.

Yi-Tae Kim mentions three major features of the theology standing at the center: "comprehensive," "in tension," and "progressive rather than sensational." By "comprehensive" Kim means that theology standing at the center is not a narrow theology but a broad theology. Kim says, "theology standing at the center should absorb the river of tradition, which has a long history; therefore, it should be comprehensive in nature."[71] Also, theology standing at the center is a theology "at the center of biblical teaching," for while recognizing that there are different teachings in the Bible and they are not uniform but complex and diverse, it accepts and digests them as a whole.[72]

By "in tension" Yi-Tae Kim means that theology standing at the center is, first of all, in tension between tradition and renovation. "The desirable theology is one that always remains in tension between tradition and renovation."[73] Kim continues to say:

When the tension is loosened or broken, such theology may adhere only to tradition, be solidified in the name of

---

[70] Late Yi-Tae Kim's Writings Publication Committee (ed.), *Jungsime seoneun sinhak* 『중심에 서는 신학』 [Theology Standing at the Center] (Seoul: PUTS Press, 1994), 209-240.

[71] Ibid., 222.

[72] Ibid.

[73] Ibid., 212

so-called conservatism, degenerate into exclusive dogmatism, and finally make itself distanced from the gospel that makes people free and alive. On the contrary, theology that avoids this tension may degenerate in the name of so-called progressivism into liberal theology of opportunistic relativism that lacks any standard.[74]

In short, theology standing at the center is one that makes harmony between tradition and renovation, while not resolving the tension between them. The important thing is that here the center "does not refer to the arithmetical mean which is neither left nor right."[75] By the center Yi-Tae Kim means "the great way of the truth that the church has taught for two thousand years, comparable to the concept of the middle way (Jung-yong) in Eastern thought."[76] This great way of the truth may look sometimes left and other times right, but the point is that theology should stand at the center from the perspective of the truth of the comprehensive gospel as taught in the Bible.

By "progressive rather than sensational" Yi-Tae Kim means that PUTS' theology pursues a reliable and responsible theology. According to Kim, when someone argues that the Tan-gun mythology is a model of Christian trinitarian theology, then she or he may provoke sensation and become famous for that. However, such an argument destroys the Christian truth and lets the church fall into confusion. Thus, he says, the important thing is not to make an unprecedented

---

[74] Ibid.
[75] Ibid., 226.
[76] Ibid.,

theological argument but to walk along the great way of the truth by rediscovering the forgotten truth and correcting what needs to be corrected in the tension between tradition and renovation.

Yi-Tae Kim's theology standing at the center as discussed above is very similar to Jong Sung Rhee's holistic theology. Just as Rhee pointed out the narrowness of both theologies that focus on either the divinity or the humanity of Christ, Kim criticizes one-sided theologies that fail to endure the tension between the true divinity and the true humanity (*vere deus, vere homo*).[77] The same logic applies to their view of the Bible. Both Rhee and Kim object to one-sided theologies that resolve the tension between the divine and human nature of the Bible.

3. PUTS' Holistic Theology Today

The holistic orientation of PUTS' theology was officially announced in the PUTS Faculty Committee Theological Manifesto in 1985. Hyung Ki Rhee prepared the draft, which was then revised in the Faculty Seminar. The final document was officially approved by the Faculty Committee presided by Chang-Whan Park. The so-called PUTS Theological Manifesto was officially published in *Gidokgongbo* 「기독공보」 [Christian Information], the official weekly newspaper of the Presbyterian Church of Korea (PCK), on September 14, 1985. The manifesto contained seven theses:

---

[77] Ibid., 228.

Thesis 1: Our theology is evangelical and biblical.

Thesis 2: Our theology is reformed and ecumenical.

Thesis 3: Our theology serves the church and the kingdom of God.

Thesis 4: Our theology supports evangelism and social-historical participation.

Thesis 5: The field of our theology is Korea, Asia, and the global world.

Thesis 6: Our theology ought to respond to current social issues.

Thesis 7: Our theology is dialogical.

As these theses make clear, PUTS' theology takes seriously both evangelism and social-historical responsibility, integrates both ecumenical and evangelical theology, and seeks to walk along the great road of the right biblical theology. In short, it pursues holistic theology. In order to develop holistic theology, according to the second proposition of the manifesto, "patristic theology, medieval theology, Reformation theology, Protestant Orthodox theology in the seventeenth century, Pietistic theology, liberal theology in the nineteenth century, contemporary Catholic theology, Greek and Russian Orthodox theology, and all of the Protestant theologies in the late twentieth century" are critically appropriated for a biblically-grounded constructive and creative theology. This statement reflects and makes explicit the method of Rhee's holistic theology.

In 2002 the PUTS Faculty Committee announced a new manifesto for the twenty-first century, the so-called PUTS Manifesto for

Theological Education. In its preamble the manifesto defines the gospel of God's kingdom as the gospel of salvation of the world and of the entire creation and then makes clear that PUTS aims to proclaim this gospel of the kingdom of God. "The gospel of the kingdom of God as fully revealed in Jesus Christ is the whole gospel concerning the salvation of humanity, society, and the entire creation." "Through this gospel the Holy Spirit aims to save humanity, the world, and the life of the Earth, which are currently under the shadow of chaos, crisis, and death." Moreover, this manifesto affirms that the task of the church is to establish the kingdom of God, that the gospel should not be reduced to an anthropocentric idea but cover the entire creation, and that the perichoretic life of the triune God is the divine model of life that can solve global conflicts in the twenty-first century. In short, the PUTS Manifesto for Theological Education is also oriented toward holistic theology.

In the final analysis, holistic theology, which began to take root in the theological soil of PUTS by Jong Sung Rhee, is now growing into a great trunk around the turn of the century. PUTS' theology does not exclude Pentecostal theology, nor evangelical theology, nor ecumenical theology, nor any other theology. While studying the broad spectrum of global theology, it seeks to develop holistic theology in light of Jesus Christ and the Bible.

Chapter 3

Holistic Ecclesiology

Myung Yong Kim

Behind the division of the church there are both theological and non-theological reasons. Theological factors undergirded the division of the global church in the twentieth century. Around the turn of the century, however, we see those once divided churches coming closer to one another, because theological conflicts among them concerning the purpose and task of the church have been gradually dissolved. Still, the theological gap between those divided churches is not to be simply dismissed. In this situation the theological task to develop holistic ecclesiology is of essential significance in overcoming the division and conflict within the global church. Hence, I propose a few essential theological spirits for the development of holistic ecclesiology.

I

Global Church, Once Divided and Now Coming Together

1. Theological Differences and Division of Global Church

In the late twentieth century, roughly speaking, the global church was divided into two parties: one that supported the ecumenical movement and the other that objected to it and instead participated in the evangelical movement. The Korean church was also divided into two camps. The one participated in the National Council of Churches in Korea (NCCK), which supported the ecumenical movement, while the other participated in the Christian Council of Korea (CCK), which was critical of the NCCK.

There are several reasons for the division of the global church in the late twentieth century, but I find different theological spirits at its foundation. In the 1952 International Missionary Conference in Willingen a new theology of mission was proposed. Johannes C. Hoekendijk, the secretary of the Department of Evangelism of the WCC at that time, defined the old view of mission as church-centric and then severely criticized it. Hoekendijk claimed that the subject of mission is not the church but God and that the church is simply an instrument of God's saving work in the world. And he continued to argue that the goal of God's missionary work is to transform this world to the world of *shalom*, the concept of which is much broader than that of individual salvation through evangelism. The world of *shalom* refers to the world filled with justice, wholeness, harmony, and peace; and the church is an instrument that God commissioned to establish this new world.

In the 1968 Assembly in Uppsala the concept of the *missio dei* came to represent the WCC's theology of mission. Mission is in essence the mission of God, and its goal is to do away with injustice and restore humanity by ensuring justice, freedom, human rights, and human dignity. Since the Uppsala Assembly the WCC made explicit that the goal of the church is humanization and establishment of a just and peaceful world. In the 1973 Conference in Bangkok, whose theme was "Salvation Today," the WCC developed a comprehensive understanding of salvation. To put it briefly, salvation does not refer only to deliverance of individuals from sin, curse, and eternal punishment through Jesus Christ, but includes also liberation from all kinds of injustice and oppression in political, economic, social, and cultural realms; therefore, the church's social participation and responsibility are naturally expected.

As the WCC developed a new theology of mission and a new understanding of salvation, it was faced with considerable opposition. One source of opposition was the Frankfurt Declaration of European evangelical theologians in 1970. German missiologist Peter Bayerhaus was a leading figure. This declaration objected fiercely to the WCC's theology of the *missio dei*. Instead, it defined mission as proclaiming the gospel of Jesus Christ, letting people know and believe in Jesus Christ, saving souls, and planting and growing churches. It was also very critical of the Catholic idea of anonymous Christians. It maintained that there is no salvation without explicit faith in Jesus Christ.

The International Congress on World Evangelization in Lausanne in 1974 clearly showed that the global church was divided into two. The Lausanne Congress objected to the theology of the 1973 Conference of the WCC in Bangkok. Despite the necessity of the church's participation in issues of social justice, the Lausanne Covenant declared that saving souls takes precedence over it. Since the 1974 Lausanne Congress the global church was divided into two. Though a majority of the global church participated in the WCC, evangelical churches were also a great power.

The theological debate that divided the global church in the 1970s may be summarized as follows: salvation of souls or salvation of society? Both parties recognized that the two are interconnected. But their positions diverged concerning which of the two issues should be regarded as the essential task of the church. These divergent theological spirits were dividing the global church.

2. "The Whole Gospel" and the Global Church Moves Closer Together

In the Frankfurt Declaration of 1970 evangelical Christians expressed little interest in the church's social responsibility. But the Lausanne Covenant in 1974 declared that both evangelism and social participation are the Christian duty, though the former claims precedence over the latter (Part V). In other words, evangelical Christians too began to recognize the importance of social participation. In 1989 evangelicals around the world gathered again in Manila for the so-called Lausanne II, in which they advocated for the importance of "the whole gospel." By the whole gospel they meant, first of all, the uniqueness and finality of Jesus Christ—i.e., there is no other savior than Jesus Christ. Since we do not have any convincing evidence that there is also a possibility of salvation in other religions, according to the Manila Manifesto, the most important thing is to proclaim the gospel of Jesus Christ to all people around the world, and every church should cooperate and work toward this goal.

The Manila Manifesto defines the whole gospel as "the good news of God's salvation from the power of evil, the establishment of his eternal kingdom and his final victory over everything which defies his purpose" (preface to Part II). In this way the Manifesto affirms the importance of those tasks to abolish evil and to establish God's kingdom. This is very close to the gospel as understood in the holistic theology. Also, the Manifesto identified the evils to be denounced as "institutionalized violence, political corruption, all forms of exploitation of people and of the earth, the undermining of the family, abortion on demand, drug trafficking, and the abuse of human rights." Furthermore, with emphasis on the proclamation and establishment of God's kingdom of justice and peace, it asked for our praxis to abolish structural evil as well as personal evil.

Meanwhile, in the Nairobi Assembly in 1975 the WCC accepted the strong request of evangelical churches and made explicit the importance of evangelism in its official statement. In this vein it coined the phrase "the whole gospel" to represent the importance of both evangelism and the establishment of God's kingdom depicted as the world of *shalom*. In the Melbourne Conference in 1980 holistic mission was emphasized. The Melbourne Conference consciously reoriented the stream from the Bangkok Conference, though it was still in continuity with it. It explicitly stressed the importance of calling on the name of Jesus. Fourteen years after the WCC adopted the phrase "the whole gospel" in the Nairobi Assembly in 1975, evangelical Christians adopted the same expression in the Manila Congress in 1989. Not only in the expression, but also in its meaning, the WCC and evangelicals came very close to each other concerning the scope covered by the whole gospel, though there still remained a difference in emphasis and priority.

Holistic theology is grounded in the whole gospel; and the church based upon holistic theology proclaims the whole gospel. The whole gospel refers to the uniqueness and finality of Jesus Christ, and the salvation that the whole gospel proclaims covers humanity, society, and all of creation. According to holistic ecclesiology, both salvation of souls and salvation of the world are equally important, while in a given situation one may claim precedence over the other.

II
Foundations for Holistic Ecclesiology

1. Love of God and Love of Neighbors as the Essence of Biblical Teaching

Matthew 22:34-40 is an important biblical text for holistic ecclesiology.

Hearing that Jesus had silenced the Sadducees, the Pharisees got together. One of them, an expert in the law, tested him with this question: "Teacher, which is the greatest commandment in the Law?" Jesus replied: " 'Love the Lord your God with all your heart and with all your soul and with all your mind.' This is the first and greatest commandment. And the second is like it: 'Love your neighbor as yourself.' All the Law and the Prophets hang on these two commandments."

Jesus summarizes the teachings of the Law and prophets as love of God and love of neighbors. Jesus' teaching is also summarized as love of God and love of neighbors. John Calvin too taught that the essence of Christian piety is love of God and love of neighbors.

The important thing is that love of God and love of neighbors, taught by Jesus and Calvin, lay important theological foundations for holistic ecclesiology. Love of God refers to the relationship between God and humanity. This concerns the vertical dimension of the task of the church. Love of neighbors refers to responsibility for neighbors, history, and the world. This concerns the horizontal dimension of the task of the church. Evangelical churches emphasize the resolution of the problem of human sin, explicit knowledge of Jesus Christ, and the glory of God as the ultimate goal, all of which concern the vertical relationship between God and humanity. Evangelical churches in Korea tended to regard those works related to the vertical relationship between God and humanity as the church's spiritual tasks, while those works related to neighbors, history, and the world as the church's worldly tasks. This is not a right attitude, because just as the church's vertical task related to love of God is a spiritual task, so is the church's responsibility for neighbors, history, and the world that is related to love of neighbors. The biblical (and Jesus') teaching concerning love of God and love of neighbors provides an important foundation on which one can holistically integrate evangelical ecclesiology that focuses on resolution of the problem of sin obstructing the relationship between God and humanity and ecumenical ecclesiology that stresses responsibility for neighbors, history, and the world as represented by the phrase "Justice, Peace, and the Integrity of Creation" (JPIC).

2. Kingdom of God in Heaven and Kingdom of God Established in the World

In the past evangelical churches put their emphasis on saving human souls. Thus, they insisted that the church should function as an ark of salvation to save souls and send them to heaven. The primary task of the church is to save unbelieving souls. Unbelieving souls are destined to perish. The kingdom of God in heaven is a resting place for believing souls. In order to enter the kingdom of God in heaven explicit faith in Jesus Christ is required. Hence, the church should make every effort to save unbelieving souls and to proclaim the gospel of Jesus Christ to the end of the world.

The crucial problem of this ecclesiology is that it neglects Christian responsibility for the world and history. No one can condemn evangelical churches which make efforts for saving souls, produce many new believers, and teach them hope for the kingdom of God in heaven. In this regard they are praiseworthy. However, their neglect of Christian responsibility for the world and history is a serious problem. The primary reason in which evangelical churches neglect social and historical responsibility is that they have an unclear hope for the kingdom of God that will be established in history. A great number of evangelical Christians have a pessimistic view of history, and thus believe that it is fundamentally impossible to transform history and establish God's kingdom in history. This pessimistic view of history necessarily weakens the idea of God's kingdom that will be established in the world and discourages Christian efforts to establish the kingdom of God.

According to the Bible, the kingdom of God should come to earth, and the new heavens and the new earth should be built up. While the kingdom of God finally comes at the end of history, it should also keep growing on earth. The kingdom of God is found not only in heaven where the triune God dwells, but also in human flesh in which God's love and power drive out evil spirits and heal sickness and also in places that the Holy Spirit fills with love, joy, and peace. The kingdom of God continues to grow like a mustard seed. Just as a yeast raises the whole bread, the kingdom of God transforms the whole world. While the kingdom of God is a divine gift that will be given at the end of history, it is also the responsibility and duty of God's people to seek to establish God's kingdom in history. For this reason Jesus taught his followers to "seek first God's kingdom and righteousness" (Matt. 6:33) and commanded them to pray and work for the coming of God's kingdom and the realization of God's will in the world.

The fact that the Bible mentions not only God's kingdom in heaven but also God's kingdom established on earth is extremely significant for holistic ecclesiology. Liberal theology of the nineteenth century rightly grasped the historical dimension of God's kingdom when it emphasized that God's kingdom should be established in history, though it failed to consider the seriousness of the evil that is at work in history. Also, old evangelical churches rightly recognized the importance of God's kingdom in heaven and individual salvation, though they failed to recognize the kingdom of God that should be established in history. Holistic ecclesiology affirms that each of them has a legitimate biblical foundation and seeks to integrate them.

3. God of the Poor and God Revealed in the Cross

One of the false ideas that prevails in the Korean church today is the idea that the God of the poor is not identical with the God revealed in the cross. Conservative Christians often distance themselves from people who describe God as the God of the poor, while accusing the latter of having a radical or dangerous faith under the influence of liberation theology or minjung theology. A pastor who frequently preaches and writes about the God of the poor is hardly requested by a conservative church.

However, the point is that the Bible explicitly describes God as the God of the poor. According to the Old Testament scholar In-Seok Seo, in the Old Testament the law defined the rights of the poor, prophets defended the poor, and holy writings were songs of the poor.

Psalms 68:5 declares that the heavenly God is the father of orphans and the judge for widows.

> When you reap the harvest of your land, do not reap to the very edges of your field or gather the gleanings of your harvest. Do not go over your vineyard a second time or pick up the grapes that have fallen. Leave them for the poor and the alien. I am the LORD your God. (Lev. 19:9-10)

The divine will to save the poor and protect their rights is engraved in the Old Testament law. In addition, in the prophecies of the Old Testament, one more often than not hears the voice of God who demands justice for the poor:

> The LORD enters into judgment against the elders and leaders of his people: "It is you who have ruined my vineyard; the plunder from the poor is in your houses. What do you mean by crushing my people and grinding the faces of the poor?" declares the Lord, the LORD Almighty. (Isa. 3:14-15)

> Learn to do right! Seek justice, encourage the oppressed. Defend the cause of the fatherless, plead the case of the widow. (Isa. 1:17)

The God of the poor who seeks to save the poor is most explicitly revealed in the life and ministry of Jesus Christ as portrayed in the New Testament. In the Parable of the Sheep and the Goats (Matt. 25:31-46) Jesus says that the good work done to the hungry and the thirsty is done to the Lord, and in the Parable of the Good Samaritan (Luke 10:25-37) we read the same message. The point of the former parable is that people who have done good to one of "the least" will enter eternal life, while the point of the latter is that people who love their neighbors like the good Samaritan in the parable can enter into eternal life. Jesus mentioned the Parable of the Good Samaritan in response to a question from an expert in the law, who asked, "What should I do to inherit eternal life?" Many conservative Christians regard service for the poor as a worldly work, but Jesus interpreted it in terms of eternal life.

The God who reveals Godself in the cross is the same as the God of the poor. The cross is an event of God's radical grace, through which God saves humanity who is possessed by poverty, sickness, darkness, and the power of sin and death. The event of the cross is a saving event that has a cosmic dimension. According to Jürgen Moltmann, the cross is a cosmic event of God's salvation through which God wills to save humanity and the entire creation from the power of darkness and death, while the preferential option for the poor is a concrete event of God's salvation in history. According to Pentecostal Christians, on the cross Jesus took upon himself our sickness, poverty, sins, shame, and death in our place. They believe that Jesus' public ministry of healing the sick and feeding the poor and his redemptive death on the cross are not two events but one with the same nature. The God who in the cosmos destroyed the root of human agony on the cross is the God who in history saves people who are suffering in their concrete lives from severe poverty and affliction.

Therefore, it is wrong to distinguish between the God revealed in the cross and the God of the poor and then to regard only the former as the God of the gospel, while dismissing the latter as having nothing to do with the gospel. Such an idea contradicts biblical teaching. God wills to save both humanity and creation in groaning. The event of the cross represents the cosmic dimension of God's gracious saving work, whereas the same God works in our concrete history to save the poor. Hence, the church that proclaims the gospel of the cross should participate in God's work to save the poor.

4. The Threefold Office of Christ and the Unity of the Church

Jong Sung Rhee discerns two streams within the Korean Presbyterian Church.[1] Churches in the first stream have a dualistic worldview. In ministry they focus on saving individual souls, while concerning social or national works they tend to obey authority. Meanwhile, churches in the second stream assume that the church should take responsibility for society and the human race. Thus, Christians should engage themselves actively in social issues. By developing social policies, promoting social welfare, and participating in social actions, the church should function as the light and salt of the world.

According to Jong Sung Rhee, the Presbyterian Church of Korea

---

[1] Jong Sung Rhee, *Hangukgyohoeui hyeonsilgwa isang* 『한국교회의 현실과 이상』 [The Reality and Idea of Korean Church], 211-212.

(PCK) has not chosen either of the two streams but remained critical towards both of them. One may unduly criticize that this is an opportunistic attitude. The church is the body of Christ that inherits the threefold office of Jesus Christ as prophet, priest, and king. Thus, Rhee argues, the church should carry out all three functions in society. To be specific, as a prophet she should proclaim the Word of God; as a priest she should promote peace; and as a king she should fight against every injustice and unrighteousness until the day of the final victory. According to Rhee, proclaiming the gospel, saving souls, and establishing social justice are all connected and intertwined in the ministry of the one person Jesus Christ. With the idea of Christ's threefold office Rhee suggests a theological vision in which Korean Presbyterian churches, now divided, may be united again.

From the perspective of holistic theology the threefold office of Christ implies that the Korean church should be united. Churches that stresses saving souls are inclined to the priestly office of Christ. With their focus on the atoning death of Christ they take most seriously the problem of sin obstructing the relationship between God and humanity, which Christ resolved by his atoning death as the high priest. Church ministry for establishment of social justice has much to do with the kingly office of Christ. To drive evil and the devil out of the world is an important aspect of Christ's kingly reign. Christ's kingly reign is an essential concept in the biblical witness to the kingdom of God. Christ's prophetic office is concerned with proclamation of the gospel of God's kingdom. The gospel of the kingdom of God is not just the good news of forgiveness of sins, but also the good news for the poor concerning the new world of justice and peace. For this reason the division between soul-centered and social-justice-centered churches is tantamount to tearing apart the one person who is Jesus Christ. It is wrong to look only at any one aspect of Christ and overlook the others.

5. Individuals and Social Structure Possessed by the Power of the Devil

Is it personal change or structural transformation that should take precedence for the realization of God's reign in the world? There has been much debate about this either-or question, but in vain. In order to make God's reign realized in the world we should make efforts not only to change individuals, but also to transform the structure of the world. According to Jürgen Moltmann, while individuals affect society, society also affects individuals. While transformed individuals may change social structures, evil social structures may transform individuals into an instrument of evil.

The theology and ministry of evangelical Christians overall put more emphasis on individuals' conversion and transformation. Many of them often raise a counter-question: is it not individuals, rather than social structure, that convert? Since social structure is incapable of repentance, they argue, the ministry of the church should focus on the conversion and transformation of individuals. And social change takes place when transformed individuals bring their renewed ideas to action within the society. In short, individual change takes precedence, and social change then follows.

However, this evangelical perspective is far from holistic. Due to its one-sided narrowness it does not grasp the whole, but only part of it. Think of one of the greatest events in the twentieth century, the Second World War. All of the German people were Christians. But once Adolf Hitler gave an order, they became killing machines and took shots at their neighboring countries. No German soldier could dare to resist Hitler's order. According to John 8:44, the devil is a murderer. Behind the history of murder, war, and death that take place all around the world the devil is at work.

It should be noted that not only individuals but also the structure of the world are possessed by the devil. Not only in the political and economic structures of the world, but also in the evil culture of the world and in atheistic ideology the spirit of evil is at work. The devil is the power over the world. According to the Book of Revelation, the Emperor of Rome and the Roman Empire ruled by him are the harlot and the power of the devil.

Today public education in Korea is dominated by atheistic ideology. The government does not allow science textbooks written from the perspective of creation, because it is regarded as espousing a particular ideology. Meanwhile, only such science textbooks written from the atheistic perspective are considered as objective and rational. As a consequence, the more children learn about science, the more deeply they are convinced of atheism and finally leave the church. John 8:44 says that the devil is a liar; and according to 1 Timothy 4:1, the devil is a deceiving spirit. As a deceiving spirit the devil is at work behind atheistic ideology that denies the existence of God the creator. By means of this ideology the devil convinces people of atheism and deprives them of a worshipping heart.

In the name of communist ideology communists slaughtered many innocent people. Possessed by the communist theory of hatred-based revolution, a number of young people filled with a sense of justice hated and executed capitalists, landlords, property owners, and religious people. What is at work behind this murder and hatred? The devil as the spirit of hatred and murder is at work.

On September 11, 2001, terrorists from al-Qaeda, which was led by Osama bin Laden, hijacked aircrafts and flew them into the Twin Towers of the World Trade Center in New York City. What is at work behind the structure of deep hatred between the United States and the Arabic world which resulted in this horrible terror? Not until the structure of hatred between them is broken down will the continuing terrorism of suicide bombing cease. The devil propagates distorted ideas and ideologies among different races, cultures, and religions. He also promotes unjust economic order based upon national interests and supports oppressive governments that commit murder. In this way the devil fosters hatred in the world and keeps the history of war, murder, and death continuing.

In order to make God's reign realized in the world, the church should drive out not only the power of evil that possesses humanity, but also the power of the devil that is at work in politics, economics, military system, ideology, and culture. The problem of individual and structural evil is not an issue of either-or. The church should make efforts not only to save individuals from the power of evil, but also to transform the order of the world according the divine will. This is the direction that holistic ecclesiology pursues.

6. The Spirit's Holistic Activities for Individual and Social Salvation[2]

The Holy Spirit is the One who establishes the kingdom of God. In order to establish God's kingdom the Spirit acts first of all to save individuals. "No one can say, 'Jesus is Lord,' except by the Holy Spirit" (1 Cor. 12:3). It is the work of the Spirit to help us know who Jesus is and thus confess that Jesus is the Son of God and our Savior. It is only by the Spirit that we call God "Abba, our Father." The Holy Spirit calls unbelievers to faith in Jesus Christ and creates the people of God who know God and call God "Abba Father." As God's people the church is a community created by the Holy Spirit.

The Holy Spirit enables the church as the people of God to proclaim the gospel: "you will receive power when the Holy Spirit comes on you; and you will be my witnesses in Jerusalem, and in all Judea and Samaria, and to the ends of the earth" (Acts 1:8). The church devoted to evangelism is the church of the Spirit. For its holy and great work the Spirit makes use of individuals and churches that have great enthusiasm for the gospel.

However, when one confines the work of the Holy Spirit to individual salvation and evangelism, one fails to see the whole picture of the work of the Spirit. In the Old Testament Isaiah makes explicit that the Holy Spirit is the Spirit of Justice:

---

[2] For the holistic pneumatology, see my early writing: Myung Yong Kim, "Seongryeongronui bareun gil" [The Right Way of Pneumatology], in *I sidaeui bareun gidokgyo sasang* 『이 시대의 바른 기독교 사상』 [Today's Right Christian Thought] (Seoul: PUTS, 2001), 72-101; Myung Yong Kim, "Reformed Pneumatology and Pentecostal Pneumatology," in Wallace M. Alston Jr. and Michael Welker (eds.), *Reformed Pneumatology* (Grand Rapids: Eerdmans, 2003), 170-189.

A shoot will come up from the stump of Jesse; from his roots a Branch will bear fruit. The Spirit of the LORD will rest on him ... with righteousness he will judge the needy, with justice he will give decisions for the poor of the earth. He will strike the earth with the rod of his mouth; with the breath of his lips he will slay the wicked. (Isa. 11:1-5)

According to this messianic prophecy, the one on whom the Holy Spirit rests will eradicate the evil of the earth, defend the poor, and establish justice. In Isaiah 42:1 we also read: "Here is my servant, whom I uphold, my chosen one in whom I delight; I will put my Spirit on him and he will bring justice to the nations." The one given the Spirit of God is commissioned to establish justice among all nations.

In the Old Testament, when the Spirit of God came upon the prophets, they confronted the kings or those in power, denouncing their unrighteousness and demanding that they should establish justice. In short, the coming of the Spirit of God and the establishment of justice are closely connected.

The connection between the coming of the Holy Spirit and the establishment of a peaceful world is well demonstrated in the ministry of Jesus Christ, too.

The Spirit of the Lord is on me, because he has anointed me to preach good news to the poor. He has sent me to proclaim freedom for the prisoners and recovery of sight

for the blind, to release the oppressed, to proclaim the year
of the Lord's favor. (Luke 4:18-19)

In the passage the category of the poor covers the prisoners, the
blind, and the oppressed. In other words, the good news proclaimed
to the poor is connected with liberation of the prisoners, release of
the oppressed, and recovery of sight of the blind. When the Spirit
rests upon Jesus, he devotes himself to these works. This biblical passage clearly shows what the work of the Spirit is. The year of the Lord's
favor refers to the jubilee, which in the Old Testament is the year of
joy in which people who lost their ancestor's land recovers it and experiences the joy of social-economic liberation. This means that when
the Spirit rests upon Jesus, he frees from oppression and resolves conflict and makes a new world of peace, freedom, and joy in which our
bodies also enjoy health and peace.

According to Galatians 5:22, the Holy Spirit makes the world
of love, peace, and joy. The Spirit does not only save humanity to become the children of God, but also helps them to establish the kingdom of God. Both the salvation of individuals and the establishment
of God's just and peaceful kingdom belong to the essential work of
the Holy Spirit. It is not a right understanding of the Holy Spirit to
give priority to either one over the other.

III
Church's Saving Work according to Holistic Theology

1. Church and the Kingdom of God

The goal of the church is to proclaim the gospel of Jesus Christ and embody the kingdom of God. The church should proclaim the gospel of Jesus Christ so that unbelievers may have explicit faith in Jesus Christ that leads to eternal life. The church that does not proclaim the gospel of Jesus Christ is not a true church. Nor is the church that neglects or dismisses the gospel of Jesus Christ only for the sake of a political movement. Since there is no salvation without the gospel of Jesus Christ, every human person should believe the gospel of Jesus Christ. Hence, the church should not neglect the mission of proclaiming the gospel of Jesus Christ to the end of the world.

While the ultimate goal of the church consists in embodying the kingdom of God, to proclaim the gospel of Jesus Christ is very important for fulfillment of this goal. The people of God play an important role in establishing God's kingdom. Without soldiers that can fight against the enemy in battle it is basically impossible even to start fighting, and the battlefield will be immediately overtaken by the enemy. In order to destroy the power of the devil, likewise, we need soldiers of God's kingdom who can fight against it. It is incredibly important for the establishment of God's kingdom that the church proclaims the gospel of Jesus Christ, brings up the people of God, plants churches, and sends believers all around the world.

By proclaiming the gospel of Jesus Christ the church makes God's people and then trains them to become workers for the kingdom of God. This is important not only for increasing the number of soldiers who will fight against the power of the devil, but also for the qualitative growth of God's kingdom. For instance, Marxists have struggled for humanism and economic justice in history for a long time. But one may wonder whether humanism espoused by Marxists is a true humanism. According to Jong Sung Rhee, humanism in its genuine sense is "the humanism of Christ."[3] True humanity was revealed in Jesus Christ; therefore, true humanism is found in Jesus Christ. For this reason Rhee stressed that all other forms of humanism, whether classical or Marxist or modern secular, are only "preliminary stages for true humanism."[4] When the church sends to the world workers for the kingdom of God, she is sending people who know true humanism. They need to realize the true values of God's kingdom by embodying the true humanism.

When the church aims to establish the kingdom of God, her focus consists in the spiritual dimension of the goal. But this does not mean that the church should concern herself only with the so-called religious affairs having nothing to do with world history. Since the reign of God should be established within the world, the task of the church is necessarily connected with everything in the world. That the church is concerned primarily with its spiritual task means that the church should proclaim to the world the divine will to establish

---

[3] Jong Sung Rhee, *Gyohoeron* 『교회론』 [Ecclesiology] I, 509.
[4] Ibid.

the kingdom of God, raise for that kingdom spiritual workers, as contrasted with secular workers, and send to the world people who will transform the humanism of the world to the humanism of God's kingdom. The church should raise and send to the world workers devoted to God's politics, God's economy, and God's culture for the kingdom of God. In other words, the institutional church brings up God's people and sends spiritual workers prepared for God's kingdom so that they may transform the world. According to Jong Sung Rhee, the justice and righteousness of the world are themselves insufficient to establish God's righteousness. Thus, Rhee says, "because their judgment from time to time changes within limitations of philosophy of law, social reality, and human ability, it is very dangerous to rely exclusively on their judgment and evaluation."[5] He then insists that "the church should not appeal to any statute or philosophy of law that has only a temporary value, but to the Word and Law of God as the unchanging foundation of every statute and philosophy of law."[6] According to Rhee, "the church's judgment should be put over the judgment of the Supreme Court; the church should play the role of the spiritual Supreme Court that reviews the decisions of the secular Supreme Court."[7] This is what I mean by the spiritual task for establishment of God's kingdom.

Rhee proposes a significant thesis that "every humanistic socialism fails because it lacks a transcendental foundation."[8] Those worldly

---

[5] Ibid., 520.
[6] Ibid., 520-521.
[7] Ibid., 521.
[8] Ibid., 533.

movements unconnected with the fountain of spiritual life, which derives only from the church, cannot endure for long. In this vein, Rhee argues, it would be very hard to establish a true welfare society if Christians did not take the central position.[9] The establishment of God's kingdom is closely connected with the church; without the spiritual service of the church it would be virtually impossible to establish the kingdom of God. Therefore, the church should proclaim the gospel of Jesus Christ, make the people of God, raise many spiritual leaders for God's kingdom, and send them to the world.

2. Church and State

If the church should play the role of the spiritual Supreme Court that reviews the decisions of the secular Supreme Court, then does it imply that judges should be pastors or priests and the Chief Justice of the Supreme Court should be a pope or any representative of the church? Then, can we expect that they would judge fairly and the true righteousness of God would be realized on earth very soon? If a pope or any representative of the church would become the president of the country, then would it ensure that the politics of God's kingdom would be realized and the reign of God would be embodied in the world as quickly as possible?

I would say "No!" to all three questions. We need to be reminded of the medieval history, often called the Dark Ages. Even when the pope claimed to have authority in secular politics the world did not

---

[9] Ibid.,

become a bright world in which God's glory shined forth, but a dark world in which many unfortunate events took place. How can we explain this fact?

Holistic theology fully recognizes the distinction between the duty of clergy and that of lay people. The radically one-sided theology that confuses the two and encourages clergy to engage in politics is not a holistic theology. The temptation of medieval theocracy is still roaming all around the world. One can find it in the church's radical social and political movements supported by a one-sided theology. However, the temptation of theocracy is only a temptation; it should be distinguished from the right way to establish God's kingdom.

Why is theocracy not the right way? It is not difficult to find the reason. If a pope or any representative of the church became the Chief Justice of the Supreme Court, then would her or his judgment be fair enough? Neither the pope nor a representative of the church would be an expert in legal statutes. Knowledge of legal statutes is a prerequisite for a justice. Then, how can the pope or the representative of the church who does not know the Statute Books make a fair judgment? Today one of the most important duties of a national president is to foster economic growth. However, to our regret, neither the pope nor the representative of the church would know much about today's economic theories. They may preach on the fundamental spirit of God's righteousness and economic justice as revealed in the Bible, or proclaim that a specific policy or law violates the divine will. However, how to embody the righteousness and will of God in concrete laws and orders in today's complex society or in the complex economic order of the world is not an issue for them but for lay lawyers and lay economists.[10]

Holistic theology takes seriously and stresses God's calling of laypersons to establish God's kingdom. The culture of God's kingdom is also a locus of laypeople's ministry. To make music or works of art for God's kingdom is not a duty of clergy but a duty of musicians and artists. Holistic ecclesiology emphasizes not only that every layperson is commissioned to proclaim the gospel of Jesus Christ but also that every lay person has been called to a specific occupation. Therefore, holistic ecclesiology demands study as well as prayer within the church.

3. JPIC and Culture of God's Kingdom

In order to proclaim the gospel of Jesus Christ and embody the kingdom of God, what should the church specifically do? In contrast with old ecclesiologies, holistic ecclesiology regards justice, peace, the integrity of creation (JPIC), and the formation of the culture of God's kingdom as new tasks of the church today.

Traditionally, the tasks of the church were mission, education, worship service, and fellowship. These traditional tasks are still important in holistic ecclesiology. According to Jong Sung Rhee, the tasks of the church are proclamation of God's Word (preaching), administration of liturgies (baptism and the Lord's Supper), pastoral care, the mission of the church, and the mission of God. The first four of them are identical with the traditional tasks of the church

---

[10] Myung Yong Kim, *Yeollin sinhak bareun gyohoeron* 『열린 신학 바른 교회론』 [Open Theology and Right Church] (Seoul: PUTS, 1997), 80-82.

(mission, education, worship service, and fellowship), though slightly revised and newly organized. Meanwhile, the fifth task—the mission of God—is a new important task of today's church. It is closely related with the global church's pursuit of JPIC and formation of the culture of God's kingdom.

Since 1983 the World Council of Churches (WCC) has regarded justice, peace, and the integrity of creation as important tasks of the global church. In this regard holistic ecclesiology is in total agreement with the ecclesiology of the WCC. The Bible teaches justice, peace, and the integrity of creation as important values; also, they are essential to the establishment of God's kingdom. Hence, not only institutional churches but also all lay Christians should pray for and make an effort to accomplish these tasks in their life and work.

The church's task to embody the culture of God's kingdom is more emphasized within the evangelical circle than within the WCC. It is praiseworthy that evangelical theology stresses the culture of God's kingdom and makes every effort to embody it. In general, evangelical theology rightly recognizes that the gospel of Christ should transform the culture of the world. Jong Sung Rhee too regards such a transformative view of the relation between gospel and culture as holistic. But the important thing is to distinguish between the culture of God's kingdom and the culture of Western Christianity. Of course, in the Western Christian culture one may find many valuable things that correspond to the culture of God's kingdom. Yet the culture of God's kingdom may also contradict and challenge the existing Western Christian culture. It is also to be noted that the Korean church, located in the Korean Peninsula in East Asia, should embody the culture of God's kingdom within East Asian and Korean cultures. For this reason, Rhee engages in serious dialogue with Asian religions such as Confucianism, Buddhism, Taoism, and Hinduism. The Taoist idea of the harmony between humanity and nature is much closer to the culture of God's kingdom than the Western Christian idea of conquering nature.

4. Cooperation with Good Neighbors for God's Kingdom

For the task of establishing the kingdom of God the church should cooperate with good neighbors outside the church.[11] The church's cooperation with good neighbors outside the church is especially important, given that in Korea Christians are still a minority. In order to preserve living creatures and save the natural world, for instance, the church of Christ needs to, and ought to, cooperate with many other good neighbors who agree with this purpose. Cooperation with them may accelerate the realization of the divine will to preserve life in creation. In some cases Buddhists may be good neighbors. Though the Korean church tends to be very reluctant to cooperate with Buddhists, she ought not to refuse to do so if it helps to establish God's kingdom.

According to Moltmann, the Holy Spirit, who is the Spirit of Life, is at work behind every effort to save the life of all things. If our good neighbors are trying to save the life of the created world, then

---

11 Ibid., 124-126.

we can assume that the Holy Spirit as the Spirit of Life is at work behind their good efforts, even though they are not aware that they are possessed and influenced by the Holy Spirit. While recognizing that the Holy Spirit is working behind their good works, the church should cooperate with them.

Christians always ought to remember that the kingdom of God can be established only by God. The subject who establishes God's kingdom is neither humanity nor the church, but God. The church may be regarded as the subject of establishing God's kingdom, but only in the secondary sense. In order to establish God's kingdom God builds up the church, raises God's people, and sends them into the world; also, God makes use of good neighbors outside of the church. The church sometimes realizes that many things of God's kingdom have already come closer to her little by little, since the Holy Spirit has been at work broadly and deeply within history and the cosmos.

In the Book of Isaiah the pagan king Cyrus is described as a worker of God and God's hands. He was a pagan king who had no idea of God. But he fulfilled the divine plan much more successfully than many Israelite kings who knew God. He sent the Jewish people back to their homeland and allowed them to build the temple of God and even to use tax for its construction.

According to Jong Sung Rhee, divine providence through the church is one thing, and divine providence through the world is another. But both of them are used for the ultimate goal of God's kingdom. Even if the pagan king Cyrus accomplished the divine plan to a considerable extent, he still had no idea of God. In this sense he was not a child of God who would inherit the kingdom of God. Nonetheless, the marvelous plan of God was at work behind his rule.

Holistic theology teaches us a holistic view of history. Churches and Christians that fail to recognize the work of the Holy Spirit behind our good neighbors outside of the church do not have a holistic view of history. The church should cooperate with her good neighbors in order to embody the kingdom of God. Meanwhile, she ought not to speak too highly of their value. We have many times witnessed that without Christian participation social actions for the poor or the disabled did not endure for long. For this reason, in Germany the government commissions the church to do such works. Since our good neighbors outside the church are lacking the transcendental dimension based upon an encounter with God, their original spirit easily degenerates, and thus it is hard to ensure continuity of the work. Therefore, the church should neither speak too highly of, nor totally ignore, the value of those good neighbors outside the church. The important thing is to remember that when they do good work in the Holy Spirit, they are our precious co-workers for establishing God's kingdom.

IV
Holistic Ecclesiology and Church Growth

There is no doubt that the quantitative growth of the church is closely connected with her commitment to evangelism. For this reason many church leaders who are interested in church growth stress evangelism and plan special events like a gathering for evangelism or a special Sunday for mobilization and evangelism. In addition, for the growth of the global church they send missionaries all around the world so that they may proclaim the gospel and plant churches. It is certain that evangelism and missionary works are essential to increasing the number of Christians.

However, many church leaders in Korea do not recognize that the church's social responsibility also has significant effect on church growth. Today, growth of the Korean Catholic Church has not resulted from her enthusiastic evangelism, but from her commitment to social-political responsibility from the 1970s to the 1990s. These days Korean people think of the Catholic Church as more trustworthy than the Protestant Church. In their view the Catholic Church loves her neighbors, takes care of the marginalized people, devotes herself to justice and democracy, acts like a fortress of human rights, and has a strong social conscience. This positive image of the Catholic Church is the decisive reason for her growth. Thanks to the Catholic image symbolized by Myungdong Cathedral and Cardinal Su-Hwan Kim, many Korean people trust the Catholic Church and believe that she suggests a right way for the Korean society and government.

The same is true of the explosive growth of the Korean Protestant Church after independence from Japan and the Korean War. At that time the Korean Protestant Church cared for war orphans, distributed relief food to the poor, built hospitals and schools, taught with an honest conscience, and drove out superstitions. Thus, she was regarded as a cradle of the advanced spirit that would guide the future of Korean society. During the dark ages of Japanese colonialism, the

Protestant Church produced sixteen out of thirty-three national leaders in the March 1st Independence Movement, worked hard for the edification and independence of the nation, and raised many respected national leaders for the suffering people. The history of the Korean Protestant Church as a national conscience and a national torch led to her rapid growth. Since then the Protestant Christians in Korea overwhelmingly outnumbered the Catholic Christians.

From the early period of the Korean mission the Korean Protestant Church focused on education, medical care, social welfare, and women's enlightenment, all of which in combination then resulted in her remarkable development. According to Mu-Yeol Choi, the mission of the Korean Protestant Church from its early phase was a holistic mission comprising education, medical care, social welfare, and women's enlightenment.[12] Such a holistic mission brought about rapid growth and remarkable development of the Korean Protestant Church within a very short time.

However, these days the stagnation of the Korean Protestant Church is closely connected not only with the lack of enthusiasm for evangelism, but also with church activities that provoke social criticism: for instance, existence of too many different denominations, use of non-evangelical means for church growth, neglect of responsibility for poor neighbors, helplessness of the majority of the Protestant Church with regard to historical-political responsibility, superstitious exorcism that contradicts modern science, and exclusive attitude towards other religions and cultures. For these and other reasons the so-

---

[12] Mu-Yeol Choi, "Tongjeonjeok seongyomodelloseoui hangukchoiseongyo" [The Early Korean Mission as a Model of the Holistic Mission], *Mission and Theology* 98/2, 137-162.

cial image of the Korean Protestant Church has fallen to the ground. In this context it is very difficult to expect church growth.

For the sake of church growth we need to stress not only evangelism but also the church's social responsibility. And the latter is connected with responsibility for the kingdom of God. Both proclamation of the gospel and social responsibility are essential, like two wheels of a wagon. They are two hands of God for the salvation of the world. With one of them missing, the church would stop growing or face serious difficulty.

Chapter 4

Holistic Spiritual Theology

Myung Yong Kim

In the Korean church, as in the global church, there are as many different spiritual movements. Each spiritual movement has its own distinctive characteristics, emphasis, and lifestyle that it promotes. In what direction should the global church seek to move spiritually? What is the right spiritual movement?

I

Various Spiritual Movements[1]

1. Pentecostal Spiritual Movement

The Pentecostal spiritual movement is one that emphasizes baptism in the Holy Spirit as well as the power of the Holy Spirit. One of the important goals of Pentecostal church activities is to train God's workers who have received the power of the Holy Spirit. In this vein the Pentecostal church stresses prayer meetings and revival gatherings as an occasion for experiencing the Holy Spirit. Speaking in tongues is regarded as evidence of baptism in the Holy Spirit, while people who make prophecy or heal the sick are considered spiritual persons.

Pentecostalism is overall inclined to the possession of something: for instance, driving out poverty and gathering wealth, overcoming failure and making success, washing away humiliation and shame and gaining glory, healing sickness and gaining health, reviving a shrinking church and making her grow in number, and overcoming coldness within the church and making her a hot and voluntary community. Spiritual power, or spirituality, is believed to be found in the place where these events happen. In this vein the pastor who succeeds in making a mega-church through such spiritual movement is respected as a spiritual pastor.

However, the spirituality that Pentecostalism pursues is often indistinguishable from that of shamanism. Too close a connection between supernatural wonders and spirituality leads the church to mysticism and frenzied enthusiasm. The importance of human reason

---

[1] Myung Yong Kim, "Yeongseonge daehan bareun ihae" 영성에 대한 바른 이해 [The Right Understanding of Spirituality], in *I sidaeui bareun gidokgyosasang* 『이 시대의 바른 기독교사상』 [Today's Right Christian Thoughts], 56-60.

is often overlooked. Also, it lacks the awareness of Christian historical responsibility; i.e., it does not recognize that genuine Christian spirituality should shine forth in society and history.

2. Catholic Monastic Spiritual Movement

One of the characteristic features of the Catholic monastic spiritual movement is self-reflection on one's inner world. By reflecting upon one's inside the monastic movement seeks to suppress sinful desires within humanity and attain to the whole measure of the fullness of Christ. In *The Imitation of Christ*, a classic textbook for Catholic spirituality, Thomas à Kempis encourages Christians to throw away worldly greed, continuously meditate upon Christ, deny oneself, live a simple life, and thus attain to the whole measure of the fullness of Christ. In general, the Catholic monastic movement tends to emphasize self-denial, asceticism, labor, and honest poverty. In particular, the Franciscan friars put great emphasis on honest poverty.

> Brothers, think of money as a privilege given to help you live together with those forsaken in the world, including the sick, the weak, the poor with leprosy, and beggars on the streets. When you need money, do not feel shameful to ask alms. ... Jesus was as poor as Mary and his disciples, and he was a stranger. He never refused hospitality offered to him. ... Traditionally, almsgiving is the right given to the poor. Jesus ensured it for them.[2]

While Pentecostalism, which is strongly connected with a theology of blessing, encourages its adherents to obtain something and succeed and connects wealth, health, and honor with spiritual power and blessing, the Catholic monastic spiritual movement is more concerned with the beatitude through self-denial and honest poverty. For the latter, to follow Jesus means to attain to the poverty of Christ. St. Francis of Assisi, who had such a vision, distributed all his possessions to the poor and followed Christ.

Catholic monastic spiritual movement prefers to distinguish different stages of spiritual growth. For instance, Bernard of Clairvaux describes Christian beginners as animal-like, Christians with growing faith as rational, and mature Christians as spiritual.[3] Each of these three stages of spiritual life corresponds, respectively, to what he understands as the three aspects of humanity: *soma* (flesh), *psyche* (soul), and *pneuma* (spirit). The first, animal-like stage refers to that in which one remains in a physical state and is dominated by desire and lust. In the second, rational stage one stands between flesh and spirit, thus sometimes dominated by flesh and sometimes by spirit. Still, the person is not completely liberated from carnal desires. In the third, spiritual stage one enjoys complete fellowship with God. It refers to the state of supreme bliss whereby one transcends physical limitations, including space and time, and encounters God.

However, the Catholic monastic understanding of spirituality contradicts today's biblical anthropology. Contemporary biblical the-

---

[2] Hae Yong You, Hananim cheheomgwa yeongseong suryeon 『하나님 체험과 영성 수련』 [Experience of God and Spiritual Training] (Seoul: PUTS Press, 1999), 33.

[3] Ibid., 61.

ology understands humanity as the whole person. Behind the Catholic monastic movement lies the Platonic idea that human flesh is inferior and, as such, the origin of sin. But this Hellenistic view of humanity is not biblical at all. The Bible does not know much about Hellenistic philosophy, which regards human flesh as inferior. Holistic spiritual theology does not despise human flesh in favor of the spiritual world. It denies soul-body dualism. According to holistic theology, it is the human being as whole person, consisting of body and soul, that encounters God, is possessed by the Spirit of God, and moves to God's kingdom filled with life, love, and peace.

3. Liberation Spiritual Movement

While Pentecostalism and Catholic monasticism are concerned primarily with personal blessing or the individuals soul (or inner world), liberation theology stresses social, political, and historical contexts. The God who was revealed in the event of Exodus is the God of liberation. This is an important insight in liberation spirituality. The Exodus event, which formed the core of Israelite religion, reveals the God of liberation who overthrew injustice, broke the stick of the oppressor, and delivered Hebrew people out of bondage. Thus, according to liberation spirituality, genuine Christian spirituality encourages participation in God's liberating acts in history.

Liberation spirituality was first proposed by liberation theologians in Latin America. However, its influence has not been confined to Latin America but has reached the church all around the world. Korean minjung theology, which has a similar spirituality to liberation theology, claimed that genuine Christian spirituality consists in activities for minjung. Liberation theology developed into a spirituality in solidarity with the poor, and in political and economic realms emerged as spirituality combined with socialism that fosters a socialist world.

With its emphasis on historical responsibility, liberation spirituality proves that it belongs among the great Christian spiritualities. Also, its insistence that the kingdom of God should be established within history shows that liberation spirituality has solid biblical and theological foundations. However, there are also several problems with it. Liberation spirituality too hastily identifies Christian spirituality with a particular ideology. This reflects its too narrow methodological commitment. And it has become overly politicized so that one can hardly discern whether it is a Christian spiritual movement or simply a political movement. Finally, it more or less neglects the importance of personal encounter with God and personal experience.

4. Piety and Spirituality of the Reformed Church

The Reformed Church, which holds a quite negative view of medieval Catholic monasticism, underlines the importance of God's Word and teaches that studying God's Word is the essence of piety and of the faith and life of Reformed Christians. This is a strong point of the Reformed Church. Also, she rejects the otherworldly Catholic spirituality of self-denial and world-denial and, instead, argues that true spirituality is found in our concrete life where God's glory is revealed. To put it another way, according to the Reformed Church, true piety and spirituality of Christianity consist in temperate living and stewardship in our concrete life for God's glory.

In *The Protestant Ethic and the Spirit of Capitalism* Max Weber explicated the relation between Calvinistic piety and the development of capitalism. His explanation helps us understand what Reformed piety and spirituality are. Calvinists lived diligently for God's glory, denied themselves luxury, humbled themselves, and saved money. Weber observed that the development of capitalism in the area where Calvinists were living had much to do with their diligence, frugality, and saving. As demonstrated by Calvinists' diligence, temperance, and stewardship for the glory of God, Reformed spirituality is far from otherworldly. Rather, it pursues God-centered life at the very center of the world.

Reformed spirituality does not despise the world but emphasizes responsibility for the world before God. Reformed emphasis on the life for God's glory in the world was further developed in the twentieth century by several Reformed theologians, who reformulated Reformed spirituality in terms of life for the kingdom of God. This is a very important development for the right spirituality. True Christian spirituality should be oriented toward the world in which God's glory is revealed. Genuine Christian spirituality takes place in the world where God's glory shines forth and Christians make efforts to build God's kingdom as God's co-workers.

II
A New Theological Perspective for Holistic Spiritual Theology

1. Whole-Person Experience of God and Spirituality for the Whole Person

Once Plato was highly regarded as "a Christian before Christ." A number of Church Fathers believed that Plato's idea of the spiritual world is quite similar to that of Christianity. According to Plato, the body is vulgar, while the soul is noble. Salvation takes place when the soul, which is now suffering inside of the body, is liberated from the prison of the body. The human body is the enemy of the soul, which ceaselessly afflicts the latter. Bodily desire brings about the soul's agony and sin.

This idea of Plato's is not biblical at all, but it has influenced Christian theology and spirituality to a considerable extent. For a long time the Christian Church identified sin with bodily pleasure and regarded bodily dissipation as the root of sin. Hence, Christian spirituality began with controlling bodily passions and assumed that God is experienced in something non-sensory—that is, far away from worldly beauty. However, God is not experienced in a non-sensory world but is recognized through human senses. God is not experienced only by souls but by the whole person, consisting of soul and body. True experience of God's grace and salvation is possible in the human body, and world history where God's saving history unfolds.

In many religions one finds great efforts to attain deep spirituality by mortifying one's body. Behind such efforts lies the idea that body contradicts the soul, and thus one cannot attain deep spirituality without controlling one's bodily passions. In many world religions, therefore, one can easily find efforts to attain to spiritual satisfaction by ascetic practices like self-mortification, fasting, and eliminating sexual desire.

The idea that the body is opposed to the soul and that the mysterious experience of God is possible only from deep inside the soul is also found in many Christian spiritual movements. According to Augustine, one can find a way to God when one is deeply immersed in one's inner world, or in one's soul. He says that God is not found in the sensory world; rather, God is found deep inside the human soul. Catholic spirituality, which took over Augustine's idea, emphasizes soul's inner journey to encounter God. According to Teresa of Avila and Thomas Merton, there are seven stages in the soul's journey, of which God is experienced at the peak of the lonely soul that has passed through suffering and trials.

However, this idea that the body opposes the soul and that God is spiritually experienced in the immaterial and non-sensory world is a Platonic idea, but not a biblical one. In the Bible conflict between spirit and flesh does not refer to conflict between body and soul but to conflict between spiritual power and fleshly power. Paul never taught that the human body is inferior or sinful. Rather, according to Paul, our body is "the temple of God." Moltmann says:[4]

---

[4] J. Moltmann, *The Source of Life* (Minneapolis: Fortress, 1996), 73.

The origin of the life that has missed the mark and miscarried—that which is traditionally called 'sin'—is not located in the sensuality of the body at all, with its allegedly lower drives and needs. It is to be found in the disorientation of people as a whole, and therefore pre-eminently in their souls and wills, if these have surrendered to the death-drive of evil... The origin of true life, on the other hand, is not the soul with its feelings, nor the mind with its reasoning power, nor the will with its determination. It is a person's life as a whole, which comes to its flowering in the nearness of God which that person experiences, and in the warmth of God's love. This touches the body with its senses as well as the soul with its feelings and understanding and will. We could talk about a rebirth to true life out of the life-drive of the Holy Spirit.

The origin of human sin is not the human body with its senses but the human soul, which surrenders to the power of sin and death. The origin of murder, alienation, jealousy, adultery, and all greed is the human soul and the power of sin and death to which the human soul surrenders. The core of the gospel proclaimed by Paul is not the holy soul being liberated from the sinful body but destruction of the power of sin and death through the cross of Christ ["Where, O death, is your victory? Where, O death, is your sting?" (1 Cor. 15:55)], liberation of the human being as a whole person, body and soul, from the power of flesh, and possession by the power of the Holy Spirit.

The power of the Holy Spirit liberates the human body from the power of death. Jesus Christ drove out demons and healed the sick by the power of the Spirit. The spiritual theology that locates the place of human encounter with God deep inside the soul or at the mountain peak of soul's journey has a very narrow perspective. For God is experienced not only at the mountain peak of the soul's journey but also in the human body when the power of the Spirit heals the sick body. The resurrection of the body—the essence of Christian gospel—fundamentally contradicts the spiritual theology of the soul alone. When our body is liberated from sickness and death we truly experience God. Jesus' resurrection convinced his disciples that Jesus is God. Also, the new heaven and new earth that Christians are awaiting in hope are connected with the renewal of nature and creation. God is more truly experienced in beautiful nature and joyful creation than in the deep closet of a lonely soul separated from beautiful nature and creation.

Holistic spiritual theology does not separate the human soul from the human body. It does not despise the body and sense, nor depart from nature and creation, nor enter the deep closet of a monastery. Traditionally, spirituality was understood as dealing with the inner world or the deep inside of the human soul, and God was thought of as being experienced only in that deep inner world. Holistic spiritual theology recognizes that God is not experienced only in the human soul but also in the human body. Also, it recognizes that God is experienced not only in the deep closet of a monastery but also in joyful nature and beautiful creation. When Pentecostalism witnessed to the power of the Holy Spirit that is experienced in the human body, it overcame the prejudice of the past spiritual theology of the soul alone. However, it failed to further develop the idea of bodily experience of the Holy Spirit in terms of the socio-historical dimension of spiritual experience. The Israelites experienced the God of liberation and freedom through the Exodus. It was a social and historical experience in which the whip of the oppressor was broken down and the yoke of the slave was thrown off.

2. False Dichotomy of Spirituality and Reason

It is false to place spiritual theology in opposition to reason. Reacting to medieval rational scholastic theology, Catholic spiritual theology was once strongly oriented toward anti-intellectualism. Even in Pentecostalism today one can detect an anti-intellectual inclination. However, human reason is a valuable instrument of the Holy Spirit, and the Holy Spirit is a personal God who has intellect, emotion, and will.

On the other hand, it is also false to confine the work of the Spirit of God within the limit of human reason. In the nineteenth century liberal theology failed to see the transcendent aspect of the work of the Holy Spirit and, as a consequence, confined it within the limit of human reason. Meanwhile, it is important to note that human reason possessed by the Spirit of God can recognize the work of the Spirit that transcends worldly limitation. Jong Sung Rhee rightly stressed the power of human reason within faith. The Spirit works through human reason, whereas human beings recognize God and put into practice the divine will in history through the clear and distinct Word of God that is rationally grasped. On the day of Pentecost, according to Michael Welker, people from Greece, Libya, Rome, and Pontus who gathered in that place were enabled to know clearly in their own language—i.e., explicitly and correctly with their own reason—the marvelous work of God's salvation as revealed in Jesus Christ. In this way Welker emphasizes clarity and correctness through human reason in the work of the Holy Spirit. Holistic spiritual theology objects to the false dichotomy between spirituality and reason. Human reason born again through the Holy Spirit is of great significance to right Christian spirituality. A spiritual movement that lacks right rational judgment based upon the Word of God is susceptible to mysticism or even heresy.

However, excessive trust on human reason may lead to barren intellectualism. Since the Holy Spirit uses our intellect, emotion, and will, the right Christian spiritual movement also should encompass human intellect, emotion, and will. The experience of God through music should also be taken seriously. Spiritual revival movements in general neglected the experience of God through human reason, while stressing experiencing God through emotion—e.g., by means of music. The Holistic spiritual movement does not divide, but perceives as a whole, human reason, emotion, and will. In the history of Methodism and the Pietist movement one also finds a one-sided emphasis on the experience of God through the human heart, which is regarded as separate from the brain.

Medieval scholastic theology, Pietism, and American revivalism—all of them fell far short of the integrity of Christian spiritual formation due to their respective one-sidedness. In contrast, holistic spiritual theology insists that the Spirit of God encompasses human reason, emotion, and will, and therefore God is experienced in all of them; hence, it stresses the harmony between them.

3. Spirituality for Land and Nature

Holistic spiritual theology encourages love of land and nature. The spirituality that does not love land is not a true Christian spirituality. Holistic spiritual theology recognizes that the land is groaning and the entire creation is hoping to be liberated from its bondage to decay. Hence, holistic spiritual theology tries to protect the land, the Earth, and all life in the entire created world.

According to the Bible, the land should enjoy its Sabbath every seven years. In this commandment of the land's Sabbath we observe the concern and activity of God's Spirit to bring the land and the creation to life. Concerning the land's Sabbath, Leviticus 26:33-35 says:

> I will scatter you among the nations and will draw out my sword and pursue you. Your land will be laid waste, and your cities will lie in ruins. Then the land will enjoy its Sabbath years all the time that it lies desolate and you are in the country of your enemies; then the land will rest and enjoy its Sabbaths. All the time that it lies desolate, the land will have the rest it did not have during the Sabbaths you lived in it.

To infringe upon the health of the land is a sin against the land.

Paul the Apostle mentions the crying and suffering of creation (Rom. 8:19-21). Creatures subjected to futility are groaning in the entire cosmos. True Christian spirituality should listen to the groaning of creatures, take care of nature, and make efforts to liberate creation.

The Old Testament laws of the Sabbath and the sabbatical year are a source of spirituality that encourages us to love our body. "Six days you shall labor and do all your work, but the seventh day is a Sabbath to the LORD your God. On it you shall not do any work, neither you, nor your son or daughter, nor your manservant or maidservant, nor your animals, nor the alien within your gates" (Exod. 20:9-10). The laws of the Sabbath and the Sabbath year command that human beings, animals, and the natural world should all take rest to recover health in fullness of vitality. The right spirituality does not allow us to mistreat our bodies, animals, or nature but encourages us to take care of them for the sake of the world filled with life.

According to Moltmann, the land and nature are not simply the environment for humanity, but "the environment of God."[5] Creation is the environment for God's joy, while "a new heaven and a new earth" refers to the completion of God's indwelling environment. According to Revelation 21:1-4, the entire world will become the Temple in which God's glory dwells and rests. The cosmos in which the Spirit of God becomes all in all and all things perfectly reflect the glory of God—this is the ultimate goal of God's work. Still, creation is subjected to futility, and the entire world does not perfectly reflect God's glory. The Spirit of immortality who dwells in all things (Book of

---

[5] Ibid., 118.

Wisdom 2:1) wills to drive the power of futility and death away from all thing and fill them instead with eternal life. In the final analysis, true Christian spirituality encourages us to love the land, to protect the natural world, and to drive out the power of futility and death with the help of the Spirit of God.

4. Spirituality that Loves the World

In many religions spirituality is concerned with renouncing the world, and loving the world is regarded as incompatible with religious piety and spirituality. For this reason many people take spiritual training deep inside a mountain, on the peak of a cliff, or in the midst of a desert. To renounce the world and depart from it may be common in other religious spirituality, but it is not a true Christian spirituality.

Christian spirituality does not encourage us to renounce the world but to love the world. John Bunyan's *Pilgrim's Progress*, first published in England in 1678, has been an important guidebook for Protestant spirituality that encourages people to renounce the world. However, true Christian spirituality encourages us to love, rather than denounce, the world. Jesus Christ so loved the world that he came to the world (John 3:16). In his entire life and even in his death Jesus aimed to save humanity and the world. The eternal ground of Christian spirituality is Jesus Christ. Spirituality not founded upon Jesus Christ is not a true Christian spirituality. Spirituality that is grounded upon Jesus Christ encourages us to save the world.

In the early twentieth century German theologian Dietrich Bonhoeffer taught people all over the world a spirituality that loves and saves the world. He taught what genuine Christian spirituality is through his whole life until he was executed. He stressed the meaning of Christ's suffering for the sake of saving the world and on following Jesus (or discipleship) as the true spirituality of Christianity.

Catholic priest Oscar Romero, who was appointed Archbishop of Sal Salvador in El Salvador in 1977, was also a man of the Holy Spirit. He followed the way of Bonhoeffer. While spending one night in the church of a priest who had been killed for protesting against the fraudulent election by the military regime, the Archbishop found Christ suffering amidst the suffering people. Afterwards he became a "bishop of the people," making every effort to save the suffering people in El Salvador. Not until he was killed in front of the altar by a hired assassin did he stop helping people who were suffering and dying under the dark history of El Salvador.

Christian spirituality does not encourage us to leave the world for the desert. Holistic spiritual theology does not entirely deny the attempt to experience loneliness in a mountain or desert—temporarily for personal spiritual training—and encounter God in such an extreme situation. However, according to holistic spiritual theology, the attempt is meaningful only when it finally leads to participation in the Spirit's work to save the world. The power of darkness is still at work in the world, and human history is staggering due to the Satanic power that dominates the world.

Holistic spiritual theology recognizes that the devil is behind wars. The devil is the spirit of murder (John 8:44) and the one who makes the history of hatred, murder, war, and death. When the World

Trade Center in New York collapsed on September 11, 2001, the devil as the spirit of murder was working behind it. Spirituality that fails to recognize this fact is not true Christian spirituality. Also, spirituality that does not recognize that the dark power of the spirit of death is at work globally in terror and war and also in the structure of hatred that underlies them is a dead spirituality.

Holistic spiritual theology is a theology for the land and for the world. We find spirituality that renounces the land and the world deeply seated in many world religions. Even in the history of Christian spirituality we find such false spirituality. Holistic spiritual theology takes seriously the will of God who so loved the world as to send the Son (John 3:16), and seeks to participate in the Spirit's work to make a new heaven and a new earth. Spirituality for the land and the world is well articulated in the theologies of Dietrich Bonhoeffer, Jürgen Moltmann, Johannes Metz, and Jan Lochman.

III
Characteristics of Christian Spirituality

1. Knowledge of God and Wisdom

The Reformed Church was built upon the foundation of the Word of God and pursued pastoral ministry and Christian education based upon God's Word, which is essential to true Christian spirituality. For the knowledge of God and wisdom are the first foundation of Christian spirituality.

The devil is a deceiving spirit (1 Tim. 4:1), and false spirituality is found in many religions all around the world. In some religions it is justified to sacrifice one's children to please God, while other religions promote self-mortification until one's body is paralyzed. To attain a right knowledge of God is the first step of true spirituality. Without the knowledge of God it is not possible to discern false ideas prevailing in the world, nor to see and judge history rightly, nor to take right actions for historical responsibility.

The church that fails to understand the depth of divine grace as revealed in the cross easily degenerates into a legalistic community. A legalistic, non-evangelical church is already covered by the spirit of darkness. Spiritual training based upon legalism is false, for it kills human beings; its final outcome is disastrous.

The Crusades of the medieval church were a tragic event. The Crusades illustrate the false spirituality that possessed the medieval Catholic Church. Spirituality that kills pagans is possessed by the spirit of murder; it is not a Christian spirituality. The cross on shields of the crusaders did not ensure that the Crusades were an event guided by the Holy Spirit. As well, numerous inquisitions and witch hunting further confirm that the spirituality of the medieval Catholic Church was far from sound. All things considered, the right knowledge of God and wisdom are most important for genuine Christian spirituality.

The Word saves human beings and transforms them to give glory to God. The Word is the means through which the Holy Spirit works. For this reason it is called the sword of the Holy Spirit. The

Holy Spirit works through our knowledge of God and wisdom. And people who deeply know God, God's will, and the history of God's salvation are in fact great people of the Holy Spirit. In 1 Corinthians 12:28-31, therefore, Paul refers to apostles, prophets, and teachers, who all witness to the Word, as the first, the second, and the third duty. Paul refers to the knowledge of God and wisdom as gifts of the Holy Spirit, and encourages believers to make efforts to obtain these gifts (1 Cor. 14). The knowledge of God is the source of the power that helps the church, makes the world upright, and saves humanity and the world. For this reason the first foundation of Christian spirituality is the knowledge of God and wisdom.

2. Faith and Hope

People of faith are people of the Holy Spirit and people of deep spirituality. Faith has the power to move mountains, to force evil spirits to surrender, and to break through the power of darkness. Faith makes light amidst darkness, transforms despair into hope, creates new history, and makes a world in which God's glory shines forth. Christian spirituality does not escape from hopeless situations. Christian spirituality breaks down the unbreakable walls of Jericho and walks through the Red Sea as if it were dry land. The Book of Hebrews mentions many spiritual people in the Old Testament:

By faith Abraham, when called to go to a place he would later receive as his inheritance, obeyed and went, even though he did not know where he was going. ... By faith

Abraham, even though he was past age—and Sarah herself was barren—was enabled to become a father because he considered him faithful who had made the promise. And so from this one man, and he as good as dead, came descendants as numerous as the stars in the sky and as countless as the sand on the seashore. ... By faith the people passed through the Red Sea as on dry land; but when the Egyptians tried to do so, they were drowned. By faith the walls of Jericho fell, after the people had marched around them for seven days. By faith the prostitute Rahab, because she welcomed the spies, was not killed with those who were disobedient. And what more shall I say? I do not have time to tell about Gideon, Barak, Samson, Jephthah, David, Samuel and the prophets. (Heb. 11:8-32)

Faith determines characteristics of Christian spirituality. The faith of Abraham, Gideon, David, and Daniel is the eternal model of Christian spirituality. David was not afraid even in front of Goliath and finally threw him to the ground. He threw down the enemy and gave glory to God. Faith is the essence of Christian spirituality and reveals the glory of those who call upon God.

Pentecostal spirituality has much to do with faith. From the very beginning the Pentecostal church stressed the power of the Spirit that works through faith, and thereby gave hope to people who were suffering from poverty, sickness, and the darkness of life. "If you can? Everything is possible for one who believes." (Mark 9:23) This is the favorite biblical passage in the Pentecostal church, for it highlights the power of the Holy Spirit who works through faith.

Along with faith, hope is another important axis of Christian spirituality. Faith and hope are not separate, but in fact two interconnected sides of the same reality. This is why the Book of Hebrews mentions hope with regard to the people of faith:

> All these people were still living by faith when they died. They did not receive the things promised; they only saw them and welcomed them from a distance. And they admitted that they were aliens and strangers on earth. People who say such things show that they are looking for a country of their own... By faith Moses, when he had grown up, refused to be known as the son of Pharaoh's daughter. He chose to be mistreated along with the people of God rather than to enjoy the pleasures of sin for a short time. He regarded disgrace for the sake of Christ as of greater value than the treasures of Egypt, because he was looking ahead to his reward... Some faced jeers and flogging, while still others were chained and put in prison. They were stoned; they were sawed in two; they were put to death by the sword. They went about in sheepskins and goatskins, destitute, persecuted and mistreated... God had planned something better for us so that only together with us would they be made perfect. (Heb. 11:13-40)

Hope helps us to endure today's suffering and to walk along the way of discipleship. It is an important aspect of Christian spirituality.

People of faith and hope speak more highly of their suffering for the sake of Christ than every treasure in Egypt. The deepest Christian spirituality is hidden in suffering for the sake of Christ. Christians who endure suffering in daily life and serve others in hope of heaven are people who possess great Christian spirituality.

Moreover, Christian spirituality shines forth in efforts to realize God's reign within dark history, with belief in the ultimate victory of Christ. Hope for history is also an important aspect of Christian spirituality. Jong Sung Rhee taught hope for history by saying that, however strong the evil may be in the darkness of history, it is Christ who will gain the victory. Hope for history and the final victory of incarnation is an essential part of true Christian spirituality that will shine forth, especially in the darkness of history.

3. Love and Justice

According to Jong Sung Rhee, the essence of the work of the Holy Spirit is faith, hope, and love. Michael Welker says that faith and love are the means through which the power of the Spirit reveals itself, or the field of the power of the Spirit. In addition to faith and hope, love is also a very important aspect of Christian spirituality. Paul says, "And now these three remain: faith, hope and love. But the greatest of these is love" (1 Cor. 13:13).

Johann Heinrich Pestalozzi, the father of orphans in Switzerland, was a great man of the Holy Spirit who possessed deep Christian spirituality. With deep spirituality of love he saved lives of numerous war orphans and educated them. Behind love, great power that saves humanity and the world is at work. Behind hatred that brings about war and death, the devil, or the evil spirit, is at work, whereas behind love that makes the world full of life and peace the Holy Spirit, or the Spirit of life, is working. Mother Teresa was also a great woman of the Spirit who lived and the twentieth century and who possessed deep Christian spirituality. The life of the Earth will be protected by people of such spirituality that loves the Earth and takes responsibility for creatures before God. Christian spirituality that loves humanity should develop into a spirituality that loves the natural world and takes responsibility for the entire creation before God. Danish pastor Nikolaj F. S. Grundtvig advocated a threefold love. This is a valuable legacy of Christian spirituality that should be highly appreciated and restored today. Briefly speaking, when we love God, love our human neighbors, and responsibly love the natural world, genuine Christian spirituality will shine forth.

Justice stands in the same line with love. It is also an important aspect of Christian spirituality. For a long time conservative churches have ignored it. When the Spirit of God came to prophets of the Old Testament, they proceeded to those in power and demanded that they stop oppressing the poor and the powerless with violent means and create a just society. In short, justice stood at the center of the spirituality of the Old Testament prophets. According to In-Seok Seo, they were defenders of the poor. Their love towards the poor expressed itself through their request of justice:

> the LORD ... upholds the cause of the oppressed and gives
> food to the hungry. The LORD sets prisoners free, the

LORD gives sight to the blind, the LORD lifts up those who are bowed down, the LORD loves the righteous. The LORD watches over the alien and sustains the fatherless and the widow, but he frustrates the ways of the wicked. (Ps. 146:6-9)

The coming of the Spirit of God is directly related to liberating the oppressed, supplying the poor with food, and helping people who are unfairly suffering. The church that is insensitive to social justice and blind to the reign of God's righteousness in history is a very hopeless church. According to Luke 4:18-19, Jesus summarized the essence of his ministry as proclaiming the gospel to the poor—namely, people in prison, the blind, and the oppressed. It is in order to liberate the oppressed and make a world of jubilee that Jesus came to the world.

True Christian spirituality is found where the Spirit of Christ shines forth. Spiritual theology that focuses on the inner world of human beings is narrow in scope. Holistic spiritual theology pays attention not only to the inner world of humanity but also to God's kingdom of righteousness, peace, and life that is coming to the world. Unlike spirituality that affirms the unjust world order and focuses on spiritual elevation through resignation, holistic spiritual theology pursues solidarity with people who are suffering from poverty and oppression in the unjust world and seeks to build a new world in which true humanism shines forth.

IV
The Kingdom of God as the Goal of Spirituality

The final goal of Christian spirituality is to build the kingdom of God. The joy that Christians experience in their encounter with God should lead them to live for the kingdom of God. Spirituality that encourages only individuals' blissful life within a monastery falls short of wholeness. So does spirituality that seeks only personal blessings like healing and overcoming poverty. Christian spirituality should lead to driving out the power of darkness that is still at work in the world and seek to transform the world into the stage of God's glory.

Christian spirituality is at work where one plants and grows a tree and also where judges struggle alone for the righteousness of God. It is also found in the love of teachers who spend nights taking care of erratic students. The goal of spirituality is the kingdom of God. It means that the will and reign of God should be realized in all realms of the world, including politics, economy, society, culture, and the environment. Furthermore, Christian spirituality is at work in every thoughtful effort to break down demonic atheism and nihilism and to proclaim that there is God the Creator and that the world and human beings exist in the light of Christ's grace. Holistic spiritual theology discerns different forms of true Christian spirituality around the world. According to holistic spiritual theology, the spirituality of a street cleaner who recognizes her or his vocation in relation to God's kingdom is as great as the spirituality of a monk in a monastery.

Chapter 5

A Hermeneutical Reconstruction of Holistic Christology

Chulho Youn

I define Christology as an explication of Jesus whom the Christian Church confesses as Christ and Lord, or Jesus Christ. The primary task of Christology is to explain and defend for what reason and in what sense the Church confesses Jesus of Nazareth as Christ and Lord. This task covers the following three interrelated issues concerning the person and work of Jesus Christ: incarnation, atonement, and the relation between the historical Jesus and the Christ of faith. First, the doctrine of incarnation, which deals with the person of Jesus Christ, originally formed in the ecumenical councils of the ancient church. Next, the doctrine of atonement, which discusses the salvific meaning of the work of Jesus Christ and focuses on his cross, developed primarily during the medieval period. Finally, the relation be-tween the historical Jesus and the Christ of faith emerged as an im-portant issue, owing to the development of modern historical consciousness and the historical-critical approach to the Bible. In this chapter I aim to explore the prospect and task of holistic Christology in our context today from a hermeneutical perspective, with a special focus on the above-mentioned three topical dimensions.

Since theological discourse today develops in the postmodern context, I will deal with the relation between the historical Jesus and Christ of faith as the first step of reconstructing a holistic Christology. Prior to delving into this issue, however, I will explain my method-ological commitment and thereby disclose the hermeneutical nature of the holistic Christology that I will reconstruct. In the following discussion I will summarize and further develop my earlier discussion of major Christological issues in my two-volume work, *Jesus Christ*,[1] and at the same time make even more explicit than in my earlier books the holistic and hermeneutical nature of Christology. Reconstructing holistic Christology from a hermeneutical perspective involves hermeneutical and theological reflections upon the process of forma-tion and development of Christology from the early church on. Also, it does not allow us to take the neutral stance of an outsider when we describe the hermeneutical development of Christology; rather, we are required to understand, by participating in, the hermeneutical process through our historical imagination and empathy under the il-lumination of the Holy Spirit, as well as to experience and describe

---

[1] Chulho Youn, *Yeosu grisdo* 『예수 그리스도』 [Jesus Christ], vol. 1, rev. ed. (Seoul: Publishing House of the PCK, 2003); *Yeosu grisdo* 『예수 그리스도』 [Jesus Christ], vol. 2 (Seoul: Publishing House of the PCK, 1998).

Jesus Christ anew from our own initiative in the contemporary world.

I
Methodological Commitment for Holistic Christology

1. Three Dimensions of Christology

Christology has three interrelated dimensions: theological, historical, and practical. The first dimension of Christology is a theological or dogmatic one. Christology is not a purely rational, value-free discourse on the historical figure named Jesus of Nazareth from a purely phenomenological or historical perspective. It is above all a theological discourse relating to practical reason about Jesus whom the Christian faith community confesses as Lord and Christ. Just like theology in general, Christology is also faith seeking understanding (*fides quaerens intellectum*), not *vice versa*. This is in fact the original intention of the New Testament. The authors of the New Testament in the early church did not intend to hand down biographical records about Jesus' life but to witness to the one whom they believed was Lord and Christ. Likewise, the proper task of Christology is not to describe Jesus from a phenomenological viewpoint but to explain the significance of Jesus who is already experienced and confessed in faith as Lord and Christ and, furthermore, to proclaim that Jesus is our Lord and Christ.

The second dimension of Christology is a historical one. Christology can be neither reduced to, nor independent from, a phenomenological work of the historical dimension. Although faith cannot be established on the basis of reason, faith that does not seek understanding is vulnerable to the danger of blind fideism. Dogmatic ideas without historical verification may result in authoritarian dogmatism. Hence, it belongs to the proper task of Christology to investigate as earnestly as possible the validity of the historical foundations of traditional Christological doctrines and thereby justify or, if necessary, revise and reconstruct them.

The third dimension of Christology is a practical one. Every discourse on Jesus as Christ, or Jesus Christ, pursues the actual unity with him, and the unity with Jesus Christ is accomplished through faith, knowledge, and practice in the Holy Spirit. Knowing Jesus Christ is believing and trusting him, which in turn means witnessing to him through practices in life. This practical dimension includes not only our existential belief in Jesus Christ within the church and our proclamation of the gospel in the world, but also our sharing of Jesus Christ's vision of the kingdom of God in the Holy Spirit, our following of the way of Jesus Christ for the sake of God's kingdom, and our efforts to accomplish the divine will in our social and historical reality today.

Holistic Christology is possible only through the integration of these three dimensions—theological, historical, and practical. The first, the theological dimension, depends on the traditional deductive approach from above; the second, the historical dimension, depends on the inductive approach from below, primarily through modern historical criticism; and the third, the practical dimension, depends on individuals and the church's history-transforming praxis for the proclamation of the gospel of Jesus Christ and the embodiment of the kingdom of God. The practical dimension of Christology is called, on the one hand, "Christology from ahead," in the sense that it participates practically in the embodiment of God's kingdom, which comes from the eschatological future, and, on the other hand, "Christology from the bottom," in the sense that it pursues in the process solidarity with and service for the poor, the marginalized, and the oppressed. The theological dimension of Christology originates primarily from traditional piety within the realm of the church; the historical dimension derives from academic science within the realm of theological schools; and the practical dimension derives from practice within the realm of society. All three of these realms are interconnected and overlapped in the internal and external life of every Christian. Therefore, *pietas* (piety), *scientia* (science), and *praxis* (practice), in the above-mentioned three distinct yet interconnected realms, are three pillars for the reconstruction of holistic Christology.

2. Four Hermeneutical Circles

Holistic Christology consists dialectically of four hermeneutical circles. The first circle is formed between Christology and soteriology. Traditionally, Christology and soteriology are distinct from each other. Soteriology deals with the redemptive work of Jesus Christ, while Christology deals with the personal identity of Jesus Christ. In other words, Christology is expected to respond to the question of "Who is

Jesus Christ?" while soteriology answers the question of "What did Jesus Christ do for us?" The Christological question is answered by the doctrine of incarnation, while the soteriological question is answered by the doctrine of atonement.

In general, Christology in its broad sense includes soteriology. In this regard one can discern a twofold circular relationship. First, there is a circular relationship between the person and work of Jesus Christ, which are distinct but not separate from each other. By understanding the work of Jesus Christ one perceives his person, and by understanding his person one perceives his work. In addition, there is another circular relationship between the objective historical reality of the person and work of Jesus Christ, on the one hand, and its subjective existential significance, on the other. They are distinct but not separate from each other. Kant once said that "thoughts without contents are empty, intuitions without concepts are blind." In Christology, likewise, present subjective meaning without foundation in past objective reality is empty, while past historical fact that is not combined with present existential interpretation is blind.

In short, on the one hand, there is a hermeneutical circle between the doctrine of incarnation concerning the person of Jesus Christ and the doctrine of atonement concerning his work. On the other hand, there is another hermeneutical circle between the historical Jesus as an objective reality of the past and the Christ of faith as the former's present existential meaning. The name of Jesus Christ itself implies this twofold hermeneutical circle. To put it another way, "Jesus" refers to the person and work—which in themselves consist in a hermeneutical circle—of an objective reality or event of the past, while "Christ" denotes an existential meaning that the present faith community attains to through spiritual experience and confessional interpretation of the person and work of Jesus Christ. The former offers a particular, concrete, and factual foundation for the latter, while the latter bestows universal theological meanings on the former. To use Edward Schillebeeckx's expression, the two form one reality, Jesus Christ, in the reciprocal relationship of offer and response.

The second hermeneutical circle integral to holistic Christology is found in its ontological dimension. It concerns a circular relationship between a pre-structure or horizon of Christological understanding of Jesus and a Christological experience or interpretation of Jesus. In the Christian community of the New Testament era, to be specific, the pre-structure or horizon of Christological understanding was primarily the Jewish tradition based upon the Old Testament, and secondarily Hellenistic religions and thoughts. Our subjective experience or interpretation of an objective reality is not possible in a vacuum or on a blank paper, nor is it a product of an individual person's purely psychological subjectivity. It is possible only in a subjectivity of *Dasein* as "being-in-the-world," or within a pre-structure, horizon, or effective history of understanding at the ontological level. The first Christological experiences and interpretations of Jesus were made possible above all within the horizon of the Old Testament and Judaism. The first Christians experienced, understood, and represented Jesus within the effective history of the Old Testament and Judaism. By employing different messianic names and models found in the Old Testament, therefore, they described Jesus as Christ (Messiah), the Son of David, the Prophet, the Son of Man, the Son of God, Wisdom, the servant of Yahweh, and so forth. Meanwhile, their experiences and interpretations of Jesus themselves were made possible by such names and models. When the locus of the church moved to the Hellenistic world, the Christian Church reinterpreted and represented Jesus within the horizon of Hellenistic culture and thought. In the process the earlier Christological names and models that belonged to the Jewish tradition had gradually been deprived of their meaning and thus forgotten or even suppressed; instead, new Christological names and models such as Logos, lord (*kyrios*), and savior (*soter*), which were derived from the Hellenistic tradition, emerged as dominant and normative Christological names and models.

However, the relationship at the ontological level between the pre-structure of understanding and the experience and interpretation of Jesus is not one-sided but reciprocal and circular. The early Christian community not only experienced and interpreted Jesus in light of the Old Testament, which determined the horizon of their own understanding and thought, but also reinterpreted the Old Testament in light of their experience of Jesus. Indeed, several messianic names in the Old Testament could not be simply attributed to Jesus. Hence, it was required to reinterpret the Old Testament. The early Christian community began to employ such terminology as the Old and New Testament, which resulted from reinterpretation of the Jewish canon in light of the current experience of Jesus—that is, typologically in terms of promise and fulfillment. In this regard, of course, the relation between promise and fulfillment is not one of simply continuity but involves discontinuity that is not easily connected. Given such discontinuity, then, reinterpretation implies formation of a unique and authentic—namely, Christological—Christian identity. So does the early church's reinterpretation of Hellenistic thought. In the process of the formation and development of the Christological identity of Christianity, Christianity became Hellenized and Hellenism became Christianized. In other words, there was a reciprocal and dialectical fusion of two horizons.

In the process of formation and development of Christology we should note that the hermeneutical circle and dialectical fusion between the pre-structure of understanding and the actual experience and interpretation were not completed once and for all in the early church. Rather, the hermeneutical circle has always been at work in the ancient, medieval, modern, and even contemporary church—i.e., throughout the history of Christianity. Furthermore, it is essential to the subsequent development of Christology today and tomorrow. The task of Christology is not to escape from the hermeneutical circle (from an epistemological viewpoint every hermeneutical circle is regarded as a vicious one), but to enter into the right circle (from an ontological viewpoint the hermeneutical circle is an inevitable condition) and to make the fusion of horizons dialectical and creative (or productive).

The third hermeneutical circle of holistic Christology lies between tradition and experience. The first Christological representations that the early church made through reinterpreting the Old Testament resulted in the canonical status of the New Testament, for they were grounded upon the original Apostolic tradition. As a result, they became the norm for every subsequent church. The church tradition as the secondary tradition (*norma normata*) was derived from the New Testament as the objective deposit of the original Apostolic tradition (*norma normans*). From then on, therefore, the Christian tradition with the inclusion of the New Testament forms the normative horizon or pre-structure of every Christological experience and interpretation. There is no Christian experience possible apart from the effective history of this Christian tradition.

However, the relationship between Christian tradition and Christian experience in a new context is not one-sided but reciprocal and dialectical. There is a reciprocal circle between them, just like the relationship between the Old Testament and the first Christian experiences of Jesus. The task of Christology is to bring about a fusion of two horizons—i.e., the past tradition and the present experience. A desirable hermeneutical fusion of horizons takes place above all by the inspiration and guidance of the Holy Spirit. Its concrete process demands both the hermeneutics of retrieval within the structure of the effective history of tradition and the hermeneutics of suspicion which is critical of the tradition. In Christianity, indeed, the Christological tradition, with the inclusion of the Bible, represents the confessions, interpretations, and descriptions of the first and subsequent experiences of Jesus that were inspired by the Holy Spirit and then formalized and normalized through consensus within the church. Tradition not only offers a horizon for today's Christological experience, but also becomes a criterion by which one judges the appropriateness of experience; meanwhile, Christological experience within today's context enables a critical reinterpretation of tradition for the sake of its intelligibility to contemporaries. When a certain part of tradition loses its intelligibility and turns out to be inappropriate within a new context, it needs to be revised and reconfigured in light of today's experience. For instance, one may refer to systematic distortion within an oppressive sexist tradition that reflects a despotic or patriarchal social structure. Thus, there is a dialectical hermeneutical circle between the past tradition and the present experience within which the mutually critical correlation between tradition and experience, through the hermeneutics of retrieval and suspicion, not only transforms present experience but also reforms tradition so that it becomes a new tradition. It is in this sense that the Reformed Church is always being reformed (*ecclesia reformata semper reformanda*). In short, the primary task of holistic Christology is to bring about the hermeneutical fusion of horizons, in a right and continuous way, through the mutually critical correlation between tradition and experience.

Finally, the fourth hermeneutical circle that lies at the foundation of holistic Christology is concerned with the threefold relationship between faith, knowledge, and praxis. Praxis is not simply an application of a theory, nor an enactment of belief. Praxis can neither take the place of faith or knowledge, nor be reduced to one or both of the latter. Just as faith and knowledge require praxis, faith and knowledge are put to the test, revised, and actualized through praxis. Praxis is in itself the power of the transforming truth. "For the kingdom of God is not a matter of talk but of power" (1 Cor. 4:20). One attains to praxis through knowledge and faith; at the same time one attains to true knowledge and faith through praxis. As St. Augustine once said, we come to know by loving. We do not interpret Jesus Christ simply to believe and understand him, but ultimately to follow him in transforming the world and embodying the kingdom of God.

Hence, holistic Christology pursues not just orthodox doctrine and orthodox faith, but also ortho-praxis. These three consist in a perichoretic hermeneutical circle, leading to a practical love and wisdom. The goal of holistic Christology is not simply to establish a theoretical and speculative system of Christology, but to transform the historical reality of the present world in the light and power of God's kingdom, which comes from the eschatological future. Therefore, holistic Christology leads us to the service of, and love for, Jesus Christ and to the way of the cross and self-denial. "If anyone would come after me, he must deny himself and take up his cross and follow me" (Matt. 16:24).

II

The Historical Jesus and The Christ of Faith

With the dawn of the Age of Enlightenment traditional dogmatics of the Christian church were increasingly put into question, though biblical studies emerged as an independent theological discipline, thanks to the development of modern historical science and philology. While earlier tradition of dogmatic biblical exegesis assumed the Bible as the a-temporal and literal revelation or Word of God, modern biblical studies regarded the Bible as historical documents and thus employed historical-critical method. From then on official doctrines of the church had to be verified and judged by more thoroughgoing historical-critical biblical exegesis. With the development of biblical criticism the historical quest for the life of Jesus became the main task of biblical theology. The investigation of the historical Jesus then appealed to historical reality in order to obtain liberation from traditional dogmatics. Through the historical approach Enlightenment thinkers attempted to prove that the historical Jesus was different from the Christ of traditional faith, and that Jesus himself did not claim divine authority.[2]

1. Quest for the Historical Jesus in the Nineteenth Century

The historical approach to the Bible, which attempted to disprove or at least reinterpret traditional doctrines by demonstrating a substantial difference between the historical Jesus and the Christ of orthodox faith, was intensified and proliferated under more advanced historical-critical methods in the nineteenth century.[3] The first scholar who gave lectures on the life of Jesus was Friedrich Schleiermacher, and yet his primary interest was more theological than historical or biographical. In other words, he was not concerned with demonstrating the falsity of traditional Christological doctrines but with reinterpreting and defending them through historical and psychological approaches—i.e., in a way intelligible to his contemporaries.

Meanwhile, Friedrich Strauss was a Hegelian. In his book, *The Life of Jesus*,[4] Strauss distinguished between the historical Jesus and

---

2 The quest for the historical Jesus began with Gottfried Lessing's publication of Hermann Samuel Reimarus' posthumous essays under the title of *Wolfenbüttel Fragments Drawn from the Papers of an Anonymous Writer* (1774-1778).

3 Two representative studies of the historical Jesus in this period are David Friedrich Strauss' *The Life of Jesus* (1935) and Ernest Renan's *The Life of Jesus* (1863).

4 David Friedrich Strauss, *The Life of Jesus: Critically Examined* (London: SCM, 1972).

the Christ of faith and then regarded the latter as a product of mythological interpretation. According to him, each Gospel's records of Jesus' life contain mythological elements. However, he understood mythology as representing, in a form of historical story, religious ideas that formed by age-old creative unconsciousness and were made concrete in a specific historical figure. At the time of Jesus, he believed, the Jews in Palestine lacked historical consciousness and, as a result, their thought took a mythical or poetic form. If we fail to see the fact that the Jews contemporaneous with Jesus thought mythically, then it means that we fail to think historically. While arguing that mythology was a widespread form of knowledge in the pre-scientific and pre-historical world, Strauss made efforts to convince his contemporaries of the truth of biblical writings by explaining their mythical thought and language in an intelligible way. From the historical-positivistic viewpoint, on the one hand, he tried to demonstrate the historical reliability of Jesus' stories recorded in the Gospels; from the viewpoint of Hegelian rationalistic idealism, on the other hand, he argued that the truth of Christianity is in essence philosophical and thus has no necessary connection with historical events. In short, there was a logical inconsistency between these two positions. In the end, Strauss diverged from the orthodox teaching of the church by claiming that Jesus of Nazareth was a historically existent yet ordinary person and that after his death his followers bestowed on him a divine nature, or an image of the idealized Christ drawn from the Old Testament passages about the Messiah.

In the late nineteenth century, neo-Kantianism took the place of Hegelianism and, as a consequence, anti-metaphysical historicism became influential. Speculative philosophy was denied, and increasing attention was given to empirical and historical phenomena. During this period historical studies of the biblical texts and church dogmas appropriated the remarkable development of historical-critical methods. Albrecht Ritschl endeavored to meet the demands of the times. His thinking is characterized by suspicion of metaphysics, denial of church dogmas and natural theology, interest in the historical Jesus and his ethical teaching, and emphasis on the kingdom of God as a community of spiritually liberated people. These features are regarded as typical of Protestant liberal theology.[5] In his work *The Christian Doctrine of Justification and Reconciliation*,[6] Ritschl discussed the theory of value judgment, the historical Jesus, and the person and work of Jesus Christ from the perspective of Immanuel Kant's practical reason. According to Ritschl, religion does not belong to the realm of factual judgment but to that of value judgment. The object of religious experience is not perceived by rational inference (Hegelian idealism) or mysterious feeling (Schleiermacher); rather, it is revealed in concrete historical events. Meanwhile, Jesus Christ, who is the norm for these historical events, is not inferred from historical facts but is accessible by the value judgment of faith. Unlike historical positivists, on the one hand, Ritschl believed it would be impossible to attain to the historical Jesus as a purely objective reality detached from faith

---

[5] One can observe the widespread influence of the Ritschlian school in the German Protestantism from 1875 until the break of the first World War and also in the American theology from the late 19th century to 1930. In the late 19th century most of the mainline theological schools in Germany were dominated by Ritschl's students or his books. Wilhelm Hermann, Julius Kaftan, and Adolf von Harnack represent the Ritschlian school, and in the Unites Walter Rauschenbusch, well known for his social gospel movement, belongs to the same school. 9

[6] Albrecht Ritschl, *The Christian Doctrine of Justification and Reconciliation*, 3 vols, trans. H. R. Mackintosh and A. B. Macaulay (Edinburgh, 1900).

experiences of the early church. One can reach Jesus' historical reality only from the perspective of the faith of the Christian community. Every judgment about the person and work of Jesus Christ is a value judgment. On the other hand, however, Ritschl did not claim that one should accept uncritically the pictures of Jesus Christ that are found in the early Christian tradition and the Gospels. Rather, he insisted that a thoroughgoing historical-critical research is in need in order to reconstruct the historical Jesus out of the different layers of Christological traditions. In short, while Ritschl's contribution consists in his recognition of the reciprocal relationship between the historical Jesus and the Christ of faith, he failed to suggest a way out of the dilemma inherent in this circular argument.

Martin Kähler tried to solve the dilemma from the perspective of the so-called Kerygma Christology. In his book *The So-called Historical Jesus and the Historic Biblical Christ*,[7] Kähler aimed to criticize the quest for the historical Jesus by the nineteenth century liberal theologians—above all, Strauss and Ritschl. According to Kähler, the essence of the Bible is neither history out of which the historical Jesus is to be reconstructed, nor dogma which can be immediately translated into the language of the Chalcedon creed; rather, it is found in kerygma or proclamation. He says, "It is as kerygma, as a deliverance of the divine commission to his heralds and messengers, that the ancient word of Scripture acquires its significance in the church." "The genuine Christ is the proclaimed Christ."[8] In this way Kähler attempted to overcome historicism. By separating history from kerygma

---

[7] Martin Kähler, *The So-called Historical Jesus and the Historic Biblical Christ* (Philadelphia: Fortress Press, 1964).

[8] Ibid., 60, 131.

and then claiming that the latter, not the former, is the essence of Christianity, however, he opened the way to a radically existentialist interpretation of the Bible as found in Rudolf Bultmann.

Another significant criticism of the quest of the historical Jesus in the nineteenth century was raised by New Testament scholar Johannes Weiss, who wrote *Jesus' Proclamation of the Kingdom of God.*[9] While Kähler was critical of the project of drawing a reliable picture of the historical Jesus itself, Weiss pointed that it failed to bring the historical task to completion. From his careful study of the historical Jesus Weiss concluded that Jesus' proclamation was neither ethical nor political, but apocalyptic and eschatological in nature. The Ritschlian concept of the ethical kingdom of God, according to Weiss, is not grounded upon Jesus' teaching but upon the ideas of Immanuel Kant. The imminent kingdom of God that Jesus proclaimed did not refer to an ethical, political kingdom to be established on earth by human efforts but to an apocalyptic kingdom that would be brought about only by the transcendent power of God. In short, Weiss believed that thorough historical research would disclose the eschatological and apocalyptic nature of Jesus' proclamation of the kingdom of God.

This idea was accepted by Albert Schweitzer, who then came to the radical conclusion that Jesus expected the end of history immediately after his death. It was from this perspective, often called "thoroughgoing eschatology," that Schweitzer understood the New Testament as well as Jesus' movement. Thus he believed that Jesus walked along the path of death to advance the date of the coming of God's kingdom. In 1906 he published his work *The Quest of the His-*

---

9 Johannes Weiss, *Jesus' Proclamation of the Kingdom of God* (London: SCM, 1971).

torical Jesus,[10] which brought to an eventual end the liberal quest for the historical Jesus in the nineteenth century. In this book Schweitzer pointed out that liberal theologians of the nineteenth century failed to take into proper consideration the historical context of Jesus' proclamation—that is, the Jewish thought world that was then dominated by apocalypticism. The primary subject of Jesus' teaching, according to Schweitzer, was the imminent end of the world. However, the post-Enlightenment scholars were not good at dealing with such mythological ideas. Instead they described Jesus as a teacher who taught a bourgeois ethics of the nineteenth century. In other words, they were interested in history, but failed to retain a thoroughly historical stance. Instead, they were possessed by an a-historical, idealistic preunderstanding.

Though Kähler, Weiss, and Schweitzer brought to an end both historicism and the quest for the historical Jesus that dominated the nineteenth century, no one succeeded in suggesting a convincing alternative. The problem of "the scandal of particularity," derived from "the ugly ditch between the historical, contingent truth and the rational, universal truth," was still left unsolved.

2. Discussions of the Historical Jesus and the Christ of Faith in the Twentieth Century

At the dawn of the twentieth century the issue of the historical Jesus and the Christ of faith entered a new phase with the develop-

---

[10] Albert Schweitzer, *The Quest of the Historical Jesus: A Critical Study of the Progress from Reimarus to Wrede* (A&C Black, 1954).

ment of form criticism in biblical exegesis. In the old quest for the historical Jesus in the nineteenth century scholars focused on the authenticity of Jesus' teaching recorded in the Gospels. Meanwhile, in the twentieth century form criticism presupposed that it is almost impossible to extract Jesus' authentic words from the later addendum, for the Gospels are not historical documents in the modern sense but faithful witnesses reflecting the *Sitz-im-Leben* of each faith community. The Gospels are not concerned primarily with the historical Jesus but with the proclamation of the gospel and the worship service in each faith community and also with Christ who is present in everyone's life. Hence, form critics concluded that it is impossible to historically reconstruct Jesus' biography.

The major New Testament scholar who represents this position is Rudolf Bultmann. As a leading form critic Bultmann believed that the historical reality of Jesus is in itself inaccessible. Following the way of his teacher Martin Kähler, he developed an existentialist kerygmatic Christology starting from Christ who is present in the proclamation of the gospel. On the basis of his own existentialist interpretation of the Bible he stressed divine revelation through kerygma and existential response to it. In this vein he demythologized the doctrine of the divinity of Jesus Christ, the atonement theory, eschatology, and so forth, and proposed a reductive reinterpretation of them as an event of faith from the existentialist perspective. According to his existentialist biblical interpretation, Jesus Christ does not save us because he is the Son of God; rather, Jesus Christ is the Son of God because he saves us. The revelatory value of the death and resurrection of Jesus Christ does not derive from their effect on bringing about the eternal atonement as an objective event that occurred then and there, but from the transformation into a new being they bring about here and now through existential response. When one realizes the death and resurrection of Jesus Christ as an existential possibility of our self-understanding here and now, it becomes an eschatological moment.

Meanwhile, some systematic theologians attempted to rescue theology from history by returning to traditional dogmatics. Karl Adam in Catholicism and Karl Barth in Protestantism are two major figures representing this position. They rejected to start from below—that is, from the historical reality of Jesus, but decided, following traditional dogmatics, to start from above—i.e., from the revelation of the Word of God. In this way they intended to renew their commitment to traditional doctrines of the church and convince their contemporaries of their truth. Barth did not deny the need for historical criticism, but in reality he made little use of it in his theological interpretation of the Bible.

But the situation changed in the middle of the twentieth century. There was an increasing awareness that the problem of historicity raised by modern reason cannot be solved in this way. The problem Lessing once proposed was still unsolved. Barth's supra-historical positivism of revelation transcends history for the sake of heavenly realm called "primal history" (Urgeschichte), whereas Bultmann's historical skepticism and theological existentialism allow him to escape from objective history to historicity (Geschichtlichkeit) of the existential inner world. They all tried to listen to God's Word coming from the realm of a-historical revelation but failed to offer a convincing solution to the problem of the scandal of particularity. Thus there remained "the ugly ditch" between the historical Jesus and the Christ of faith, between historical particularity and theological universality, between objective reality and subjective faith, between fact and meaning, and between history and interpretation.

Theologians after Barth made significant revisions to Barth's theology of the Word of God. Wolfhart Pannenberg and Jürgen Moltmann, while criticizing the vertical and a-historical nature of Barth's theology, restored the historical horizon to theology from the perspective of eschatology and universal history. As a philosophical theologian Pannenberg insisted that today's Christology cannot start from above—that is, from traditional dogmatic presuppositions, but it should start again thoroughly from below—i.e., from history. He carried out an historical-critical investigation of the concrete historical reality of the Bible and then connected it to the project of eschatological universal history in terms of a Hegelian idealistic philosophy of history. This is how Pannenberg solved the problem of the scandal of particularity. Of course, his Hegelian idealistic philosophy of history was Christologically baptized. In other words, Pannenberg understood the event of Jesus Christ as an anticipation within history of the ultimate fulfillment of history and, therefore, as a decisive revelatory event for the hermeneutics of universal history. For Pannenberg, in particular, the resurrection of Jesus Christ, regarded as a concrete historical reality, is the essence of revelation, for it proleptically anticipates the universal resurrection which will take place as the ultimate consummation of universal history in the eschatological future. It is because Pannenberg understood the event of the resurrection as the key to the hermeneutics of universal history that he made every effort to demonstrate the historical factuality of Jesus' resurrection.

Meanwhile, Moltmann, standing in the Reformed tradition, developed a vision of the consummation of the eschatological kingdom of God in the socio-political and cosmic dimension. Assuming that the eschatological kingdom of God was proleptically realized in Jesus Christ, he stressed our obligation to participate in the messianic work for the eschatological kingdom of God through our solidarity with the poor, the oppressed, and people who are suffering, and through our transforming and liberating praxis. Moltmann's Christology emphasizes the proleptic nature of the event of Jesus Christ as a sign of God's kingdom coming from the eschatological future. In addition, it requires us to participate in the history-transforming praxis in hope for the eschatological consummation of the kingdom of God. In this sense, his Christology is called Christology "from ahead." However, he had little interest in reconstructing the earthly life of the historical Jesus through the historical-critical approach.

Latin American liberation theology, in solidarity with European political theology, sought a more radically praxis-oriented theology. Liberation theologians—such as Gustavo Gutierrez, Jon Sobrino, and Leonardo Boff—attempted to reinterpret the meaning of Jesus Christ within the context of Latin American people who were poor, alienated, oppressed, and suffering. Starting from the historical Jesus they preferred Christology from below to traditional Christology from above. But they did not aim simply to draw a picture of the historical Jesus, but to find in the historical Jesus a vision and motivation for the transformation of, and liberation from, the historical reality of poverty and oppression. In this sense, Latin American Christology may be called Christology "from the bottom." Broadly speaking, the praxis-oriented theological paradigm of Latin American liberation theology also applies to Third World theologies (including Korean minjung theology), feminist theology, and ecological theology.

In the meantime, a group of biblical scholars in Europe and North America, called "the Post-Bultmannian school," tried to overcome the weakness inherent in Bultmann's existentialist kerygmatic theology.[11] Awakened to the theological importance of historical reality, they renewed the quest for the historical Jesus. The so-called "New Quest" began with Ernst Käsemann's lecture at Marburg University in 1953, entitled "The Problem of the Historical Jesus."[12] In this lecture Käsemann proposed that the old quest for the historical Jesus in the nineteenth century should be renewed on the ground of today's new theological context. The renewed interest in the historical Jesus was provoked not just by the theological motivation to overcome both a-historical dogmatic Christology with no historical basis and enthusiastic, existentialist Christology devoted to present experiences of salvation, but also by biblical exegetical studies. Experts in biblical exegesis came to increasing agreement that historical-critical studies may bring about a reliable picture of the historical reality. Günther Bornkamm said that "the Gospels do not give us any reason for resignation or suspicion. Rather, they show us an impressive historical figure named Jesus, if in a different way than other chronicles or his-

---

[11] After Bultmann many Protestant biblical scholars participated in the new quest for the historical Jesus: Ernst Käsemann, Ernst Fuchs, Günter Bornkamm, Hans Conzelmann, Herbert Braun, James M. Robinson, Gerhard Ebeling, Friedrich Gogarten, and Willi Marxsen. Also, several Catholic scholars also joined in it.

[12] Ernst Käsemann, "Das Problem des historischen Jesus," in Käsemann, *Exegetische Versuche und Bestimmungen* I, 6th ed. (Gottingen, 1970), 182-214.

toriography."[13]

Unlike the "old quest" of the nineteenth century, the "new quest"" attempted to arrive at the historical Jesus by passing through, rather than bypassing, the kerygma of the early Christian community. Käsemann said, "The historical Jesus comes to us as the Lord of faith community through the community."[14]

According to the new quest the function of history is neither to prove the validity of kerygma, nor to lay the foundation for a higher level of Christology but to serve as a critical standard and corrective for them. It did not intend to establish the historical ground of faith but to critically discern right proclamation from wrong proclamation. While the old quest presupposed separation between the historical Jesus and the Christ of faith and forced theologians to choose either one or the other, the new quest affirmed substantial continuity between the two and suggested a hermeneutical circle between them— i.e., to interpret the historical Jesus in terms of the kerygma and the kerygma in terms of the historical Jesus. In the following I too attempt to understand Jesus in light of the faith of the church and at the same time to reconstruct the faith of church in light of Jesus.

3. Recent Discussions of the historical Jesus and Christ of Faith, and A Hermeneutical Approach for Holistic Christology

Today's theological trend after Barth and Bultmann suggests the

---

[13] Günther Bornkamm, *Jesus von Nazareth*, 9th ed. (Stuttgart, 1971), 21.
[14] Ernst Käsemann, *Essays on New Testament Themes* (London: SCM, 1964), 23, 46.

task and direction of holistic Christology in the twenty-first century. The primary task of holistic Christology is to solve the problem of the scandal of particularity by combining the historical Jesus and the Christ of faith into a whole. The two should not be separated from each other, nor should they be reduced into one or the other. On the one hand, if the historical Jesus were dissolved into the Christ of faith, then the human face of Jesus as an objective fact would be forgotten. Then, little attention would be given to the soteriological dimension as revealed in the realty-transforming works of Jesus who was willing to sacrifice his own life in order to embody God's kingdom and righteousness on earth. Also, Jesus' teaching, "If anyone would come after me, he must deny himself and take up his cross and follow me" (Matt. 16:24), would lose its validity. This explains the need for the new quest for the historical Jesus. On the other hand, if the Christ of faith were dissolved into the historical Jesus, then we would lose sight of the divine face revealed in Christ. Then, the ground of Christian belief in Christ's statement that "Anyone who has seen me has seen the Father" (John 14:9) would be weakened, and one would not be able to speak of God who sacrificed Christ to save the world. Therefore, the historical Jesus and the Christ of faith can neither be directly identified nor reduced to one or the other.

There is another convincing reason why one should understand the relation between the historical Jesus and the Christ of faith as one of substantial continuity rather than one of separation. Our Yes or No to the kingdom of God that Jesus proclaimed correspond to our Yes or No to Jesus Christ, and the other way around. For the kingdom of God was proleptically present and realized in the person and work of Jesus Christ. In our attempt to understand the historical Jesus we should remember that the historical Jesus is accessible to us only through the first Christians' subjective experiences and faithful interpretations, because it is only through the New Testament that we can have access to the historical Jesus. In the strict sense, therefore, the historical Jesus refers to the historical-critically reconstructed Jesus. In the new quest, furthermore, the historical-critical approach does not bypass, but passes through, the kerygma of the early Christian community. As a result, the historical Jesus in the historical-positivistic sense does not exist.

In the New Testament the historical Jesus and the Christ of faith are mediated by the appearance of the resurrected Jesus. This does not mean that the Christ of faith is not historically grounded upon the teaching and ministry of the pre-Easter Jesus, but that the experience of the appearance of the resurrected Jesus marked the decisive turning point in faith in Jesus as Christ and Lord. The pre-Easter historical Jesus became Lord and Christ after Easter. Jesus, who was filled with the Holy Spirit before Easter, became a spiritual reality after Easter. In fact, the appearance of the resurrected Jesus, as recorded in the New Testament via oral traditions, is in itself a combination of an objective reality and an existential, i.e., faithful interpretation of it, rather than a purely objective, value-neutral event. Experiences of the resurrection appearance are given to us as on object of intention (*noema*), or a fact (*Sache*) grasped in the pre-structure of understanding, through different forms of resurrection traditions and in the written form of the New Testament.

Thanks to Edmund Husserl's epistemological phenomenology

and Martin Heidegger's phenomenological ontology, today we are more clearly aware that it is impossible to make a dualistic distinction between external object and intentional object, between objective reality and semantic reality, and between being and interpretation. Hence, it is an impossible possibility to completely separate the historical Jesus as an objective realty from the Christ of faith as a semantic reality. Thus, one should reject both modern alternatives to traditional metaphysical dogmatism: namely, the historical-positivistic objective realism of the old quest in the nineteenth century which sought to find the historical Jesus as a pure, value-free fact, on the one hand, and existentialist subjective idealism which reduced the reality of Jesus Christ to the Christ of faith, on the other. Moreover, supra-historical transcendental revelationism, which was suggested as an alternative to historicism of the nineteenth century, cannot provide us with a genuine alternative.

A purely objective fact (*Sache*) does not exist—at least in the human existence as *Dasein* (Being-there). Today's hermeneutics clearly shows that the fact (*Sache*) itself contains the pre-structure of understanding and the models of interpretation, both of which are derived from the ontological horizon of being-in-the-world. They should not be confused with a simply psychological subjectivity. The world, horizon, pre-structure of understanding, pre-understanding, and models of interpretation are fundamental conditions of the understanding and existence of a human being as *Dasein* (Being-there). The hermeneutical circle, which is regarded as a vicious circle in the epistemological dimension, now becomes the fundamental structure of *Dasein* (Being-there) in the ontological dimension. Hence, the real issue is not how to overcome the circularity between the historical Jesus and the Christ of faith in the epistemological dimension, but how to enter into the circle in a proper way in the ontological dimension. This points to the methodological task for the hermeneutical construction of holistic Christology.

In 1985 a group of scholars gathered together to renew the quest for the historical Jesus in "the Jesus Seminar," which was founded by Robert W. Funk. Tom Wright calls it "the third quest for the historical Jesus," and Marcus Borg terms it "Jesus Renaissance."[15] According to Borg, who once participated in the Jesus Seminar, the Jesus in the Gospel stories is not the historical Jesus but the Jesus who is confessed as Christ. Thus, the search for the historical Jesus is nothing but the attempt to draw a picture of the historical Jesus from the Gospel stories of Jesus. Borg embarked on this study with two assumptions.[16] First, the Gospels contain developing traditions. As time passed the Jesus traditions in the Gospels continued to develop in the new contexts and with the new experiences of Jesus (for example, resurrection). In the Gospels, therefore, one can discern the early strata derived from the historical Jesus and the late strata produced by the early Christian

---

[15] The Jesus Seminar has two tasks. The first is to collectively and systematically study how many of the Gospel records are in reality ascribed to the historical Jesus, and the second is to exalt biblical consciousness among people so that people may find the Bible convincing to them. Marcus J. Borg, "The Search for the Historical Jesus," Online Interview, http:www.cathedral.org /cathedral/cathedral-age/borg.html, 1. Participants in it reconstructed Jesus' words and acts. In the process they thought the biblical documents are not sufficient enough. So they employed research of other neighboring disciplines—including the study of the social world of the first century Palestine. By disclosing the dominant culture of the social world at that time they attempted to reconstruct the meaning of Jesus' words and acts as a whole. Scholars of Jesus Seminar claimed that they made two new discoveries: (1) Jesus was not an eschatological prophet who proclaimed the imminent end of the world, and (2) Jesus was a teacher of subversive wisdom who overthrew the established wisdom and order. Marcus J. Borg, "Jesus and Eschatology: Current Reflections," trans. Jun-Woo Kim, "Yesuwa jongmalon: choigeunui donghyang," *Segyeui sinhak* 「세계의 신학」 [Global Theology] 51 (2001.6). In this regard E. P. Sander is an exception.

community. In order to reconstruct the historical Jesus one should distinguish one (the voice of Jesus) from the other (the voice of the church). Second, the Gospels contain both history remembered and history metaphorized. The Gospels do not simply transmit the remembered Jesus but also make use of metaphorical language and stories in order to represent the meaning of Jesus. As a result, the task to reconstruct the historical Jesus requires making a distinction between history remembered and history metaphorized.

Instead of distinguishing between the historical Jesus and the Christ of faith, Borg prefers to make distinguish between the pre-Easter Jesus and the post-Easter Jesus. The former refers to Jesus as a historical figure who lived in the first century (the historical Jesus), while the latter refers to Jesus in the Christian tradition and experience (the Christ of faith). The pre-Easter Jesus is the historical Jesus, a person of the past who lived from 4 BCE to 30 CE. As a Jew, named Jesus of Nazareth, he was a physical, finite, and mortal human being. Meanwhile, the post-Easter Jesus is a person of the present who has lived from 30 CE until today. As Jesus Christ the Savior of the world he is a spiritual, infinite, and eternal divine being.[17]

Since the scheme of the historical Jesus and the Christ of faith suggests that the former is true and the latter is simply a vague hypothetical reality that demands our faith, Borg tried to avoid such a misunderstanding by underlining that the post-Easter Jesus refers to Jesus in the Christian tradition and experience. To put it another way, the

---

[16] Marcus Borg and N. T. Wright, *The Meaning of Jesus: Two Visions* (New York: Harper Collins, 1999), 4-6.

[17] Marcus J. Borg (ed.), *Jesus at 2000* (Oxford: Westview Press, 1998), 8. Marcus Borg, *The God We Never Knew* (New York: HarperSanFrancisco, 1997), 85-87.

post-Easter Jesus is not just an article of faith but an experiential reality. He denies regarding either the historical Jesus or the Christ of faith as the true Jesus. Despite decisive discontinuity between the pre-Easter Jesus and the post-Easter Jesus, Borg emphasizes that they are in fact the same Jesus. In other words, Borg argues, the historical Jesus is the same as Jesus in the Christian tradition and experience.

In order to reconstruct the pre-Easter Jesus Borg employs historical-critical, inter-cultural, and interdisciplinary methods. In this way he reconstructs the historical Jesus as a Jewish mystic, a spiritual man, a charismatic healer, a teacher of subversive wisdom that overthrows conventional wisdom, a social prophet who criticized the contemporary ruling system represented by Jerusalem and the Temple and envisioned an alternative social structure of the kingdom of God, and a movement initiator who had a concrete vision of the inclusive, egalitarian society as demonstrated by his sharing a table with sinners.[18] This is what Borg draws from the earliest strata of the Gospel traditions. And it is not Jesus metaphorized but Jesus remembered.

Borg regards the Gospel stories about the post-Easter Jesus as metaphorical representations of the Easter experience. They do not refer to facts that should be read literally, but to metaphorical representations of both the early Christians' experience of the post-Easter Jesus and their conviction that God raised him from the dead, both of which are historical facts. In this sense they are true. After Easter the Jewish mystic became the Messiah of Christianity.[19] The essential meaning of Easter does not lie in the literal, historical reports but in

---

[18] Borg, *Jesus at 2000, 11; The Meaning of Jesus: Two Visions,* 60; *The God We Never Knew,* 89-90; *Meeting Jesus Again for the First Time* (New York: HarperCollins, 1994), 29-30.

the fact that Jesus' disciples continued to experience Jesus even after his death. In the post-Easter Christian tradition and experience Jesus was experienced as a spiritual reality who is not confined by space and time but is always and everywhere present—i.e., as the still living Jesus. The early Christians understood their experience of Jesus' resurrection from the following two perspectives: first, God vindicated and approved the pre-Easter Jesus, and, second, God raised Jesus to his right hand, or Jesus became Lord.[20]

Borg argues that the experience of Jesus as a spiritual reality developed into the conviction that God raised Jesus and the confession that Jesus is the living Lord, which then developed into traditions of the empty tomb and resurrection appearances.[21] Finally, these traditions developed into a theology of resurrection. In the process of Christological formation one finds that experience gives birth to symbol (or metaphor), which in turn gives birth to thought, as Paul Ricoeur once said. Of special significance in the process is metaphor. Borg proposes to understand Jesus as a metaphor. When "the Son of God" is understood as a metaphor, he argues, the other different Christological metaphors will disclose their own fruitful meanings.[22]

In short, Borg's contribution consists in his proposal of a good alternative to the age-long dilemma between the historical Jesus and Christ of faith, which he reconfigured as the relation between the pre-Easter Jesus and the post-Easter Jesus, and convincingly demonstrated the unity (as well as difference) between them. In contrast with the

---

[19] Borg, *The Meaning of Jesus*, 54.
[20] Borg, *The God We Never Knew*, 94.
[21] Borg, *The Meaning of Jesus*, 136-37.
[22] Borg, *Meeting Jesus Again for the First Time*, 110.

old quest for the historical Jesus and the recent Jesus Seminar, he does not ignore or overlook, but takes seriously, existential experience of spiritual reality. In this vein he takes seriously the Christian tradition and experience of the post-Easter Jesus as a spiritual reality. And he does not condemn the development from experience through metaphor to doctrine. He accepts metaphor and doctrine as truth based upon Christians' spiritual experience, though not in their literal sense. What is important here is their relation to the spiritual reality they refer to.

The essence of the resurrection experience is that Jesus' disciples continued to experience Jesus as a spiritual reality even after his death. In other words, the pre-Easter Jesus, as a man of the Holy Spirit, became the post-Easter Christ as a spiritual reality. To become a Christian means to become a person of the Holy Spirit who experiences God like Jesus and to become a person who experiences Jesus as a spiritual reality.

In short, Borg attempts to solve the dilemma between the historical Jesus and the Christ of faith in terms of the Spirit Christology. According to Borg, the idea of Jesus as a man of the Holy Spirit means that Jesus is a man possessed by the Holy Spirit in the presence of the transcendent-immanent God and lives in direct relationship with God. Jesus is filled with God as the Holy Spirit. As a man of the Holy Spirit Jesus heals the sick, teaches alternative wisdom, becomes a social prophet, and makes an alternative community. The idea that the post-Easter Jesus is not just a man of the Holy Spirit but a divine being as a spiritual reality corresponds to the reverse relationship between the Holy Spirit and Jesus. According to the New Testament, before Easter

Jesus was conceived, performed his ministry, and was raised from the dead by the Holy Spirit, while after Easter Jesus became the giver of the Holy Spirit. However, Borg fails to give a sufficiently intelligible explanation of the development from Jesus as a man of the Holy Spirit to Jesus as a spiritual reality.[23]

Developing further Borg's distinction between the pre-Easter Jesus and the post-Easter Jesus, Sandra Schneiders discerns four dimensions of Jesus in the Gospels: the actual Jesus, the historical Jesus, the proclaimed Jesus, and the textual Jesus.[24]

1) The Actual Jesus

The actual Jesus refers to the ontic being in its factuality, or the personal Jesus. Jesus existed actually in the first century Palestine, yet no longer in the same way. The actual Jesus in God's glory is the one who once existed actually in the first century Palestine and has now absorbed that actuality into the current Jesus. The actual Jesus today is the glorious Christ with whom we communicate through the Holy Spirit; regarding him we do not make historical statements in the strict sense but theological statements. The actual Jesus, therefore, refers to Jesus Christ who once lived in Palestine in the first century and now is at work among us in God's glory through the Holy Spirit. The

---

[23] Another problem in Borg's discussion of Jesus is that just like other participants in the Jesus Seminar he also overlooks the model of Jesus as an eschatological prophet and in this way makes the picture of the pre-Easter Jesus quite unhistorical. If it is because he believed the eschatological is a purely other-worldly category having nothing to do with our social-political reality that the eschatological aspect of the historical Jesus was excluded from his discussion, it is a great misunderstanding. In fact, as an eschatological prophet Jesus proclaimed a vision of the reality-transforming and future-oriented kingdom of God that overthrows the established order.

[24] Sandra M. Schneiders, *The Revelatory Text: Interpreting the New Testament as Sacred Scripture* (Collegeville: The Liturgical Press, 1999).

Gospels intend to inform us of the human existence of the one in whom we believe and thus of the life of the earthly Jesus (or his life before resurrection as interpreted in light of resurrection). And through the resurrection stories the Gospels aim to tell us who the Jesus that we believe in is as he exists now in his glory.[25]

The strong point of this approach is that one no longer needs to "return" to the "purely historical" Jesus (whom Jesus' disciples, and even Jesus himself, did not regard as divine), nor is there a need to explain the disciples' resurrection faith that produced the glorious "Christ." Every knowledge of Jesus Christ, both the pre-Easter Jesus and the post-Easter Jesus, is penetrated by the resurrection. It is impossible to "reconstruct" the pre-Easter Jesus as if he would not become glorified at last. The pre-Easter or earthly Jesus who would never be raised from the dead is not the real Jesus. The real Jesus is the living Jesus Christ who is now transformed and glorified through resurrection but incorporates the pre-Easter experiences as his past.

In fact, there is no past as an objective reality or state that is isolated in itself. The past always exists as one that has been incorporated into the experience (including interpretation activities) of the current subject. The Gospel authors did not first look back on the life of the earthly Jesus and then interpret it in light of their resurrection faith, but they approached the "past" as a part of their present. We have four Gospels that are not easy to harmonize. Each Gospel shows the events of Jesus who was incorporated into the experiences of a particular community within a particular context. Thus, the Jesus stories are incorporated into very complex experiences (or interpretations) of the

---

[25] Ibid., xxi.

present. From this very complex web of interpretations it is impossible to separate the "pure history of Jesus."[26]

The actual Jesus is currently in God's glory and works in the world through the Holy Spirit. The actual Jesus cannot be reduced to the pre-Easter Jesus, nor to any one statement in the New Testament, nor to any later scholarly reconstruction. The New Testament texts do not allow a faith-neutral approach to the person of an isolated past. Those texts were written in faith for the purpose of mediating faith to faith.[27]

2) The Historical Jesus

"The historical Jesus" refers to a historian's literary construction or representation of the pre-Easter Jesus out of the Gospel stories and other sources. As regards "the historical Jesus," however, one cannot deal with the supra-historical aspects of the Jesus event or the church's faith in Jesus. Nor can one speak of the divine origin of Jesus far back beyond his physical birth, nor of his resurrection, ascension, sending of the Holy Spirit, or glorious life "at the right hand of God" far beyond his death. In other words, the historical Jesus does not refer to a person; it falls short of the pre-Easter Jesus who "actually existed." It is simply a literary representation of a certain aspect of the pre-Easter Jesus.

The Gospel authors did not intend to suggest the historical Jesus in this sense. Though their stories of Jesus contain historical documents, they are also full of theological interpretations, faith confes-

---

[26] Ibid., xxiii.
[27] Ibid., xxvi.

sions, and experiences in the Christian community, of the post-Easter Jesus. "The historical Jesus" (or the earthly Jesus before Easter), as reconstructed in a similar form to Jesus' biography, is not "the real Jesus" but an imaginary representation. The unhistorical aspects, with which the Gospel texts are filled, are missing in the historical Jesus. Thus, the historical Jesus is not the Jesus of faith and does not tell anything about the real Jesus that is necessary for our faith.[28]

Instead of the expression "the historical Jesus" Schneiders proposes to use "the actual, ontic pre-Easter Jesus." This is useful when one distinguishes between the pre-Easter Jesus and the post-Easter Jesus. She says that we would do better to talk about "the historical documents about the pre-Easter Jesus as linguistically represented in the Gospel texts."[29]

3) The Proclaimed Jesus

"The real Jesus" whom Christian believe in is "the proclaimed Jesus." The proclaimed Jesus refers to the post-Easter Jesus in glory, who is the same as the pre-Easter Jesus who walked in the Palestinian land. This is the actual, ontic Jesus whom today's church witnesses to and in whom Christians believe. The proclaimed Jesus includes not only every historical document about the pre-Easter Jesus but also the supra-historical dimension of Jesus' ministry, as well as his enduring life in God and in the church. But whenever church falls into dogmatism or controversy, the proclaimed Jesus does not represent the real Jesus.[30]

---

[28] Ibid., xxvi.
[29] Ibid., xxvii.

4) The Textual Jesus

While the proclaimed Jesus appears in different forms throughout the history of Christianity, the textual Jesus refers to the proclaimed Jesus in the first Christian communities. In other words, the textual Jesus is the normative Jesus contained in the canonized New Testament texts. The proclaimed Jesus in each period should be evaluated by this norm. Schneiders says, "Christian faith does not terminate in the historical reconstruction of a first-century preacher, social activist, or thaumaturge who is dead, but in the real, actual, living Jesus who is accessible to us through the church's proclamation, insofar as that proclamation is faithful to the textual Jesus."[31] To follow Jesus faithfully does not mean to blindly "copy" the thought and practice of the first century, but to creatively develop what she calls "following Jesus in the present." Therefore, continuous and elaborate study of the textual Jesus is of essential significance. Faithfulness does not prohibit further development of Christian faith in response to today's new interests. The textual Jesus promised to send his disciples the Holy Spirit "who will guide them to the truth" (John 16:13). In each new period the Holy Spirit will help Christians creatively respond to new challenges that the Gospel writers never imagined.[32] In retrospect, in the textual Jesus the actual pre-Easter Jesus is incorporated into the proclaimed Jesus; in prospect, the textual Jesus in the New Testament functions as the norm of continuously developing

---

30 Ibid., xxviii.

31 Ibid., xxix.

32 Ibid., xxx.

proclamation of Jesus as the actual, glorious, and living Lord.

Schneiders' understanding of Jesus as discussed above represents a recent, more advanced form of hermeneutical approach for holistic Christology. Instead of the framework of the historical Jesus and the Christ of faith, she thoroughly stresses the textual Jesus as derived from the New Testament texts. The textual Jesus shows us the actual Jesus—namely, both the pre-Easter Jesus on Earth and the post-Easter Jesus in glory. Both dimensions of Jesus reflect a post-Easter perspective, and thus objective facts and subjective interpretations are combined in the textual Jesus. The textual Jesus in the New Testament is in its essence the proclaimed Jesus, but does not exhaust the reality of Jesus. For the post-Easter Jesus in glory has been present even in church history following the New Testament period, and he is also living among us today. In short, the textual Jesus who is proclaimed in various ways in the New Testament is the same Jesus whom each church after the New Testament era attempts to proclaim in different ways.

This understanding of Jesus is based upon the hermeneutical framework of Paul Ricoeur, who proposed to overcome the romanticist or historical-critical approach that seeks the world behind the text and to appropriate the reference or the world disclosed in front of the text on the ground of the inner structure (sense) of the text. Thus, both the pre-Easter Jesus on Earth and the post-Easter Jesus in glory are found in the dialectic between the sense and reference of the text. In the New Testament era the text itself witnesses to the proclaimed Jesus. But since then and even still today the church in her different life settings proclaims and appropriates in various ways the glorious post-Easter Jesus as the reference disclosed in front of the text and on the basis of the sense of the text. Meanwhile, not only the literary criticism of the inner structure within the text, but also the romanticist historical-criticism of the world behind the text and the hermeneutics of suspicion, including various critical theories, offer valuable criteria and correctives to ensure both relative adequacy and responsible diversity of those diverse meanings and worlds disclosed in front of the text (proclaimed Jesus). Therefore, when we combine Ricoeur's hermeneutical theory with these other approaches we can contribute to developing an even more holistic Christology.

III
The Doctrine of Incarnation

Just as Jesus asked his disciples, "Who do you say I am?" (Mark 8:29), the problem of Jesus Christ's personal identity has been at the very center of Christological discussions from the very beginning. In fact, this question was raised not only to his disciples but also to many others. "Are you the one who is to come, or should we expect someone else?" (Matt. 11:3). This passage clearly shows that the question about the personal identity of Jesus Christ is inseparable from another question concerning the soteriological significance of his works. Since the messianic ideas first formed within the context of Israel's suffering and oppression and then developed into a national hope during the period of colonization, Israelite people expected that some day the Messiah would come to save them. With such an expectation they came to Jesus and asked, "Are you the one who is to come?" In other words, the personal identity of Jesus Christ is not an abstract or speculative issue but one that has real soteriological significance. The primary concern of the first Christians, as well as of the authors of the New Testament, was not only to answer the question of who Jesus is, but also to defend and witness to the reasons for their confession of Jesus as the Messiah, Christ, and Lord. "But these are written that you may believe that Jesus is the Christ, the Son of God, and that by believing you may have life in his name" (John 20:31).

1. Christology of the New Testament

The process of Christological understanding of Jesus was not completed once and for all; nor does it show a linear, progressive development. Christological ideas developed by employing different titles and models available within the horizons of the early Christian communities and through a very complex process of mutual interactions between them. Immediately after Jesus died on the cross his disciples scattered. But after the appearance of the resurrected Jesus they began to proclaim that Jesus is the Messiah for whom the Israelite people had been awaiting a long time. In the process, however, the traditional Jewish concept of the Messiah had to be revised and reinterpreted. The concept of the Davidic, kingly Messiah who has a political and military power to liberate Israel from the domination of other nations had to be replaced by the concept of the suffering Messiah who dies for us. When the first Christians applied the messianic concept to Jesus, they represented it as an image of the prophet or the suffering servant of Yahweh rather than as an image of a kingly ruler. In Peter's preaching, which is regarded as one of the oldest traditions, Jesus is represented as an eschatological prophet filled with the Holy Spirit.[33]

The image of the eschatological prophet filled with the Holy Spirit became the matrix out of which all other Christological titles and models emerged and developed through a complex process of reciprocal interactions. Of the Synoptic Gospels, the Gospel of Mark retains relatively faithfully the image of Jesus as an eschatological prophet filled with the Holy Spirit. As the first written Gospel it begins with the event of Jesus' baptism in the Jordan River rather than with the divine origin of Jesus' life. This shows the first understanding of Jesus' personal identity in the early period. The Markan report that Jesus was appointed to the messiahship through the presence of the dove-like Spirit in the Jordan River implicitly suggests that Jesus began his messianic ministry as an eschatological prophet filled with the Holy Spirit. Of course, one can also find other Christological models in the Gospel of Mark—e.g., the model of a divine person (*theois aner*) that emphasizes Jesus' supernatural power of performing miracles (Mark 5:30; Luke 1:35).[34] In the Gospel of Mark, just as in the other

---

33 "But he was a prophet and knew that God had promised him on oath that he would place one of his descendants on his throne... Exalted to the right hand of God, he has received from the Father the promised Holy Spirit and has poured out what you." (Acts 2:30,33). "For Moses said, 'The Lord your God will raise up for you a prophet like me from among your own people; you must listen to everything he tells you. 23 Anyone who does not listen to him will be completely cut off from their people.'" (Acts 3:22-23).

34 According to Edward Schillebeeckx, early Christians accepted, though in a revised form, the Hellenistic idea of a god man. Schillebeeckx called Jesus of this model a "divine miracle worker," and this Christology "Christology of the Solomonic son of David." For the details, see Edward Schillebeeckx, *Jesus: An Experiment in Christology*, trans. Hubert Hoskins (New York: Seabury Press, 1979), 424-28.

Gospels, diverse, sometimes incompatible Christological models co-exist. Nonetheless, the most distinctive Christological model in the Gospel of Mark, whose story reaches its climax in the suffering of Jesus, is the eschatological prophet, who in the power of the Holy Spirit, proclaimed and brought to practice the gospel of God's kingdom, was persecuted, and, finally, executed.

As time passes, the story of Jesus' divine origin develops into a clearer form. In the Gospel of Mark Jesus' genealogy starts from Abraham, and the divine origin of Jesus is represented by the story of the virgin birth through conception by the Holy Spirit. In the Gospel of Luke Jesus' genealogy goes further back to God, and the story of the virgin birth is further elaborated by including the story of the birth of John the Baptist. Meanwhile, the original Markan tradition ends up with the story of the empty tomb. But the Gospel of Matthew adds to the story of the empty tomb a short story of the appearance of the resurrected Jesus in Galilee. And the Gospel of Luke contains even more details of Jesus' appearance, including his appearance to two of his disciples on the way to Emmaus, his appearance to the apostles in Jerusalem, and his ascension to heaven.

The Gospel of John, written latest of the four Gospels, does not begin with Jesus' genealogy or the story of Jesus' virgin birth through the Holy Spirit, but with the story of the incarnation of the Word (*logos*) of God. While the Synoptic Gospels overall represent bottom-up Christology, the Gospel of John shows an example of top-down Christology. Of course, since the latter is the only book written by one of Jesus' direct disciples, it contains many concrete and correct records about the historical Jesus. At the same time, however, it is the

Gospel that most reflects the religious culture of the Hellenistic world in the late first century—sometimes even Gnosticism. In the Gospel of John, hence, one finds that the Jewish-historical and Hellenistic-metaphysical features coexist more so than in the other Gospels. The Gospel of John contains not only the story of the empty tomb but also the story of Jesus' appearances; in particular, it tells that the resurrected Jesus appeared to his disciples in Galilee, ate with them, and talked with Peter in great detail. All things considered, I think that by the late first century, when the Gospel of John had been already written, the development of the bottom-up Christology came to its final form in the Christian community.[35]

Noteworthy is the fact that the life setting of the church changed from Jewish to Hellenistic religious and intellectual culture. The new context demanded the Hellenization of Christianity in order to defend Christian truth in the Hellenistic world. In other words, the gospel of Christianity transformed the Hellenistic world, while the Christian identity was reconfigured within the religious, intellectual, and conceptual contexts of Hellenism. In the process traditional Jewish titles of Jesus Christ—such as Messiah, Son of Man, Servant of Yahweh—were replaced by Hellenistic titles—e.g., Word (*logos*), Lord (*kyrios*), and Savior (*soter*). The title of the Son of God was originally a family metaphor in the Jewish context, but its meaning changed and came to have a metaphysical connotation in the Hellenistic context. The Synoptic concept of the kingdom of God, which refers to historical,

---

[35] The development of Christology parallels that of the understanding of the relation between Jesus and the Holy Spirit. At first one finds the stories of Jesus' birth, baptism, ministry, and resurrection by the Holy Spirit, and then the reference to the Holy Spirit as the Holy Spirit of Christ and our Helper.

communal salvation in the Jewish religious-cultural tradition, was replaced by the Johannine concept of eternal life, which refers to suprahistorical, individual salvation in the Hellenistic world. One should also note that the Logos Christology of the Gospel of John functioned as an almost exclusive paradigm and norm for the orthodox Christological doctrines in the ancient church.

Meanwhile, the issue of Jesus' personal identity was not dominant in the letters of Paul. Instead, Paul concentrated his attention on the salvific meaning of Jesus' death on the cross. He laid the foundation for the Christian doctrine of atonement, which I will discuss in detail in the next section. The important thing to be noted is that Paul's theology of atonement, which concerns the significance of Jesus' death on the cross, inevitably implies a Christological understanding of Jesus' person. Paul rejected the divine-man Christology, according to which Jesus demonstrates his divinity by his power performing supernatural miracles. Paul was convinced that God's saving power was revealed exclusively in the sacrificial love of Jesus Christ who suffered for us (1 Cor. 1:18). As an expert in the Jewish law Paul thought strictly in monotheistic terms. One can hardly expect from him a Johannine (or trinitarian) concept of the incarnation, which developed much later. The basic framework of Paul's Christology is the Adam Christology (Rom. 5:17-18; 1 Cor. 15:45-49). While the first Adam brought sin to humanity, Paul believes, Jesus Christ as the second or last Adam brought salvation to humanity. Also, he proclaims that Jesus Christ became our savior through the dialectic of cross and resurrection.[36] Thus, in Paul one finds the same development of bottom-up Christology as in the Gospels. However, for Paul the divinity of Jesus

Christ does not refer to the pre-existent Logos as a distinctive divine Person different from God, but to the physical presence of the divine wisdom (*hokma*) in the Holy Spirit.

Thus far I have discussed the formation and development of Christology in the New Testament. For holistic Christology the following points should be remembered. First, the formation of Christology was not completed once and for all, but progressively, though relatively rapidly, through a complex hermeneutical process. In the early Christian community there was a process of dialectical fusion of horizons in the hermeneutical circle between different traditions derived from different experiences and memories of Jesus, on the one hand, and different pre-structures of understanding, or Christological concepts and titles, originating from both Jewish and Hellenistic tradition. In the process different Christological models were formed and developed in different ways. But the early Christian community was not concerned primarily with describing the divine origin of the incarnation but with reinterpreting and proclaiming the salvific significance of Jesus' ministry—in particular, his cross—in light of the appearance of the resurrected Jesus. Even in the New Testament, incarnation Christology, as found in John 1:1-14, developed quite late. But the subsequent development of incarnation Christology was as fast as the change of the church's life setting from its Jewish to its Hellenistic context.

---

36 "... and who through the Spirit of holiness was declared with power to be the Son of God by his resurrection from the dead: Jesus Christ our Lord." (Rom. 1:4). "And being found in appearance as a man, he humbled himself and became obedient to death-- even death on a cross! Therefore God exalted him to the highest place and gave him the name that is above every name, that at the name of Jesus every knee should bow, in heaven and on earth and under the earth." (Php. 2:8-10).

Second, the hermeneutical development of Christology overall moved from bottom upward as time passed. Christological models developed first from the model of the eschatological prophet filled with the Holy Spirit, through the models of Messiah and Son of Man, to the models of Lord and Logos. The process was not a monolithic, evolutionary process, as if according to a natural law. It was a very complex process resulting from the combination of historical causality, contingency, and theological finality. Once the bottom-up Christology was established, the top-down model of the incarnation of the Word became the dominant paradigm and norm. The incarnation model, as described in the Gospel of John, was the paradigmatic model for the classical Christology in the ancient church within the context of the Hellenistic world. And this model dominated both the (pre-modern) Orthodox and (modern) neo-Orthodox Christology in the Western Church.

Third, It is neither possible nor desirable to say that any one of the various Christological models is absolutely right or normative. One cannot argue from a historical-positivistic or cultural-anthropological perspective that the first model is the authentic and, thus, true model. Nor can one argue from the evolutionary or idealistic perspective that the last model is the best. Each Christological model in the Bible, if it is an outcome of a faithful response through the process of the dialectical fusion of horizons in the given hermeneutical circle, can claim its own normativity and relative adequacy. Each model should be understood within the context of the life setting in which it formed, and whether it is true or false should be judged first of all in that context. From the hermeneutical perspective, therefore, we need to critically reflect upon the fact that the incarnation Christology in the Gospel of John played the role of an exclusive paradigm or norm for the first as well as later Christological discussions in the Western church. Arguably, it was natural for the Christian church in the Hellenistic world to adopt John's incarnation model as the normative paradigm. However, such an exclusive normativity was possible only by suppressing other—especially Jewish—Christological models. Be that as it may, one cannot demand to substitute it with another exclusive model. Our criticism of the exclusive normativity of one certain model does not aim to replace it with another exclusive model, but to establish the vision of a more holistic Christology by taking into account the relative adequacy of other models as well.

Fourth, on the basis of hermeneutical awareness, holistic Christology pursues unity in diversity rather than uniformity, as well as universality through diverse concrete individuals rather than through abstract generalization. Thus, in pursuit of unity and universality we do not simply exclude conflicting elements, even if it is not easy to harmonize them, but critically embrace them for the sake of wholeness through the conciliar unity of the Holy Spirit. Furthermore, holistic Christology recognizes the task of a new fusion of horizons in today's new life setting. The Christological process is not completed in a certain period. It is not closed to itself. Just as in the New Testament, so is it open to the continuous fusion of horizons in the ancient, medieval, modern, and postmodern times. Through the fusion of horizons today's holistic Christology is necessary to construct a new One out of the Many against the horizon of the postmodern world and to enrich the Many through the new One.

2. Theory of Incarnation in the Ancient Church.

Since the first century the ancient church was institutionalized and systematized in the Hellenistic world. Remarkable in the Christological models of the ancient church is the shift from the Jewish historical paradigm to the Hellenistic metaphysical paradigm. The metaphysical paradigm was established in essentially dualistic and substantial categories—with a focus on the model of the incarnation of the Logos. The original meaning of incarnation is found in the first witnesses' confession that everything in Jesus' person and life and every salvific grace given to us through him come from God (2 Cor. 5:17-19). Within the metaphysical framework of Hellenism this authentic confessional interpretation developed into the idea of incarnation as the act or state whereby a non-physical divine being takes the physical human body, referring to the mysterious union between divinity and humanity in the one person of Jesus Christ.

In the ancient church the formation of the doctrine of the incarnation took the following three steps, centering around the debate between the Antiochene School and the Alexandrian School. In the first step the key issue was the divinity of Jesus, or Jesus' relationship with God: namely, the trinitarian issue; in the second step the humanity of Jesus; and in the third the way of union of two natures, divinity and humanity, in one person. In the first step Arius and Athanasius were in debate. Adhering to the concept of Logos as generally understood in the Hellenistic dualistic and substantial worldview, Arius regarded the Logos as the secondary God who mediates between the transcendent One and the world. In this way Arius represented Hellenistic rationality and argued that the divinity of Jesus Christ is "of similar substance" with that of God the Father. In contrast, Athanasius represented the opinion more faithful to the soteriological piety in the apostolic tradition. Following Irenaeus' teaching that the savior must be the creator, he argued that the one who saves us should be "of the same substance" with God the Father. In the first ecumenical council in Nicaea (325) the latter understanding was adopted as orthodox.

Then, as the second step, the Council of Constantinople (381) established Christ's humanity by adopting the anthropology of Apollinarius, who asserted that Christ's humanity consists in his flesh and animal-like soul, while his spirit or mind is replaced by the divine Logos. In particular, Gregory of Nazianzus' soteriological thesis that that which he has not assumed he has not healed was crucial in ensuring Christ's humanity.

In the third step there was a controversy regarding the manner of the union between the divinity and humanity of Jesus Christ: the Antiochene School supported the indwelling model, while the Alexandrian School argued for the model of hypostatic union. It should be noted that both models used Hellenistic categories. When Nestorius argued for the indwelling model along with Theodore, he tried to ensure not only Jesus' humanity but also his divinity. In his judgment, on the one hand, if Jesus' humanity were hypostatically united with the infinite, immutable, eternal, incorruptible, and immortal divinity, then the former would be absorbed by the latter; on the other hand, if his divinity were hypostatically united with the finite, mutable, temporal, corruptible, and mortal divinity, then the former would be damaged by the latter. In ensuring Jesus' humanity the position of the Antiochene School was in agreement with the Jewish historical model of the eschatological prophet filled with the Holy Spirit.

Meanwhile, Cyril of Alexandria supported the model of hypostatic union in order to ensure the divinity of Christ. He did not explicitly deny Jesus' humanity. However, he was well aware that the model of hypostatic union necessarily weakens the concept of Jesus' humanity. For when two opposing natures, divinity and humanity, are hypostatically united, humanity is unavoidably absorbed by, or subjugated to, divinity. Cyril's successor, Eutyches, argued that after the incarnation there is only one nature—namely, divinity. In this way he made explicit the monophysite tendency that was implicit in the hypostatic union model.

The Council of Chalcedon condemned both Nestorius' model of indwelling and Eutyches' monophysitism. The Chalcedonian Creed contained four negative expressions, which was an outcome of negotiation and synthesis between the two positions represented by Nestorius and Cyril. To be more specific, the model of hypostatic union, rather than that of indwelling, was adopted, while the deification of human nature as the unavoidable consequence of the hypostatic union model was denied. Two of the four negative phrases, "indivisibly" and "inseparably," represent hypostatic union, while the other two phrases, "unconfusedly" and "unchangeably," represent denial of the deification of human nature. Still, a difficult problem was left unsolved. For the Creed of Chalcedon was formulated within the conceptual framework of the dualistic and substantialist worldview of Hellenism, in which it is a logical self-contradiction to argue for the hypostatic union in one person of two incompatible natures—i.e., the infinite, immutable, eternal, incorruptible, and immortal divinity and the finite, mutable, temporal, corruptible, and mortal humanity.[37] However, the church justified such a logical dilemma in terms of a paradoxical truth or an incomprehensible mystery of God.

This critique of the self-contradiction and related problems of the Chalcedonian Creed do not necessarily lead to denial of its validity. Nor do they mean that one should reject the Creed because it is false. Rather, they mean that one should indicate and overcome the limitations of the Creed while affirming its legitimacy and contribution. The legitimacy of the Creed consists in the fact that it was one of the best possible responses to the biblical tradition within the worldview of the time, as an outcome of the hermeneutical fusion of two horizons—namely, the biblical tradition and the worldview and experience of the time. Of course, the Creed of Chalcedon is not the final answer, which is not possible within history. By incorporating the Hellenistic worldview and concepts to the stream of the biblical tradition the Creed handed over the classical paradigm to all subsequent Christian traditions. In other words, the Chalcedonian thesis that true deity and true humanity are united in Jesus Christ has become the foundation, presupposition, and starting point for every subsequent Christological discussion.

---

[37] In medieval and modern times there were continuing debates and serious attempts to solve the problem implied in the Chalcedonian idea of two natures in one person: for instance, the theory of communication of properties *communioatio idiomatum* (Col. 2:9) and the theory of kenosis (Php. 2:6-8). But none of the proposed theories succeeded in solving the dilemma convincingly. For more details, see my book, *Yeosu grisdo* 『예수그리스도』 [Jesus Christ], vol. 1, rev. ed., 493-497.

3. Prospect of the Holistic Doctrine of Incarnation

Today's Christological discussion should neither repeat the propositional truth of the Chalcedonian Creed literally—i.e., in an uncritical and non-temporal way, nor regard it as an obsolete relic of an old age and throw it away with one-sided emphasis on a contemporary perspective. The task of today's Christology is, on the one hand, to recognize the effective history of the Creed of Chalcedon as the classical paradigm within the Christian tradition and, on the other hand, to critically point out the fundamental reason for the problem implied in it and then pursue a holistic postmodern Christological model through a new hermeneutical fusion of horizons.

Indeed, modern and contemporary theologians attempted to reinterpret the Creed of Chalcedon in their own way in a quite broad and diverse spectrum—namely, from simply imitating or repeating to radical reformulation and even abrogation. In the twentieth century Karl Barth tried to recover the traditional Christological model of the incarnation of the Word in a top-down approach. Barth accepted the Chalcedonian doctrine of two natures and then combined it with the idea of kenosis.[38] For Barth, as the act of God's free love, incarnation is a paradoxical mystery. Incarnation proves itself to be an event of divine revelation, he argued, because it is paradoxical and incomprehensible.[39]

Unlike Barth, Wolfhart Pannenberg attempted to reconstruct

---

[38] For more details about Barth's Christology, see my earlier discussion in *Yeosu grisdo* 『예수그리스도』 [Jesus Christ], vol. 2, chs. 2 and 3.

[39] This statement of Barth's provoked criticism that his position is not far from the ancient anti-intellectual fideism of Tertullian who said "I believe because it is absurd."

the incarnation Christology through the bottom-up approach—i.e., through the historical-critical approach to the reality of the historical Jesus. For Pannenberg, "the task of Christology is to establish the true understanding of Jesus' significance from his history."[40] Starting from the event of Jesus' resurrection, Pannenberg tried to confirm the eternal divinity, preexistence, and incarnation of Jesus Christ. Following Hegel, Pannenberg developed his ideas with strictly historical categories, and thus understood Jesus' divinity in terms of history rather than substantialist metaphysics. According to Pannenberg, Jesus is not a person in whom two qualitatively different substances, divinity and humanity are united; rather, Jesus' history is in itself God's history, and as such it anticipates divine revelation as the eschatological consummation of universal history. In this sense the man Jesus himself is God.

Today, in our pursuit of the holistic Christological model, we need to remember that since Christology of the incarnation of the Logos was adopted as the orthodox paradigm (and originated from the Gospel of John and then developed within the dualistic and substantialist metaphysics of Hellenism), earlier Christological models have been forgotten or suppressed. Today we need to recover these earlier Christological models. In particular, we need to recover the Spirit Christology, or the Christological model of Jesus as the eschatological prophet filled with the Holy Spirit, which was formulated in the earliest period within the Jewish tradition.

G. W. H. Lampe developed Spirit Christology on the basis of

---

40 Wolfhart Pannenberg, *Jesus—God and Man* (Philadelphia: Westminster Press, 1977), 30.

the Jewish concept of the Spirit.[41] According to Lampe, in the Hebrew context the Spirit (*ruach, pneuma*) does not refer to a substance or a personal being distinguished from God but to the creative act of God which is experienced in this world. The Spirit of God refers to the Godself who acts within humanity for humanity. The first Christians understood their experience of the Holy Spirit as the fulfillment of God's eschatological promise, and also believed that the Spirit was incarnated in Christ. According to Lampe, early Christians identified the Holy Spirit with their present experience of Christ's presence as an historical-eschatological reality. However, as the church grew within Hellenistic culture, the concept of the Spirit was substantialized in terms of Hellenistic dualism and lost the historical and eschatological meaning that it had in Hebrew culture. Sometime later in the development of Christological thought the concept of the Spirit was replaced by that of the Logos, because the latter better described Christ's substantial divinity. But Lampe asserted that Logos Christology cannot explain the relation between divinity and humanity within the one person of Jesus Christ in an intelligible way.

As Lampe said, the Israelite concept of the Spirit derived from the experience of the reality and power of God who was actively present in the world, in history, and in humanity. Hence, the full presence of the Spirit meant nothing but the presence of God, and the reality of the Spirit meant nothing but the reality of God. The presence of the Spirit and the reality of the Spirit were not separate. Thus, in Jesus Christ the presence of God and the reality of God were not separate.

---

[41] Cf. G. W. H. Lampe, *God as Spirit* (London: SCM, 1983).

When the pre-Easter Jesus, who was filled with the Spirit, and the historical Jesus, who was given the fullness of the Spirit, became, after Easter, Christ and Lord who bestowed the reality of the Holy Spirit,[42] the two statements were no longer incompatible nor contradictory. Unlike the Logos Christology of dualistic and substantialist Hellenism, Spirit Christology of the non-dualistic and non-substantialist Jewish tradition fits very well with the contemporary, postmodern relational worldview and has a great potential to develop into an intelligible and holistic Christological model.

However, the retrieval of Spirit Christology does not mean the replacement or dismissal of Logos Christology but the supplementation of its weaknesses and limitations. Our success in fully retrieving Spirit Christology in itself will bring us closer to holistic Christology, because in the contemporary postmodern world we are awakened anew to the fact that the truth is not one-sided or monolithic but many-sided and multi-dimensional. These days we do not believe that any one model can exhaust the truth in an absolute and exclusive way. Each model is essentially a sort of metaphor, and as such it uncovers and points to some of the multiple aspects of the reality and truth respectively. To use McFague's words, the metaphorical language of every religious model contains both yes and no.[43] Therefore, holistic Christology does not rely exclusively upon any one absolutized model but demands different and diverse models. Of course, it may not be easy to bring those different models into harmony, and they may ap-

---

[42] For a recent discussion of this topic, see Marcus J. Borg (ed.), *Jesus at 2000* (Oxford: Westview Press, 1998).

[43] Cf. Sallie McFague, *Metaphorical Theology: Models of God in Religious Language* (Philadelphia: Fortress, 1982), 14ff.

pear to conflict with each other. Nonetheless, holistic Christology does not allow us to abandon hope for the eschatological possibility that all of them can finally converge in one truth. This hope encourages us to pursue ecumenical spirituality as well as conciliar unity and solidarity in the Holy Spirit during the historical interim before the eschatological consummation. In ecumenical spirituality difference does not lead to mutual impoverishment but to mutual enrichment. It is not simply a crisis, but in fact an opportunity. In particular, to remember the face of the other who has been so far alienated and oppressed and recall her or his name is tantamount to liberating a new dimension of the thus far hidden truth. In this sense, as Emmauel Levinas once said, the face of postmodernity is the face of the other.

With regard to the prospect of holistic Christology, one concrete alternative model that may solve and overcome the dilemma of the Chalcedonian Creed is found in Alfred North Whitehead's relational process metaphysics and process Christology, both of which presuppose today's postmodern scientific worldview. The process view of reality provides us with a new vision of reality that overcomes the dualistic and substantialist worldview of Hellenism and integrates both the historical categories in Jewish thought and the ontological categories in Hellenistic thought. According to Whitehead's metaphysics, the essence of reality is not an independent and isolated substance but the dynamic process and relation themselves. Thus, it is "the fallacy of misplaced concreteness" to think of substantial being, meaning absolute reality, as being located in one temporal moment and in one spatial point, which is nothing but a product of abstraction. In this view of reality the subject-object dualism or immanence-transcendence dualism is metaphysically impossible. Every actual entity is a subject of prehension in the process of concretion and becomes an object immediately after it reaches satisfaction. Here experience, or prehension, does not refer to a subject's positing an object but to the self-organizing activity of a subject that forms itself by incorporating the object into itself. Therefore, the person itself is not assumed as an immutable, self-identical, and solid substance, and divinity and humanity are not understood as two mutually incompatible substantial natures. The identity of one person is ceaselessly renewed in the relationship with God and the world, and thus its creative progress never stops. The establishment of Christ's person in incarnation takes place when the subjective aim fully realizes the initial aim, or the primordial nature of God who enters the process of concretion. One may call it the fullness of the Holy Spirit or the incarnation of the Logos. For the historical is the ontological, and reality is nothing but the process in relationships.[44]

According to this relational, historical, and ontological view of reality the mystery of incarnation is explained as the harmony and unity of divine and human elements, rather than as the paradoxical union of two substantial natures. The God of love as relational in essence and authentic humanity created in God's image became perfectly united in the person and work of Jesus Christ. This is the true meaning of the Chalcedonian formulation of true God and true humanity. Only on the foundation of this relational and historical understanding of incarnation can one speak of the redemption of

---

[44] For more details, cf. my *Yeosu grisdo*, ch. 9.

humanity through God's suffering and sacrificial love as revealed in the cross of Jesus Christ. For, as Dietrich Bonhoeffer said, only the suffering God can save us.

IV
The Doctrine of Atonement

The process of formation and development of the doctrine of atonement in the ancient and medieval church parallels that of the doctrine of the incarnation. The early Christian community's soteriological understanding of the cross first formed in terms of the substitutionary suffering of Yahweh's servant, which corresponds to the early Christological model of an eschatological prophet filled with the Holy Spirit. Later, as the Christological model of the incarnation of the Logos appeared, the doctrine of atonement developed the idea that the Son of God died for all humanity. Hence, we need to look into the history of the hermeneutical process.

1. The Understanding of the Cross in the New Testament

When Jesus' disciples followed Jesus to Jerusalem, they expected that once he arrived he would become the king of the Jews and the kingdom of God would be established on earth. To their disappointment, however, Jesus was helplessly crucified and died. When Jesus was arrested and condemned by religious leaders and crucified by political power, his disciples, trembling in fear, left Jesus and scattered. But some time later they gathered again and attained to a renewed understanding of the meaning of Jesus' death after their experience of Jesus' resurrection appearance. Now they understood Jesus' death on the cross as the completion of his messianic ministry, rather than its failure. In other words, even though Jesus was crucified to death, God raised him so that he became our Christ and Lord (Acts 2:36; Rom. 1:3-4). This understanding of Jesus' death was made possible by reference to the destiny of the Old Testament prophets. "In any case, I must keep going today and tomorrow and the next day—for surely no prophet can die outside Jerusalem" (Luke 13:33). Jesus' destiny is different from that of other prophets only in one point: namely, by being raised by God he became our Lord and Christ.

The death of Jesus was basically a prophet's death. But since he was raised from the dead and became our Lord and Christ, the early Christian community's soteriological interpretation developed in a more positive direction. That is, his death was interpreted as an atoning death "for us." It is not "despite" his death that he became our Lord by resurrection, but he came to the world "in order to" be crucified and die "for" us. From then on theological teleology from above ("for") overwhelmed historical causality ("despite"). To put it another way, the historical Jesus was understood thoroughly from the perspective of the Christ of faith. However, it was too early to speak of the incarnational doctrine of atonement as found in St. Anselm of Canterbury. In this stage a doctrine stating that in order to forgive human sin the sinless Son of God should become a human being and pay for human sin still sounded strange. The early Christian community still remained within the Jewish religious tradition—to be specific, under the influence of the Old Testament ideas of the suffering of the righteous (Isa. 53), sacrifice of atonement, substitutionary punishment of Yahweh's servant, and the late Jewish theology of martyrdom. Within the effective history of these traditions the death of Jesus, a sinless human person (or to use Paul's term, the second Adam), was interpreted as an atoning death for us.

It was the Apostle Paul who decisively articulated the meaning of Jesus' death as an event of atonement. Paul's doctrine of atonement has two characteristics. First, Paul developed his interpretation of the cross within his historical and cultural context. Above all, as an expert in the law he interpreted Jesus' death on the cross as a redemptive death for us, while quoting from the Jewish tradition as well as from different passages of the Old Testament—for instance, the Old Testament ideas of substitutionary punishment (Isa. 53; Rom. 8:3; Gal. 3:13), sacrifice of atonement (Rom. 3:25), and the Passover lamb at the Exodus (1 Cor. 5:7). Furthermore, he explicated the meaning of Jesus' redemptive death by means of the social images of debt payment and slave emancipation (1 Cor. 6:19-20; Col. 2:14), as well as the mythical concept of ransom (Col. 1:13). The point Paul tried to make by these explications was that Jesus' death was a redemptive death for us. For him, redemptive death meant the death of a sinless Jesus who is the second or last Adam (Rom. 5:17-18; 1 Cor. 15:45-49), as contrasted with the first Adam who committed sin.

Second, Paul never had a direct experience of the historical Jesus. Thus, relying almost exclusively upon his experience on the way to

Damascus, Paul made an existential interpretation of the soteriological meaning of Jesus' death. For this reason his doctrine of atonement lacks the awareness of the historical causality that resulted in Jesus' death on the cross. He is little aware of the religious, social, and political reality that constructs the causal connection between Jesus' ministry for the kingdom of God in Galilee and his death in Jerusalem. This explains in part why the traditional soteriology of the Christian church, which is heavily grounded upon Paul's doctrine of atonement, has been inclined to dehistoricization, individualism, and existentialism.

However, this does not imply that Paul's doctrine of atonement is totally wrong. It simply points to its limitation. I believe that Paul faithfully carried out the hermeneutical task one would expect of his historical and cultural context, and he did so under the inspiration of the Holy Spirit. According to postmodern hermeneutics (especially of Hans Georg Gadamer and Paul Ricoeur), Paul found the meaning of the text (in this case, the cross) neither behind nor within the text, but in front of the text.[45] In other words, he found a new possibility in the secondary reference or the world disclosed by the text. However, when I indicate weak points of Paul's doctrine of atonement, I mean that today we cannot repeat it as it was, but we should find another reference that the text discloses to our life world. Hence, the holistic doctrine of atonement demands a new hermeneutical fusion of horizons in our historical and cultural context.

---

[45] The meaning behind the text is accessible through the historical-critical approach to the historical situation in which the text was written, while the meaning within the text through the structural analysis of the semiotic and syntactic sense within the text.

Then, what is the holistic doctrine of atonement that we should pursue with this hermeneutical presupposition? To say the conclusion first, the holistic doctrine of atonement should integrate both subjectivism and objectivism, both historical causality and theological teleology,[46] and both the bottom-up approach and the top-down approach. And the integration should be grounded upon the awareness of the hermeneutical circle between each of the two parties.

2. Doctrine of Atonement in Ancient and Medieval Church

In the ancient church the dominant doctrine of atonement was the classical ransom theory, which reflected the ancient mythical worldview. Irenaeus of Lyon first developed this classical theory on the basis of the biblical images of debt payment and slave emancipation, as well as on the ancient dualistic mythical worldview. It was then further articulated by Origen, Gregory of Nyssa, and others. They described the saving history depicted in the Bible as a cosmic battle between the kingdom of God and the kingdom of Satan. By paying the expensive cost, i.e., by sacrificing his Son, God, in the end, won the eternal victory in this cosmic, spiritual battle against Satan. According to the theory, there was a transaction between God and Satan, whereby God delivered people who were held captive by Satan due to their sin by paying a ransom (i.e., Jesus Christ) to Satan. In this sense, this theory is classified as an objective doctrine of atone-

---

[46] Lessing described each of them as "the historical, contingent truth" and "the universal, rational truth."

ment. Today it is hard to accept the ancient dualistic mythical world-view that underlies this theory in its literal sense. It is also problematic that according to this theory Jesus' redemptive death directly affects Satan first, and then God and humanity. Furthermore, this theory does not make room for humans' own decision-making inshaping their destiny.

In the medieval church there was a debate between Anselm's theory of satisfaction and Abelard's theory of moral influence. Anselm rejected the mythical ransom theory, for it presupposes that Satan has ownership of humanity. Rather, he believed that not only humanity, but even Satan, lies under God's control. Thus, God does not need to pay ransom to Satan in order to rescue humanity from Satan. By violating God's commandments, humans commit sin against God alone. In order to restore the divine honor and justice that was damaged by human sin, humanity should pay the penalty of sin. And the compensation should be sufficient enough to satisfy God. But humans as sinners cannot do it—only God can. In the final analysis, only one who is both divine and human could carry out this work. Thus, God became human to carry the guilt of human sin and die on the cross in submission to God. As a result, God's justice was satisfied and God's honor was restored. In his book, *Cur Deus Homo*, Anselm explained the logical necessity of the incarnation and cross of Jesus Christ in this way. This theory too belongs to an objective theory of atonement, since it asserts that Jesus' death satisfied God and produced an objective merit that is sufficient enough to save all human beings for eternity. But by assuming that Jesus died above all to compensate God's honor and justice that were damaged by human sin, it weakens the significance of God's self-sacrificial love and the soteriological meaning of Jesus' redemptive death for humanity. With its one-sided emphasis on the objective effect of Jesus' death on the cross, just like the classical theory, it not only overlooks the salvific significance of Jesus' entire life and ministry, but also weakens the importance of humanity' subjective response.

Meanwhile, Abelard understood Jesus Christ's death on the cross as the demonstration of God's infinite love toward humanity. According to him, Jesus' death arouses within the heart of people who look at the cross the love that corresponds to divine love. In other words, the love revealed in Jesus' death on the cross awakens humans to a responsive love. Thus, the primary effect of Christ's death concerns human beings rather than God, for the love of God inspires the human mind to repent and come back to God. In this sense, this is classified as a subjective theory. But with too much emphasis on human subjective responses this theory does not make explicit the objective effect of Jesus' death (namely, the redemption of human sin) and blurs the qualitative distinction between divine love, which was revealed in the cross of Jesus, and human love in general.

As I have discussed so far, in the ancient and medieval churches the doctrine of atonement formed in a different worldview and a different political-social-cultural reality than ours. For example, the classical theory reflects the ancient mythical worldview. And Anselm's satisfaction theory describes God as the monarch in the ancient monarchical system and interprets Jesus' death in terms of the Latin legal system as a means to compensate for human sin and to satisfy God. These ancient and medieval worldviews and languages are not easily acceptable or repeatable in our postmodern world. Hence, today our task is to construct a holistic doctrine of atonement that is at the same time faithful to the Bible and church tradition and adequate to today's postmodern worldview and language.

Before discussing the holistic doctrine of atonement for today's postmodern world, we need to recognize that the three above-mentioned theories of atonement have one thing in common. In each of them the top-down theological teleology is too overwhelming to pay due attention to the bottom-up historical causality. However, one may explain it, in part, by indicating that traditional theories of atonement are heavily dependent upon Paul's existential interpretation of the atonement. In other words, they do not take seriously the fact that Jesus' death in Jerusalem was an inevitable outcome of his ministry for the kingdom of God in Galilee and, thus, a political-religious event that took place in a concrete historical reality. This weakness of the ancient and medieval theories of atonement discloses the limitations and problems of the pre-modern dogmatic approach that prevailed before the development of the historical approach to the Bible.

3. Modern Theories of Atonement

In the modern (that is, post-Enlightenment) period, unlike in the pre-modern period, historical causality overwhelmed theological teleology. In the seventeenth century Faustus Socinus argued that Jesus' death was necessary in order to make his life a model for people. According to Socinus, Jesus demonstrated that it is possible for a human being to accomplish the perfect love of God. He said that

Christians should and can follow the example of Jesus' devotion. In the nineteenth century historicist theologians like David Strauss and Ernst Renan denied the traditional doctrine of atonement that speaks of divine satisfaction and human salvation through the substitutionary redemptive death of Jesus. On the basis of their studies of the historical Jesus, they understood Jesus' death as a martyrdom caused by the religious and political situation of the time. They reduced the religious meaning of Jesus' death to a purely ethical dimension. According to them, the true meaning of Jesus' death lies in the perfect example that he showed us in his total commitment. Thus, they liked to quote the following biblical passage: "To this you were called, because Christ suffered for you, leaving you an example, that you should follow in his steps" (1 Pet. 2:21).

However, Albrecht Ritschl and his followers did not agree with this position of historical positivism. In addition to the effort to ground the value judgment of the Christian faith community upon the reality of the historical Jesus, Ritschl sought to draw a picture of the historical Jesus on the ground of faith's value judgment. Hence, on the one hand, he denied the validity of traditional Christological dogmas that had nothing to do with the person of the historical Jesus and were not grounded upon experience, and, on the other hand, he refused to return to the historical Jesus behind faith's value judgment. But Ritschl drew faith's value judgment from the ethical teaching of the historical Jesus. According to Ritschl, the religious judgment that Christ is "the totally revealed God" derives from, and thus depends upon, the ethical judgment that Christ is "the totally realized man." In this way he reversed the traditional framework. Christ's work for others is necessarily connected with the accomplishment of his own goal. "Therefore, the permanent significance of Jesus Christ for his community is grounded above all upon the fact that he was the only one qualified for the special calling, or the coming of the kingdom of God, and also upon the fact that he devoted himself to accomplish this calling by proclaiming the truth and ceaselessly loving."[47] In short, Ritschl found the ground of religious value of the work of Christ in Jesus' accomplishment of his own ethical vocation, whereby he tried to connect historical causality with theological teleology through the mediation of ethical value judgment.

As I discussed earlier, Martin Kähler made the dualistic distinction between the historical Jesus and the Christ of faith and then defined the essence of Christianity in terms of the latter, which opened a way to Rudolf Bultmann's existentialist biblical interpretation. As Kähler's student, Bultmann regarded the traditional objective theories of atonement as mythical and magical, and so he reinterpreted them in thoroughly existentialist terms through demythologization and an existentialist interpretation of the Bible. According to Bultmann, the atonement in Jesus does not refer to the objective event of universal reconciliation that took place then and there, but to the faithful response and existential decision to the kerygma that is proclaimed here and now. The objective history (*Historie*) and its effect were reduced to the subjective history (*Geschichtlichkeit*) and decision.

Karl Barth attempted to rescue theology from history in a different way than Bultmann. Starting from the classical incarnation

---

[47] Albrecht Ritschl, *Instruction in the Christian Religion*, trans. A. M. Swing, in *The Theology of Albrecht Ritschl* (New York, 1901), 200.

Christology, Barth developed his doctrine of reconciliation based upon the traditional understanding of atonement as the objective event of universal salvation through Jesus Christ's death on the cross. He distinguished between the objective and subjective dimension of reconciliation. The objective reconciliation was accomplished in Jesus Christ, namely, "extra nos" (outside of us), whereas the subjective reconciliation is accomplished by the Holy Spirit "in nobis" (in us). The former refers to the "de jure" universal salvation that took place for all human beings, while the latter to the "de facto" personal salvation that takes place for each individual.[48] Also Barth explained three aspects of reconciliation—justification, sanctification, and vocation—in relation to Christ's threefold office of priest, king, and prophet. According to Barth, justification and sanctification are two distinct yet inseparable occasions of God's reconciling work in Jesus Christ. Justification separated from sanctification degenerates into "cheap grace" and quietism, while sanctification separated from justification degenerates into vain activism.[49] Meanwhile, vocation is the teleological form of justification and sanctification.[50] Justification and sanctification are the ground of vocation, while vocation is the goal of justification and sanctification. One who is justified and sanctified in Jesus Christ is called by God to move toward the end of history under the eschatological promise of God.[51]

---

[48] Karl Barth, *Church Dogmatics*, VI/4, trans. G. W. Bromiley et al. (Edinburgh: T&T Clark), 27.

[49] Barth, *Church Dogmatics*, IV/2, 507-509.

[50] Vocation denotes service for Christ's prophetic ministry as a witness to Christ. Thus, vocation is an event in which one is established to serve Christ's prophetic work, that is, to serve in God's reconciling word, and thus, to serve God and neighbors. Barth, *Church Dogmatics*, IV/3-2, 481-482.

[51] Ibid., IV/1, 108-111; IV/3-1, 212; IV/3-2, 902.

What is noteworthy in Barth's doctrine of reconciliation is that it integrates Christology (objective reconciliation) and pneumatology (subjective reconciliation), justification (priest) and sanctification (king) and vocation (prophet), and also doctrines of reconciliation and creation and eschatology. For Barth, vocation is for the universal liberation of humanity and the entire world. He defined redemption as the eschatological consummation of reconciliation. "Salvation is fulfillment ... of being. ... Salvation is [created being's] *eschaton*."[52] However, Barth attempted to rescue theology from history by beginning with the incarnation of the Word regarded as the transcendent Truth. As a result, he could not overcome "the ugly ditch" between historical causality and theological teleology, and he failed to fully develop his doctrine of reconciliation as far as it concerns the doctrine of creation and eschatology. In this regard post-Barthian theologians further developed the doctrine of atonement by broadening its horizon beyond human history to the entire nature and cosmos. For example, Jürgen Moltmann, by accepting insights from the natural theology of the Eastern church and contemporary ecological theology, discusses the doctrine of atonement in connection with the coming of the eschatological kingdom of God that will bring about the transformation and consummation of the entire cosmos in the ultimate future. This cosmic atonement, or the vision of the fulfillment of the eschatological kingdom of God whereby all things will participate in

---

[52] Ibid., IV/1, 8. In traditional theology Jesus Christ was described as God the redeemer, and redemption was defined as atonement in Jesus Christ. But Barth describes Jesus Christ as God the reconciler and atonement in Jesus Christ as reconciliation. In addition, he describes the Holy Spirit as God the redeemer and redemption as the eschatological consummation of reconciliation. Ibid., I/1, 448.

God's full glory, is called the reconciliation of all things.

In the final analysis, today's doctrine of atonement should have an integrating approach to the hermeneutical circles between historical causality and theological teleology as well as between subjectivism and objectivism, and it should also suggest a vision of holistic salvation that integrates Christological, pneumatological, creational, and eschatological dimensions of atonement. A holistic theology of the cross should understand the event of Chris's cross as both ethical and religious—in other words, as both a human event toward God and a divine event toward humanity and the world. Thus, the event of the cross affects both God and humanity and the world simultaneously. And the subject of the event of the cross is Jesus Christ as divine-human. The effect of the event of the cross, as a divine-human event, is not only objective and universal, but it is also realized through subjective and existential responses. The holistic theology of the cross aims to construct this holistic and integrative doctrine of atonement through historical and hermeneutical approaches.

4. Prospect of Holistic Doctrine of Atonement

The historical, hermeneutical starting point of the holistic doctrine of atonement is the historical reality of Jesus Christ. In other words, the cross of Jesus Christ should be understood in continuity with his ministry for the kingdom of God in Galilee (as well as in light of the event of his resurrection appearance). In this vein, the cross of Jesus is an event of the human Jesus toward God. To be specific, it is an event of a human being becoming God, a servant becoming the Lord, and Jesus becoming Christ. Jesus devoted himself to God's kingdom and righteousness and was faithful to God unto his death. Jesus' death should be understood as the final outcome of his service and sacrificial devotion for the kingdom of God. It was caused by unjust religious and political powers. A religious doctrine of atonement that overlooks this historical causality dehistoricizes and demoralizes soteriological categories. In order to prevent the doctrine of atonement from dehistoricization and demoralization and to restore its full meaning one should be sufficiently aware of the historical and ethical dimensions of the cross. In the redemptive event of Jesus' cross the historical-ethical dimension and the theological-religious dimension are not separated from each other.

However, the holistic doctrine of atonement is also explicitly oriented toward theological teleology. On the cross Jesus offered his life to God as a ransom not only for all Jews, including those who crucified him, but also for all humanity, taking up their sin. "For even the Son of Man did not come to be served, but to serve, and to give his life as a ransom for many." (Mark 10:45) Thus, the cross was not just an event that happened to Jesus as a righteous man or a prophet "by" sinful humans; but it was also a sacrifice whereby Christ, as the Son of God and the true human (*vere Homo*), offered himself to God "for the sake of / in the place of" all human beings. "Father, forgive them, for they do not know what they are doing" (Luke 23:34). With the prayer that Jesus offered on the cross historical causality that resulted in the crucifixion of Jesus turns into theological teleology that forgives the sins of all humanity. At last Jesus became the eternal high priest who sacrificed his own body for the forgiveness of human sins. "So

Christ was sacrificed once to take away the sins of many people" (Heb. 9:28).

Furthermore, the holistic theology of the cross proclaims that God is in Christ and that Christ is the true God (*vere Deus*). "All this [in Christ] is from God" (2 Cor. 5:18). Every grace of atonement that is given to us in Jesus Chris is originally from God. God is present and active in Jesus Christ. Jesus Christ is God. In this sense the cross is the starting point of the doctrine of divine revelation. The cross is not just the sacrifice that humanity offered to God, but also the sacrifice that God offered for humanity. On the cross God's righteousness and love are united. This unity is accomplished when God's sacrificial love comprehends and completes divine righteousness. Therefore, according to the holistic doctrine of atonement, the cross in its ultimate dimension is not simply a human act for God, but primarily a decisive demonstration of God's sacrificial love. When God judged human sin, God in Jesus Christ carried out the wages of sin and was judged on humanity's behalf. In this way God judged and saved humanity at the same time. In this vein Barth rejected Calvin's doctrine of double predestination but argued that divine election in Jesus Christ refers to the sum-total of the gospel—i.e., a divine "No" to Jesus and "Yes" to all other human beings. In other words, Jesus Christ is both God who judges and a human being who is judged. The judgment occurs only in Jesus Christ, while only the grace of salvation is given to us. This is the true meaning of the doctrine of election. On the cross the righteousness and life of Jesus are imputed to us, and our sin and death are imputed to Jesus. This is the "happy exchange" on the cross.[53] Barth emphasized more than anyone else God's infinite sacrificial love as revealed in Jesus Christ. He understood the horizon of reconciliation and redemption as reaching all humanity. He said that no one can restrict God's infinite love as revealed in Jesus Christ, and that one can hope for, if not claim, universal redemption.

Therefore, the holistic doctrine of atonement does not agree with the traditional objective understanding of the cross as the substitutionary punishment of a person for the sake of satisfying God's justice and compensating God's damaged honor. Behind this understanding of the cross lies the image of God as the sovereign ruler, which is a projection to God of the image of a king in an ancient monarchy. The atonement of God on the cross is not accomplished by appeasing divine wrath or satisfying divine honor through the substitutionary punishment of a representative person, but essentially by God's sacrificial love for humanity. The atonement on the cross is an objective event of universal salvation, for on the cross God in Jesus Christ took up the human destiny of sin and death, thereby fulfilling his righteousness and bringing forgiveness and salvation to humanity. On the cross of Jesus Christ it is no one but God who suffered. The cross of Jesus is the historical appearance of God's eternal essence— i.e., God's suffering love. The event of Jesus Christ as a human being for God is enclosed in the event of Jesus Christ as the God for humanity and the world. In other words, Jesus Christ's commitment to the kingdom of God in the Holy Spirit is enclosed in the reality of the presence of God and the reality of the Holy Spirit.

Moreover, the objective event of God's universal salvation on the

[53] Cf. Ibid., IV/1, 231-238.

cross demands our existential response by bringing to our heart gratitude and inspiration in the Holy Spirit. Thus, the atonement on the cross is not just a past event of the objective, universal salvation, but also a present event in which salvation is accomplished in today's life through our existential faith. To put it another way, God's sacrificial love, as disclosed in the cross of Jesus Christ, not only brings to humanity the objective reality of universal salvation and reconciliation, but also inspires us in the Holy Spirit to walk along the path of the cross in our practical life responding to divine love. The existential response in the Holy Spirit includes both justification through our inner faith and sanctification through our prophetic witness and praxis in the social-historical reality. Sanctification without justification is a vain self-righteousness, while justification without sanctification is a fanatic religious fantasy. The objective justification and salvation of God that are given through the cross are fulfilled when we take up our cross and practice the discipleship of following Jesus Christ in our socio-political situation, in addition to a personal response through our inner faith. "If anyone would come after me, he must deny himself and take up his cross and follow me." (Mark 8:34; Matt. 16:24; Luke 9:23)

We believe, understand, and then follow. But at the same time we believe and understand by following. Thus, the holistic doctrine of atonement demands a hermeneutical approach that overcomes the dualistic understanding of knowledge and practice by grasping both in a dialectical circle. Above all, today's holistic doctrine of atonement asks for a participatory and practical hermeneutics that connects our understanding of the cross to our history-transforming praxis that seeks to embody the eschatological kingdom of God in today's world. Just as we follow Jesus Christ by believing and knowing the grace of atonement in Jesus Christ, so we believe and know the power of atonement through our experience by participating in the liberating praxis that seeks to creatively transform the world as Jesus' disciples. Through our commitment, sacrifice, suffering, and cross for the sake of the coming of God's kingdom on earth we experientially understand and know the person of Jesus Christ and the meaning of his atoning work.

Given the destruction of nature and the consequent ecological crisis, furthermore, today's holistic Christology needs to reconfigure the doctrine of atonement concerning God's reconciliation and salvation in regard to the natural world and the entire cosmos—that is, beyond the human world. As a result, the transformative and liberating praxis of following Jesus should encompass the natural world and the entire cosmos as well as human history. Against this cosmic horizon holistic soteriology is to be combined with the doctrine of creation and ultimately to be integrated with eschatology. The kingdom of God that will be completed along with the coming of the new heavens and the new earth in the eschatological future denotes the salvation and consummation not only of human history, but also of the history of nature and the entire cosmos. In other words, the kingdom of God in the parousia will not be consummated by the abolition, but by the transformative re-creation, of the old heavens and the old earth. Then the salvation of humanity and the cosmos will be fully completed. The resurrection of Jesus Christ as the historical anticipation of the eschatological kingdom of God represents the divine promise of, and thus Christian hope for, the cosmic salvation and consummation in the eschatological kingdom of God. "When he has done this, then the Son himself will be made subject to him who put everything under him, so that God may be all in all" (1 Cor. 15:28). When salvation is ultimately completed in the eschatological kingdom of God, justification and sanctification will be united with deification (2 Pet. 1:3-4).[54]

Both divine promise of, and Christian hope for, God's kingdom in the eschatological future ceaselessly provide us with the ground and power for Christian vocation and praxis in cosmic, as well as human, history. The task of the holistic doctrine of atonement for today and tomorrow is to make a clear and explicit representation of the promise and hope of the eschatological kingdom of God as the ground and power of Christian vocation and praxis.

---

[54] In the Orthodox tradition the ultimate dimension of salvation was understood as *theosis*. This notion of theosis does not mean that humans become God, but that believers enter personal fellowship with God through baptism and fully participate in the divine life through sacraments. In the Orthodox Church, hence, salvation means participation, sharing, fellowship, and indwelling. In 1989 American Lutherans and Orthodox Christians made the common statement, "Christ 'in Us' and Christ 'for Us'," in which both admitted that their different interests resulted in different doctrines of salvation. The Lutherans put more emphasis on Christ "for us," while the Orthodox Christians on Christ "in us." Thus, the former understood salvation primarily in terms of justification, and the latter primarily in terms of theosis. In the final analysis, they declared that their different positions are not incompatible. Cf. John Meyendorff and Robert Tobias (ed.), *Salvation in Christ: A Lutheran-Orthodox Dialogue* (Minneapolis: Augsburg Fortress, 1992).

Chapter 6

The Spirit of Life as the Source of Life: A Proposal for a Holistic Pneumatology

Yo-Han Hyun

Many people agree that it is a difficult task to speak about God, but it is even more difficult to speak about the Holy Spirit. For talk about the Holy Spirit often sounds abstract and even mysterious. When talking about the Holy Spirit some people feel diffident, while others become confident. In one theological tradition the Holy Spirit is directly related to the knowledge of God, whereas in another tradition the Holy Spirit is connected with divine healing or speaking in tongues. One tradition emphasizes the grace bestowed through worship service and sacraments, while another tradition is emphatic about a transformed holy life. Some people stress regeneration of individuals, while others assert that establishment of social justice and peace is the work of the Holy Spirit. Some people believe that the Holy Spirit is not present among others who have not experienced the Holy Spirit in the same way that they do.

Which of these diverse views of the Holy Spirit is correct? How should we understand the Holy Spirit? In this chapter I begin with the observation that in different theological traditions one can discern a few distinct perspectives on the Holy Spirit, some of which are often regarded as mutually exclusive. They are substantialistic, sacramentalistic, intellectualistic, voluntaristic, emotionalistic, communalistic, dynamistic, and eschatological perspectives. But careful investigation of all these perspectives reveals that each has its own validity as well as some problems arising from its narrow focus. Therefore, I believe we need to pursue a holistic and biblical understanding of the Holy Spirit that evaluates each perspective's strong and weak points and then integrates every appropriate point. Of the above-mentioned eight perspectives on the Holy Spirit intellectualism, voluntarism, and emotionalism are pneumatological applications of the three elements often mentioned in traditional faculty psychology—intellect, will, and emotion—with exclusive emphasis on one of them. While Paul Tillich defines spirit as "the actualization of power and meaning in unity,"[1] the concept of spirit demands more diverse elements. In fact, it does not do justice to the reality of the Holy Spirit to divide it into such diverse perspectives or elements. In other words, each perspective is only heuristic. No one perspective necessarily excludes other perspectives. In a certain theology one finds several of them overlapping, though

---

[1] Paul Tillich, *Systematic Theology*, vol. III (Chicago: University of Chicago Press, 1963), 111.

focus on one of them may draw attention or cause problems. Also, the list of the eight perspectives is not complete in itself. The point that I want to make is this: theologians of each perspective should understand their own position in comparison and in contrast with others, grasp the problems that might be brought about by their narrow focus, and, finally, overcome their own perspective in terms of a holistic point of view.

A number of theologians expect that future theology will be reconstructed along a pneumatological paradigm. Given that there have been different perspectives from which to understand the Holy Spirit, I propose a new holistic paradigm whose organizing concept is life. In the following I attempt to bring into a whole the above-mentioned different perspectives according to the paradigm of life or holistic life.

I
The Spirit and Life

The idea that the Holy Spirit and life are connected is present in the biblical tradition. The Old and New Testament describe the Spirit and the breath of life as closely connected. The original meaning of the Hebrew word *ruach* (רוח) is wind or breath. Later its meaning changed to denote the Holy Spirit as the supernatural influence of God. The Greek word *pneuma* (πνεῦμα) also refers to wind or spirit. In the sense of breath both words, *ruach* and *pneuma*, point to the principle of life related to breath and, furthermore, to God's life-creating power. According to Wheeler Robinson, "*Ruach* is not used of the breath-soul in man in any pre-exilic documents, thought it occurs in the sense of 'life-energy' in some early passages (Gen. 45:27; Judg. 15:19; 1 Sam. 30:12; 1 Kings 10:5)." In other words, Robinson continues, "*Ruach* is not used with psychical predicates in any pre-exilic passage."[2] In the sense of breath *ruach* is specially connected with nostrils. Thus, one finds it referring to the breath of God in the nostrils of a human person (Job 27:3; Lam. 4:20), or to the breath of life in the nostrils of every living creature (Gen. 7:22). Also, in the earlier period the primary reference of *ruach* is not the breath-soul of a human being but the breath-Spirit of God (Exod. 15:8; Isa. 30:28). In other words, it is used primarily of the external influence ascribed to God. In the post-exilic period, however, it begins to refer to the mental condition of a human being. "By the time of Ezekiel," Robinson argues, "*ruach* has come to denote the normal breath-soul as the principle of life in [human beings]."[3] Furthermore, the breath-soul of a human being is identified with the *ruach* of God itself (Job 27:3, "the breath of God in my nostrils"). It is directly derived from the wind at the command of God (Isa. 42:5, "who gives breath to [the people of the earth]"; Zech. 12:1, "who forms the spirit of man within him"; Job 27:3, "the breath of God in my nostrils"; Ps. 104:29 "when you take away their breath"; Eccl. 12:7 and Ps. 31:5, "the spirit returns to God who gave it"). In short, *ruach* denotes the life power that comes from God.

In the same vein the New Testament term *pneuma* also refers to

---

2 H. Wheeler Robinson, *The Christian Doctrine of Man* (Edinburgh: T&T Clark, 1913), 18.
3 Ibid., 19.

wind, breath of life, and especially the Spirit of God, although it is occasionally used of a human spirit or an evil spirit. In the Synoptic Gospels *pneuma* means the principle of life that leaves when a person dies (Matt. 27:50, "he gave up his spirit," cf. Mark 15:37, ἐκπνέω; Luke 8:55, "Her spirit returned"; Luke 23:46, "Father, into your hands I commit my spirit"; cf. Acts 7:59, "Lord Jesus, receive my spirit"). This usage is similar to that of *ruach* in the post-exilic period. However, according to Robinson, Paul the Apostle uses *anemos* (ἄνεμος), instead of *pneuma*, to refer to the natural wind, and the latter hardly denotes the principle of life or breath-soul in a human being. In most cases Paul uses *pneuma* to refer to supernatural influences from God.[4] In fact, the most distinctive feature in the New Testament understanding of the Holy Spirit is that the Holy Spirit is described as the Spirit of Jesus Christ. In this vein, Paul understands *pneuma* as the principle of the new life that is given to us in Christ, rather than as the principle of physical life. The Spirit of Christ Jesus is "the Spirit of life" (Rom. 8:2). "If Christ is in you, your body is dead because of sin, yet your spirit is alive because of righteousness" (Rom. 8:10). "The first man Adam became a living being; the last Adam, a life-giving spirit" (1 Cor. 15:45). "He who raised Christ from the dead will also give life to your mortal bodies through his Spirit" (Rom. 8:11). Now the Spirit is the source of our life in Christ. Therefore, we are urged to live by the Spirit (Rom. 8:13, NASB): "for if you are living according to the flesh, you must die; but if by the Spirit you are putting to death the deeds of the body, you will live." According to the Scrip-

---

4 Ibid., 110.

tures, the physical body itself is not sinful. It is a fragile, yet good, creature of God. By "living according to the flesh" Paul does not mean the life of our physical body but our denial of the light of Christ's life in our whole person (Gal. 5:19-21). When he stresses living by the Holy Spirit, likewise, he neither condemns our physical body nor denies our physical needs, but simply refers to the life according to the light of life in the Spirit, which relates to our whole person, including our body. In this sense, "For the mind set on the flesh is death, but the mind set on the Spirit is life and peace" (Rom. 8:6, NASB). A similar idea is also found in John. John also understands the rebirth to new life as the work of the Holy Spirit (John 3:3-5). Putting the Holy Spirit and life side by side, he says "The Holy Spirit gives life; the flesh counts for nothing" (John 6:63). At the same time John still uses *pneuma* to denote the principle of physical life (John 19:30, "[Jesus] gave up his spirit").

The one thing to be noted is that while Paul's talks about how the Spirit of new life is concerned primarily with humanity, the new works of the Holy Spirit are not confined to human beings. Through the Holy Spirit both our soul and our body are empowered to participate in the resurrection of life, and creation itself also yearns to be liberated from its bondage to decay and brought into the glorious freedom of the children of God (Rom. 8:21). The Holy Spirit was with God the Father and with the Son in the creation of the world (Gen. 1:2; Ps. 33:6). The Holy Spirit is the creator of all things, including human beings. In particular, the Holy Spirit gives life to every living creature and renews the faith of the earth with life (Ps. 104:29-30). The Holy Spirit not only gives life to human beings (Job 33:4,

34:14), but also enables sinners to be born again to a new life (John 3:3-5). In short, the Scriptures describe the Holy Spirit as the one who creates, sustains, and governs life.

In addition to the Scriptures, the oldest doctrinal formulation concerning the Holy Spirit also describes the Holy Spirit as creating, sustaining, and governing life. According to the third article of the Nicene-Constantinopolitan Creed (381CE), the Holy Spirit is described as "Lord" and "Life-giver." In the subsequent patristic theology the Holy Spirit is overall understood as one of the three Persons of the Trinity, the Lord of Life, and the power of God who sanctifies us. Recently, the ecumenical movement, as represented by the World Council of Churches (WCC), has shown renewed theological interest in the concept of the Spirit of Life. Earlier, the ecumenical movement emphasized Christian social responsibility, social service, development, and social salvation in terms of justice and peace. Since the Vancouver WCC Assembly in 1983, however, the WCC began to pursue the integrity of creation in addition to justice and peace. The vision of Justice, Peace, and the Integrity of Creation (JPIC) was elaborated in the Seoul JPIC Convention in 1990. In the process, theology of life attracted considerable attention. With the theme of "Come, Holy Spirit—Renew the Whole Creation" the Canberra WCC Assembly in 1991 developed even further a theology of creation and a theology of life.

> The divine presence of the Spirit in creation binds us as human beings together with all created life. We are accountable before God in and to the community of life, so

that we understand ourselves as servants, stewards and trustees of the creation. (para. 13) ... The Holy Spirit, the Giver of Life, continues to breathe life into all creation. As all life emanates from God and ultimately will return to God (Ps. 104), the ethos of holiness requires an attitude towards all that exists as by nature belonging to God. (para. 90).[5]

In this statement one finds many important, connected themes: namely, every life's dependence on God, reconciliation between God and all things in Christ, the Holy Spirit and community of all living things, and human responsibility. Through these and other efforts the ecumenical movement has come to have an interest in the Holy Spirit and life. Noteworthy too is the understanding of the Holy Spirit as life-giver.[6] In some circles, however, excessive emphasis on the connection between the Holy Spirit and life and the immanence of the Spirit (or spirit) in the whole creation has faced the criticism that it weakens the inseparable relation between the Holy Spirit and Christ.[7]

---

[5] World Council of Churches, *Signs of the Spirit: Official Report, Seventh Assembly* (Geneva: WCC Publications, 1991), 238, 256.

[6] The theme of the first division of the Canberra Assembly was "Giver of Life—Sustain Your Creation!" In this division the Spirit-centered theology of creation was proposed and a ecological pneumatology was discussed. Ibid., pp. 238-242.

[7] In the Canberra Assembly Chung Hyun Kyung's speech evoked great controversy. The participants from the Orthodox churches even submitted an offical reflection paper which criticized "WCC's increasing departure from the Basis of the WCC." Ibid. 15, 279-282.

II

The Holy Spirit as the Source of Life
(Substantialistic Perspective)

As I discussed above, the Holy Spirit is the Spirit of life. God is
the source of life (Ps. 36:9) and the God of life (Ps. 42:8); therefore,
the Spirit of God is the Spirit of life. However, the Spirit of God is
not one among many spirits, but the Holy Spirit who creates every
being. Likewise, strictly speaking, as the Spirit of life the Spirit of God
is the source of every life, rather than of a certain life. Paul Tillich was
reluctant to use the word 'being' to describe God, for he believed that
God is not one being among many beings—i.e., of the same nature
with other beings—but the ground of all beings. Hence, he called
God 'Being itself,'[8] which is quite intelligible. But the distinctive feature of Christian faith is that the essence of God or the Spirit of God
is not exhausted simply by such abstract concepts as Being itself. God
is not only the creator of every being but also humbles God's self and
dwells concretely in the world as the God of Abraham, Isaac, and
Jacob. In other words, as the Spirit of God the Holy Spirit is not simply the source of life but also "the Spirit of life as the source of life."
The Holy Spirit is the Spirit of life who dwells among us as the source
of life.

When one speaks of the Holy Spirit, the most important issue
is the essence or substance of the Holy Spirit. From ancient times the-

---

[8] Paul Tillich, *Systematic Theology*, vol. 1 (Chicago: The University of Chicago Press, 1951), 235f.

ologians have delved into this issue, which I call the substantialistic doctrine of the Holy Spirit. A related topic is whether we can call the Holy Spirit "God," or regard the Holy Spirit as one of the divine Persons. If we can call the Holy Spirit "God," then a trinitarian question is raised: namely, how should we understand the relationship between the three divine Persons—God the Father, the Son, and the Spirit? Also, the *filioque* problem: where does the Holy Spirit proceed from? These are main topics at the center of doctrinal discussions about the Holy Spirit, from the formulation of the ancient ecumenical creeds to the medieval age. In the Scriptures one cannot find such metaphysical concepts as the Trinity, essence, and substance. But the Scriptures contain hints of a substantialistic understanding of the Trinity. The biblical writings themselves do not show substantialistic or metaphysical interests. They are witnesses, confessions, prayers, and praises of people who directly experienced divine revelation. Later, however, people began to use metaphysical concepts. There are several motivations for that. The ancient church had to protect the orthodox faith from the threat of various heretical ideas. In addition, in the process of the indigenization of Christianity in Europe, theologians made use of the conceptual tools of European classical philosophy for theological explanations.

Metaphysical—i.e., substantialistic—understanding of a certain substance seems unavoidable, because human beings are inclined to attain to the ultimate essence of a thing. It is also true of the Holy Spirit. Thus, people think of the substance, nature, and activities of the Holy Spirit. But this kind of metaphysical thinking is easily exposed to the danger of language that is too abstract to have contact with our concrete life. In fact, we know that in the past too much energy was spent for such non-productive theological controversies. The danger is that people, though equipped with a doctrine of the Holy Spirit, lack the dynamic work of the Holy Spirit that transforms their life and history. Meanwhile, even if we totally abandon metaphysical inquiry, it does not free us completely from the danger, because our cultural and intellectual milieu, wittingly or unwittingly, already presupposes some metaphysical assumptions. Also, such abstract ideas may affect our concrete practice by imperceptible degrees.[9] Here one should note that by imperceptible degrees they may become consolidated as uncorrectable prejudices, even though people do not know where they come from and whether they are right or wrong. This is the reason why one needs to disclose and critically reflect upon one's own metaphysical framework, while always paying attention to the danger of losing sight of concrete reality in the depth of abstract language and concepts.

---

[9] For instance, Moltmann believes our understanding of God, or doctrine of the Trinity, may affect our political activities. The Western, monarchical doctrine of the Trinity corresponds the ideology of despotism or dictatorship. Moltmann, *The Spirit of Life* (Minneapolis: Fortress, 2001), 117, 167ff. Moltmann instead proposes to understand the trinitarian relation as a democratic community, or the communion of love, according to the Eastern Orthodox tradition. This trinitarian theology implies a more democratic and equal political system. Ibid., 175-77. It does not mean that the Western trinitarian theology necessarily supports the political despotism, but is exposed to the danger of being politically misused.

III

Worship Service or Sacraments and the Spirit of Life (Sacramentalistic Perspective)

From ancient times the phenomenon of life was regarded as a wonder or a mystery. Life itself was worshiped as a divinity in many, particularly polytheistic, religions. Baal worship, frequently mentioned in the Scriptures, is one of them. However, Israel fought against divinization of the phenomenon of life itself. Also, such divinization of life itself was deeply connected with various forms of moral corruption, degeneration, injustice, and oppression. In contrast, Israel worshipped the one and only God above all living creatures, who is the creator and source of all life. In this way the God of the Scriptures transcends the world of life, but at the same time is present and working in the world as the Lord of all life. While God is present whenever and wherever life is, the dynamic work of the living God is experienced especially through special saving works of God and through worship services. Thus, the worship service was an important place where God's people encountered God as the source of life. The presence of the living Spirit in worship service was of great significance. Within the worship tradition the idea emerged that the Holy Spirit works in the worship service—especially in the sacraments through which people believed God bestowed special grace. When one emphasizes this idea in one's understanding of the work of the Spirit, I call it a sacramentalistic perspective on the Holy Spirit.

According to the sacramentalistic perspective, the sacraments are understood as important means mediating the work of the Holy Spirit. Ancient people tended to believe that a religious cult or sacrament in itself offered a real encounter with God. So did Jews and Christians. One can find this tendency in the ancient church in her efforts to protect the legitimacy of the apostolic church through the administration of sacraments in the face of heretics. But it was in the medieval age that the sacramentalistic understanding of the Holy Spirit was most prominent and was systematized in worship, institution, and theology. The faith and theology of the medieval church in general may be described as utterly sacrament-centered. In this sacramental system the Holy Spirit tended to be objectified as "grace" that is given to us, rather than understood as a subject. To make things worse, some theologians understood "grace," which is given to us through sacraments, even as "creatures."[10] "Grace that is infused to us through the sacraments" was of essential significance to medieval faith and theology. Grace was understood as something to be given by administration of the sacraments themselves (*ex opera operato*).[11] To put it another way, without baptism there is no grace of salvation; without confession there is no grace of atonement. In the final analysis, the free work of the Holy Spirit was fossilized in the sacramental system.

However, the Reformers of the sixteenth century, including Martin Luther and John Calvin, objected to the sacrament-centered reli-

---

[10] Thomas Aquinas distinguished different kinds of grace. Two of them are *gratia increata* (grace that was not created) and *gratia creata* (grace that was created). The former refers to the divine love itself, while the latter to "something" that was created in us by God. This explains the nature of the grace that is infused to us through sacraments. *Summa Theologiae*, IaIIae, q.110, a.1.

[11] *Summa Theologiae*, IIIa, q.64, a.8.

gion of the medieval Roman Catholic Church and also to the so-called *fides implicita* (implicit faith), or the lay people's blind acceptance of ecclesial faith without personal knowledge and decision. In contrast, the faith and theology of the Reformation were centered upon the Word of God—namely, the Scriptures and sermons. They also stressed personal knowledge and decision. They objected to the concept of grace fossilized in the sacramental system and rehabilitated the idea of the subjective and dynamic works of the Holy Spirit. At that time this was certainly a legitimate response to the medieval sacrificial system. Meanwhile, even if one rightly points to the Roman Church's problematic obsession with the sacraments, it is not desirable to ignore the works of the Holy Spirit conveyed through the sacraments. Today Protestant churches need to ask themselves whether their emphasis on the Word of God has not resulted in neglecting the sacraments and the Holy Spirit who works through them.

While the Spirit of life as the source of life is immediately present in all creation, including in humanity, the Holy Spirit also works through human beings and other phenomena.[12] These include the Word, the church, ministers, and also the sacraments; all mediate the works of the Holy Spirit. The Holy Spirit as the Spirit of life invigorates every participant in the sacraments, including its administrator. On the one hand, excessive emphasis on sacraments may lead to lifeless formalism, mystification of sacraments, or authoritarianism of institutional church that administers them. On the other hand, to

---

[12] I call it "the immediacy and mediacy in the works of the Spirit." Cf. Yo-Han Hyun, Seongryeong geu dayanghan eolgul 『성령, 그 다양한 얼굴』 [The Holy Spirit: The Multifaceted Reality] (Seoul: PUTS Press, 1999), ch. 9.

ignore the value and importance of the sacraments does not lead us to a balanced faith, because communication between the Holy Spirit and human souls occurs not only through words and logic, but also (and even at the deeper level) through images, our senses, and symbols. The issue at stake is how we should understand the works of the Holy Spirit through the sacraments.

IV

Personal Life

One of the characteristic features of Christian faith is belief in a personal God. Hence, the Spirit of God is also understood as personal. It is often emphasized that "the Holy Spirit is not simply a power but a Person." It is true that as the third Person of the Trinity the Holy Spirit is personal. Then what do we mean by "Person"? In what sense do we say the Holy Spirit is a Person? The concept of personhood is not as simple and clear as usually assumed. The concept of personhood has its own history of development and is a quite modern concept whose reference has not been fixed until recently. The English word "person," which is ascribed to God and the Holy Spirit, is a translation of the Latin word "persona." It was the ancient Latin Church father Tertullian who first employed the term in his discussion of the Trinity.[13] While pondering how to represent the distinctive in-

---

[13] Tertullian, *Against Praxeas*, ii.

dividuality of the Father, the Son, and the Holy Spirit in one God, he drew the term from the theater of the time, where it originally meant "mask."[14]

From then on the Western church used *persona* to represent each of the three Persons. By this term Tertullian seems to have intended to express the individual substance of each of the three Persons, but he did so in vain due to its original meaning. Tertullian's attempt failed to explain the personal relationship among the three divine Persons and was always exposed to the Eastern Church's criticism that the Western doctrine of the Trinity is modalistic. In contrast, the Cappadocian Fathers in the Eastern Church began to use "hypostasis" to refer to each of the three Persons of the Trinity—the Father, the Son, and the Holy Spirit. In ancient Greek this word denoted an individual substance, as distinct from the common essence of things of the same kind. Because it was used even for things other than humanity, it is hard to identify it with the current concept of person. Although the Cappadocian Fathers explained "hypostasis" by the analogy of three human persons, they had to face another problem—namely, how to explain that three individual hypostases are one substance.[15] For that reason the Eastern doctrine of the Trinity was always accused by the Western Church of degenerating into tritheism. Since today's English

---

[14] The primary meaning of *persona* was mask, from which derived its secondary meaning of actors or characters of the play. In a legal sense it also meant a property owner. In Tertullian's usage, however, it implied the concrete representation of an individual. At any rate it has nothing to do with today's concept of personhood related to self-consciousness. J. N. D. Kelly, *Early Christian Doctrines* (New York: HarperCollins, 1978), 115.

[15] Basil the Great, *Letters*, 214.4; Gregory of Nyssa, *Not Three Gods*. But Gregory of Nyssa suspected that the analogy of the three human persons who share the same human substance may lead to tritheism. Thus, he tried to avoid such criticism by arguing that, strictly speaking, one should speak of one person, rather than of many persons. He was aware of the weakness of the analogy. Cf. Kelly, *op. cit.*, 267.

word "person" derived from the Western concept of *persona*, one may say that it is closer to the Western concept of *persona* than the Eastern concept of *hypostasis*. In fact, however, both the Western concept of *persona* and the Eastern concept of *hypostasis* are quite far from the current concept of person.

After Augustine the Western Church tended to understand *persona* in terms of the relationship between the three divine Persons. That is to say, according to the Western view, the Father "begat" the Son, the Son "generated" from the Father, and the Holy Spirit "proceeded" from the Father. In the Augustinian tradition, the relationship among them is described as the relationship between lover, the beloved, and love itself,[16] or the relationship between mind, intellect, and emotion, or between memory, intellect, and will.[17] Here the independent personhood of each of the three divine Persons, especially of the Holy Spirit, is not sufficiently explained. The problem is that each Person is not explained as an independent center of intellect, emotion, or will, but identified with intellect, emotion, or will respectively. If the Holy Spirit is understood as love itself, then the independent personhood of the Spirit is seriously threatened. Augustine also acknowledged the weakness of the psychological analogy. Thus, he said that one cannot say that the Father is neither intellect nor love but only memory.[18] However, Augustine did not define personhood. A generation later Boethius (c.480-524) defined personhood as "an individual substance with rational nature."[19] In the medieval age

---

[16] Augustine, *On the Trinity*, Bk. VIII.

[17] Ibid., Bks. IX, X.

[18] Ibid., Bk, XV, 28.

Thomas Aquinas attempted to define the personhood of each of the three divine Persons in terms of the relationship among them. For Aquinas *persona* referred to "a subsisting relation" among the three Persons that distinguishes one from another.[20]

In medieval Scholastic theology Augustine's analogy was understood in almost a substantialistic manner. That is to say, the Son was identified with the intellectual activity of God, while the Holy Spirit was identified with the volitional activity of God.[21] As a result, the personhood of each divine Person—especially of the Holy Spirit—was hardly comprehensible. Still, the medieval concept of *persona* fell short of the modern concept of person.

In the modern period the concept of person was made explicit for the first time. Enlightenment philosophy was not so much concerned with metaphysical questions about being as with questioning human beings. In the process focus was directed toward the human mind—in particular, the knowing intellect and the acting will—and, at last, the human being was understood as a knowing and acting mind that is distinct from the body, or as the subject at the center of self-awareness and self-determination.[22] It is probably from this understanding that the current concept of personhood, which focuses upon intellect, emotion, and will, developed. Furthermore, there was

---

[19] Thomas Aquinas, *Summa Theologiae*, I. q. 29, art. 4.

[20] John H. Lavely, "Personalism," in Paul Edwards (ed.), *The Encyclopedia of Philosophy*, vol. VI (New York: The Macmillan, 1978), 107.

[21] Cf. Thomas Aquinas, *Summa Theologiae*, Ia, q. 27, aa.2, 4.

[22] Brightmann applied the Cartesian principle to his definition of person: "A Person ... is a complex unity of consciousness, which identifies itself with its past self in memory, determines itself by its freedom, is purposive and value-seeking, private yet communicating, and potentially rational." Quoted from John H. Lavely, "Personalism," 108.

a philosophical movement called Personalism (Buber, Ebner, Rosen-stock, etc.). According to personalism, Enlightenment philosophy was so possessed by the dualistic scheme of subject and object, according to which every relation is understood in terms of "I-It," that everything was devoid of personal subjectivity and regarded simply as an object ("It") at the disposal of the subject. Personalist philosophers instead proposed to see other persons in terms of "I-Thou," or the inter-subjective relation between two subjects, rather than in terms of the "I-It" relation between subject and object. One should call others "thou" rather than "it," they argued.[23] In other words, personal beings exist in relationships. Subjectivity does not exist in isolation but in the social network of inter-subjectivity.[24]

Karl Barth stands in the Augustinian tradition. Even though he incorporated personalistic insights into his own theology, Barth was reluctant to affirm the personal relationship among the three divine Persons. He hesitated to use the term "person" to refer to each of them. In his opinion, the concept of personhood is ascribed to God only one time, not three times. If it were used three times, he thought, then it would result in tritheism.[25] Instead, he coined a new terminology, a mode of being (Seinsweise), to refer to the Father, the Son, and the Holy Spirit. For this reason Barth's critics accuse his doctrine of the Trinity of falling into modalism or monarchism. In a similar vein Karl Rahner argued that we may say that one God subsists in three distinct "modes of subsistence." Rahner also stressed that God

---

23 Martin Buber, *I and Thou* (New York: Scribner, 1970).
24 J. Moltmann, *The Spirit of Life*, 14.
25 Karl Barth, CD I/1, 351f.

is one Person. The idea of three persons brings about the misunderstanding that there are three separate centers of action in God, which then leads to tritheism.[26] As regards the Trinity Rahner preferred the term "threefoldness," and understood three divine Persons as God's threefold self-communication: that is, "the self-communication of God in history of truth (Son) and the self-communication of God in spirit of love (Spirit)";[27] or "the one who is in truth uttered for himself (Son) and the one who is received and accepted in love for himself (Spirit)."[28] The Father is the subject who communicates himself in this way. Then there would be no inter-subjective "I-Thou" encounter between distinct modes of subsistence, and the distinction between the three divine Persons would be put to question. In fact, both Barth and Rahner had an individualistic concept of personhood. But modern personalists understand personhood in terms of social relationship. Moltmann asks how one could speak of the love between divine Persons of the Trinity if there would be no personal relationship between them. He criticizes both Barth and Rahner for giving up the concept of personhood due to their individualistic misunderstanding of the modern concept of personhood.[29]

In short, today a genuine concept of personhood should take into consideration not only Enlightenment insights into intellectual, emotional, and volitional dimensions, but also social relationships whereby one encounters the other as "Thou" rather than as "It." In

---

[26] Karl Rahner, *The Trinity* (New York: Crossroad, 1997), 109ff, 105.

[27] Ibid., 99.

[28] Ibid., 102.

[29] J. Moltmann, *The Trinity and the Kingdom* (Minneapolis: Fortress, 1993), 178-83; Moltmann, *The Spirit of Life*, 30.

the Scriptures, especially in the New Testament, one finds personal expressions ascribed to the Holy Spirit: for instance, the Holy Spirit "speaks," "guides," "knows," "wills," "laments," and so forth. In other words, the Holy Spirit as a personal life has intellectual, emotional, and volitional dimensions. Meanwhile, one should also note that there are both personal and impersonal descriptions of the Holy Spirit in the Scriptures. In addition to the personal expressions mentioned above, the New Testament contains impersonal expressions of the Holy Spirit as well: for example, the Holy Spirit is "given," "received," and so on. How can we explain it? Just like all other linguistic expressions of God, the term "person" should be understood analogically, since the way God is a Person is not totally same as the way a human being is a person. Analogy implies that there is both similarity and dissimilarity between the two. That is to say, there is both similarity and dissimilarity between the way God is a Person and the way a human being is a person. Therefore, it is no wonder that in the Scriptures one finds at the same time personal, impersonal, and even super-personal descriptions of the Holy Spirit. It should be noted that unlike modern people the New Testament authors did not think of such expressions as strange. Maybe whether the Spirit is a Person or not was not so much a controversial issue to them as it is to us.

1. Intellectual Dimension of the Spirit of Life (Intellectualistic Perspective)

According to the Scriptures, the Holy Spirit "speaks," "knows," "awakens," "teaches," and "witnesses." Also, the Holy Spirit is called "the Spirit of truth" or "the Spirit of wisdom." On the ground of these and other biblical passages an intellectualistic perspective on the Holy Spirit developed. I call it intellectualism. By intellectualism I mean the attempt to understand the nature of the Holy Spirit or the Spirit's relationship with us primarily in terms of "reason" or "intellect." This may sound strange to people who understand the Holy Spirit as irrational, but in Western philosophy "spirit" is essentially related to human intellectual activities. In this intellectualistic tradition the essence of humanity consists in the human soul, whose most precious part is reason. Also, God is understood as the most rational Being. Thus, Christian theologians within this tradition thought of the Holy Spirit as related to reason. Therefore, the relation between the Holy Spirit and human beings is understood in terms of theological epistemology, because knowledge of something is in general regarded as a function of reason. In this regard there are two possibilities: moving toward natural theology, with belief in the rational power of the human spirit, on the one hand, and on the other hand moving toward revealed theology, i.e., focusing on divine revelation with the recognition of the total depravity of human reason's spiritual power. In any case the Holy Spirit or spirit is thought of in relation with reason or intellect.

Medieval Scholastic theology was inclined to intellectualism and, as a result, to natural theology. According to Thomas Aquinas, God is the most rational Being. Aquinas' theological system is a massive logical construct. However, the Scholastic understanding of the Holy Spirit was not intellectualistic. During the medieval age the faith of the Roman Church overall focused on the sacraments, and little doctrinal knowledge was required of under-educated lay people. Lay people were asked simply to accept and follow what the church taught to be true. This attitude was justified in terms of "implicit faith."

However, the Reformers objected to implicit faith, arguing that every believer should have explicit knowledge of God through the Scriptures and make a personal decision to believe in God. In other words, they asked for "explicit faith." John Calvin defined faith as "a sure knowledge of God's goodness toward us."[30] For Calvin, faith is a gift of the Holy Spirit and is given to us by the Spirit's inner witness to and illumination of the Word of God.[31] Here the Holy Spirit is related to the knowledge of God. Although the Reformers did not understand the works of the Holy Spirit simply from an intellectualistic perspective, there is no doubt that they regarded the knowledge of God through the Word as of essential significance. From its very beginning, then, the Protestant Church was inclined toward an intellectualistic understanding of the Holy Spirit. Of course, the work of the Holy Spirit was not simply identified with human reason, nor reduced to activities of human reason. As the Spirit of God the Holy Spirit infinitely transcends the human spirit in intellect. Still, however, the Holy Spirit is related to human knowledge of God, or theological epistemology, and is regarded as a hermeneutical route to divine mystery. In short, as the Spirit of life the Holy Spirit is the one who renews our knowledge of God and invigorates the intellectualistic dimension of our faith.

This intellectualistic view of the Holy Spirit in relation to theo-

---

[30] John Calvin, *Institutes of the Christian Religion*, III.ii.7.
[31] Calvin, *Institutes*, I.vii.4.

logical epistemology is quite convincing. No one can deny some epistemological connection between the Holy Spirit and the human spirit. But the intellectualistic perspective tends to ignore the communal dimension and bolsters up individualism, because it is concerned primarily with the knowing process of an abstract individual person. Also, if the process of knowing God through the Holy Spirit is not firmly grounded upon an objective reality, there is a danger of subjectivism. Finally, it should be noted that the intellectualistic inclination may lead to a dry, apathetic faith and end up mired in debates over doctrinal details at the expense of the dynamic power of faith and the transformation of life.

2. Volitional Dimension of the Spirit of Life (Voluntaristic Perspective)

According to the Scriptures, the Holy Spirit "wills," "prays," "transforms" the human mind to have faith, "gives guidance" to the saints, "sanctifies" the believer's life, and so forth. Also, the work of the Holy Spirit results in love and righteous works. In short, the Scriptures indicate that the work of the Holy Spirit has an intentional dimension. This understanding of the Holy Spirit primarily in terms of volitional acts is called voluntarism. This voluntaristic perspective appeared most strongly in the Western church—especially after Augustine. Augustine compares the status of the Holy Spirit within the Trinity to the human will. It is an indirect explanation appealing to traces of the Trinity (*vestigium trinitatis*) in the world. It is noteworthy that the Holy Spirit is compared to the will rather than to intellect or emotion. Augustine explains the Trinity as memory, intellect, and will, or as mind, intellect, and love.[32] According to Augustine, the Spirit is compared to love between the Father and the Son, or to a volitional act. In other words, the voluntaristic view of the Holy Spirit is connected with the understanding of the Holy Spirit as love. Augustine says that the Holy Spirit is love itself that unites the lover (Father) and the beloved (Son). This idea made an enormous impact on the Western understanding of the Trinity and the Holy Spirit.

When one understands the Holy Spirit in terms of love and will, both the doctrine of predestination as well as ethics become important issues. The doctrine of predestination is a radicalization of the theological idea that everything is ultimately God's grace. If everything were God's grace, then God would be responsible even for the distinction between people who receive grace and people who do not receive grace. But this idea had been hotly debated with regard to the role of human will in faith and life. When the Holy Spirit is understood in connection with human will, one's concrete acts led by the Spirit become another important issue. This is an ethical issue. In the traditional understanding human acts were regarded as the work of the Holy Spirit for sanctification of the believer's life. In this vein the Holy Spirit denotes the Spirit who transforms Christians to live an ethically holy life, or the life of love. As the Spirit of life the Holy Spirit makes our faithful decision and action become oriented toward God.

Throughout history there have been many misunderstandings

---

[32] Augustine, *On the Trinity*, Bk. IX, X.

and much speculation about the doctrine of predestination. But neither predestination nor free will is as simple a question as is usually assumed. The doctrine of predestination contains a mystery concerning the relation between the Holy Spirit and our human will. It is a faith confession and a theological praise that everything is God's grace. Be that as it may, it is unfortunate to misunderstand the doctrine in terms of mechanical fatalism or determinism. The voluntaristic view of the Holy Spirit contributed to emphasizing the work of the Spirit in Christians' ethical and holy life, especially in their life of love. Also, its emphasis on will and love may help us understand the communal dimension and historical concreteness of the work of the Holy Spirit. However, the one-sided emphasis on the Holy Spirit's work for love and ethics may lead to moralistic reduction of Christian faith, and it also overlooks the Spirit's work in the knowledge of God, the relation between the Spirit and human emotion, and the Spirit's powerful works.

3. Emotional Dimension of the Spirit of Life (Emotionalistic Perspective)

By emotionalism I mean the view of the Holy Spirit that focuses on the emotional dimension. One may ask whether this emotionalistic view of the Spirit is valid or not. Koreans seem to be inclined to understand the Holy Spirit from the emotionalistic perspective, probably due to the Korean expression "성령의 감동 (gamdong [being emotionally moved] of the Holy Spirit)." In the Scriptures, however, the expression "gamdong of the Holy Spirit" has little do with emotion.

Such expressions as "in the Spirit," "by the Spirit," and "through the Spirit" were often translated into Korean as "gamdong of the Holy Spirit."[33] Nonetheless, it is not true that the work of the Holy Spirit has nothing to do with our emotion. The Scriptures suggest that as the personal Spirit of God the Holy Spirit has an emotional aspect. For instance, the Holy Spirit "groans" (Rom. 8:26) and "grieves" (Eph. 4:30). Also, the Holy Spirit sometimes evokes in our soul fear of God, joy, gratitude, peace, and comfort, as well as sorrow and grief over our sin. This emotionalistic view was the least regarded among many different views of the Holy Spirit. When somebody praises or prays enthusiastically, people often say "Do not give way to your feelings." In fact, for a long time philosophers and theologians did not have a positive view of emotions, because they believed that excited feeling often paralyzes human reason, leads to misjudgment, and causes difficult situations.

These days, however, there are many who have a positive view of emotion. The first theologian who made a positive evaluation of emotion is probably Friedrich D. E. Schleiermacher. He found the essence of religion in feeling about God, rather than in rational metaphysical theory or moral action. Confronting the intellectual challenge of the Enlightenment, Schleiermacher attempted to lay the cornerstone of our faith and theology in our feeling rather than on our reason. He defined faith as feeling or self-consciousness of absolute dependence upon God. But he did not explicitly say that the Holy Spirit is in itself the function of emotion. Instead, according to

---

33 For instance, Mark 12:36; Luke 2:27; 1 Corinthians 6:6; Revelation 1:10; 2 Peter 1:21, etc.

Schleiermacher, the Holy Spirit evokes the consciousness of absolute dependence that comes down from Christ through interactions within Christian community.[34] In Schleiermacher's definition, feeling refers to "sense"—not an emotionalistic sense, but a non-sensible intuition.

Many revivalists and theologians who engage in revivals believe that it is sometimes necessary to arouse people's feelings. Charles G. Finny was one of them. According to Finney, the work of the Holy Spirit is to bring unbelievers to repentance and thereby save them. But humans are too evil, lazy, and slow to obey the Holy Spirit. Therefore, it is necessary to excite and arouse them through emotional means that can help them overcome intellectual obstacles. In order for people to repent and believe, Finney says, their souls should be shaken and aroused to excitement so that they can overcome intractable obstacles.[35] The Holy Spirit makes use of this excited feeling. Finney asserted that without emotional excitement people seldom pursue a holy life.[36] We should admit that emotion is an integral part of our mental or believing life. However, it is not right to use artificial means, instead of accepting spiritually felt feeling, to arouse emotion. Also, it is problematic to lay the foundation of faith in emotion, for emotion is easily shaken and subject to change.

Recently we have witnessed the emergence of another perspective on the relation between emotion and the work of the Holy Spirit. With increasing interest in healing by the Holy Spirit, a new form of

---

[34] F. D. E. Schleiermacher, *The Christian Faith*, trans. and ed. H. R. McKintosh (Edinburgh: T&T Clark, 1956), 560ff.

[35] Charles G. Finney, *Lectures on Revivals of Religion* (New York: Fleming H. Revell Co., 1868), 10.

[36] Ibid., 12.

ministry appeared which is called "inner healing." This is a good example that discloses the positive and direct relation between the Holy Spirit and human emotion. Inner healing does not refer to the healing of physical disease but primarily to the healing of mental sickness or wound. Mental wound in general is related to emotional problems. The Holy Spirit works to heal mental wounds and help people become mature in personality. Our emotional problems are not solved simply by controlling our reason, but only by healing the wound and becoming mature. As the Spirit of life the Holy Spirit leads our believing life to a healthy and mature emotional state.

The emotionalistic view of the Holy Spirit may help correct wasteful debates over doctrines or legalistic inclination of moral religion. Indeed, not only is sound emotion, with a proper grounding and expression, an important aspect of true belief, but so too is emotional healing, which should be regarded as the work of the Holy Spirit. However, giving way to one's feelings, without discernment under the guidance of the Holy Spirit who is the Spirit of truth and order, may result in religious fanaticism.

V

Network of the Spirit of Life
(Communalistic Perspective)

As I discussed above, according to the Scriptures, life exists in communal relationship with other life. It is noteworthy that recent life science is discovering the network of life. In many biblical passages the Holy Spirit is mentioned with regard to this communal relationship. This understanding of the Holy Spirit I call communalism. The communalistic view of the Holy Spirit has thus far attracted little attention. People tend to understand the work of the Holy Spirit in relation to individuals. The individualistic understanding is not in itself wrong, but its one-sided emphasis on the Holy Spirit's relation with individuals may result in ignoring the communal dimension of the Spirit's work. In the New Testament the Holy Spirit is described as the one who establishes the church and enables the congregation's members to share their possessions with the community (Acts 2). When Paul speaks of the temple of the Holy Spirit, he does not mean individual Christians but the church as the body of Christ (1 Cor. 3:16). When he speaks of the gifts of the Holy Spirit, Paul stresses that each believer who has received a different gift from God should form the church as the one body of Christ and humbly serve to build the community as a member of Christ's body (1 Cor. 12:12-31; Eph. 4:11-16). But in our church the Holy Spirit is understood more often than not in connection with spiritual blessings or gifts given to each individual. But the gifts of the Holy Spirit are meant to humbly serve other members for the sake of the community. The spiritual blessing given to each individual is not just an end in itself but a means of divine blessing for others and for God's kingdom. The salvation of one individual is both an end and a means.

Augustine called the Holy Spirit the soul of the church.[37] Just as our body has a soul, so the soul of the church is the Holy Spirit. This indicates the communal dimension of the Holy Spirit's work. During the medieval age, however, this idea failed to explain the dynamic work of the Holy Spirit within the church, and the work of the Holy Spirit was fossilized within the institutional church. During the Reformation period the medieval ideas of implicit faith and sacrament-centered faith were overcome by the reformers' claim that each individual needs to recognize and believe the gospel clearly and explicitly. Given the situation of the time, this change in emphasis was quite legitimate. But as time passed the individualistic inclination grew within the Protestant church. The work of the Holy Spirit was gradually understood in relation to personal faith and salvation rather than to the church or community. The early reformers had no intention of ignoring the church community. For instance, John Calvin took very seriously the church, her ministers, proclamation of the word of God, and administration of the sacraments by the church. He said that the church is the mother of believers and there is no salvation outside the church.[38] However, in many Protestant traditions the discussion of the Holy Spirit did not clearly explicate the relation between the church and the Holy Spirit or the communal dimension of the work of the Holy Spirit.

Of modern Protestant theologians, Friedrich Schleiermacher is distinguished by his recognition of, and insistence on, the essentially communal dimension of the work of the Holy Spirit. According to Schleiermacher, the Holy Spirit communicates and evokes in the church community Christ's perfect God-consciousness through his disciples.[39] However, one may legitimately wonder whether the Holy

---

[37] Augustine, *Sermons*, 267.4.
[38] Calvin, *Institutes*, IV.i.1-4.

Spirit in Schleiermacher's view is not more like a religious community spirit immanent in the church than the Spirit of the transcendent God.

Recently the relation between the Holy Spirit and the community is attracting more serious attention. More than any other recent theologian, Dietrich Bonhoeffer emphatically stressed the communal dimension of the work of the Holy Spirit. He described the Holy Spirit as the Spirit of God who enables each believer (I) to recognize the barrier (or transcendence) of the other (Thou) as a personal being and thus to respect and love the other.[40] In other words, the Holy Spirit is the Spirit of love who builds up a true community without losing each person's individuality and uniqueness as an other. Though Bonhoeffer retained his interest in the communal dimension of the church and discipleship, he did not have an opportunity to further develop his idea of the relation between the community and the work of the Holy Spirit.

As regards Christian responsibility for the community, people began to perceive the scope of community as expanding beyond the church community to the entire society. Furthermore, with increasing emphasis on Christian social responsibility, great effort has been made to promote social justice and even to transform unjust social structures through revolution. In this vein a movement emerged that considers anew the relation between the Holy Spirit and the movement for social transformation. Liberation theologians like Gustavo Gutierrez

---

[39] F. D. E. Schleiermacher, *op. cit.*, 560ff.

[40] Dietrich Bonhoeffer, *Sanctorum Communio. Eine dogmatische Untersuchung zur Soziologie der Kirch*, hrsg. von Joachim von Soosten (München: Chr. Kaiser, 1986), 31-32.

began to speak of "the spirituality of liberation" or "social spirituality." Minjung theologians also attempted to understand the Holy Spirit in terms of liberation of minjung. In addition, in the face of the global crisis caused by ecological destruction, there are theological movements that consider the work of the Holy Spirit on a global or even cosmic scale.

Today we need to emphasize anew and develop further the idea of the communal dimension of the work of the Holy Spirit, because in many churches the Holy Spirit is often misunderstood in solely individualistic terms. Of course, personal salvation is an important issue. However, the salvation of our Lord does not end up with salvation of each of us as an abstract individual but calls us to the kingdom of God as a community. As the Spirit of life the Holy Spirit fills with life not just each individual person but also the church community and even human society and the entire created world. However, one should not stress the communal dimension so much as to make the Holy Spirit just a community spirit immanent within human groups or simply a revolutionary spirit for social transformation. One should not forget that the Holy Spirit does not call us simply to the society of human beings but to the kingdom of God, and that the one who renews the community of God is the Spirit of God, the Spirit of Christ.

VI

Power of the Spirit of Life
(Dynamistic Perspective)

In an attempt to understand life one cannot miss the power of life. Given the etymological meaning of *ruach*, this dimension seems to be most faithful to the biblical understanding of the Holy Spirit. In the Old Testament *ruach* is used to refer to God's powerful works, both natural and supernatural. In the New Testament *pneuma* is used to describe the power that enables Christ and his disciples to perform various miracles and proclaim the gospel. This view of the Holy Spirit, with focus on the Holy Spirit's power, I call dynamistism. Historically speaking, in so-called spiritual movements people experienced different gifts of the Holy Spirit as well as miracles, and therefore the dynamistic view of the Spirit dominated. Today Pentecostalism belongs to the same tradition. Pentecostal teaching does not speak of the power of the Spirit alone. It emphasizes four distinctive themes: salvation, baptism by the Spirit, divine healing, and second coming. Also, the Pentecostal church accepts the traditional doctrine of the Trinity, and understands the Holy Spirit not simply as a power but as the third Person of the Trinity. Nonetheless, it is undeniable that it is the Holy Spirit as a surprising power that stands at the front of the Pentecostal understanding of the Holy Spirit. The Holy Spirit enables sinners to repent, bestows miraculous gifts including speaking in tongues, heals the sick with divine power, and makes evangelism effective for church growth. This rapid outpouring of the Holy Spirit, according to the Pentecostal church, is a sign of the last times and implies that the time of Christ's second coming is approaching.

This dynamistic understanding of the work of the Holy Spirit has its own biblical foundation. But some traditional Protestant theologians still argue that miraculous gifts of the Holy Spirit were given only in the Apostles' times for the formation of biblical revelation. Therefore, they believe, those gifts are no longer given today since the process is now complete. In their judgment, those miracles claimed by the Pentecostal church are either untrue or demonic. However, if these miracles are understood simply as a power that helps today's church and believers, rather than as a means for a new revelation, then they are acceptable because they do not infringe on the absoluteness of the biblical revelation. Even today they may be helpful for believers and the church. It is not desirable to denounce such power simply as superstitious.

However, this understanding of the Holy Spirit primarily as a power—in particular, in relation with special gifts, including speaking in tongues and divine healing—may unduly mistreat people who have no experience of such gifts as having nothing to do with the Holy Spirit. As I have thus far discussed, the work of the Holy Spirit is very broad and diverse. Throughout church history we can find many people who worked successfully for the gospel even though they did not receive such miraculous gifts. Also, there are natural gifts as well as supernatural ones. While speaking in tongues and divine healing are gifts of the Spirit, so also are teaching, serving, comforting, and governing (Rom. 12:6-8). Despite its own validity, the dynamistic view of the Holy Spirit as a power, when excessively stressed, may lead to spiritualism or fanaticism that blindly seeks only miracles and boasts of one's spiritual gifts. Also, when one uses such power for one's own interests, one violates the fundamental reason for why the gift was given. For this reason Paul says that without love any marvelous gift is nothing.

VII

Holy Spirit and the History of New Life (Eschatological Perspective)

What is important in the biblical account of the Spirit of life is that the Holy Spirit is not just the creator of natural life but also the one who gives us new life in Christ and leads us to the new kingdom of God. This view of the work of the Holy Spirit in terms of the coming of God's kingdom and new life I call the eschatological perspective on the Holy Spirit. Given today's popular understanding of the Holy Spirit, this perspective may sound strange. Historically speaking, however, spiritual movements that had considerable historical impact generally had great interest in eschatology. For instance, one may be reminded of Montanus in the ancient church, Joachim of Fiore in the medieval church, and the Pentecostal movement today. The connection between the Holy Spirit and eschatology has a biblical basis. According to the biblical account of the outpouring of the Holy Spirit on Pentecost, Peter quotes from the prophet Joel: "In the last days, God says, I will pour out my Spirit on all people" (Acts 2:17). If one believes Joel's prophecy was already fulfilled at Pentecost, then the end has already come. In this vein the Holy Spirit is understood as the Spirit of the end times.[41] The end (eschaton) refers to the end of the old world and old person; in other words, it means at the same time the beginning of the new world, new person, and new life (2 Cor. 5:17). The eschaton was already proleptically anticipated in Jesus Christ (Luke 17:20-21). Of course, the second coming of Jesus Christ and the consummation of God's kingdom are not yet realized. But the Holy Spirit as the Spirit of new life enables us to foretaste the life and power of God's kingdom in advance (Matt. 12:28). Thus, the Scriptures describe the Holy Spirit as a deposit guaranteeing our eternal inheritance and God's seal (Eph. 1:13-14; 2 Cor. 1:22). People who have received the Holy Spirit already foretaste the eschaton and are given a deposit guaranteeing the new world and new life.

This proleptic eschatology was made explicit by Jürgen Moltmann. He rejected both consistent eschatology (Albert Schweitzer) and existentialist eschatology (Rudolf Bultmann). In his view, eschatology determines Christian theology as a whole. According to Moltmann, the ground of our hope is found in the event of Jesus Christ, for the eschatological kingdom of God was already proleptically anticipated in the event of Christ—especially in his resurrection.[42] This

---

[41] Joel wrote "afterwards"(אַחֲרֵי־כֵן). But when quoted in Acts there was a change: "in the last days" (ἐν ταῖς ἐσχάταις ἡμέραις). Joel's original intention may not have been necessarily a prophecy about "the end of the world." However, if the coming of the new era by the Holy Spirit implies the end of the old era, then the quotation in Acts may be understandable.

[42] Jürgen Moltmann, *The Crucified God* (Minneapolis: Fortress, 1993), 163, 172ff. *In Theology of Hope* Moltmann did not use the phrase "the prolepsis of the eschaton" yet, probably because his primary interest was in criticizing the existential interpretation of the eschaton in terms of the present and stressing the future-oriented hope implied in the event of Jesus Christ. Still, even in the book one can find some hints for the concept of prolepsis. But in *The Crucified God* Moltmann explicitly speaks of the prolepsis [Vorwegnahme, Prolepse] of the eschaton.

hope contradicts the reality of our present experience. Thus, this hope leads us to protest against and transform the suffering and evil in the world.[43] With this concept of proplesis of the eschaton Moltmann attempts to explicate the tension between "already" and "not yet." In other words, it is not "the eternal Spirit of heaven" but "the eschatological earnest [Angeld] of the Spirit" that is now given to believers.[44] "The 'Spirit' himself becomes the 'earnest' of the still outstanding future and therefore 'strives' against the 'works of the flesh.'"[45]

In the final analysis, the Holy Spirit is the Spirit of the last days, the Spirit of the new life, and the Spirit of the new world. Therefore, one should have an interest in eschatology when understanding the Holy Spirit. However, one should avoid pneumatology oriented toward a distorted eschatology. One should reject distorted pneumatology and distorted eschatology that claim that the end time is fixed, that no one can be saved without the knowledge of the date of the last day, that one should give up the present life for the sake of the coming end, or that only a particular group of people can receive the Holy Spirit and live in the new era of the Spirit. Already here and now the Holy Spirit enables us to foretaste the life of God's kingdom, to look forward to the consummated kingdom of God, and to proclaim the gospel and serve our neighbors and fight for righteousness in the world in hope for the kingdom of God.

---

[43] J. Moltmann, *The Theology of Hope*, 18-19, 21.
[44] Ibid., 162.
[45] Ibid., 222.

Conclusion

Thus far I discussed diverse perspectives on the work of the Holy Spirit with attention to their strong and weak points. Each of the substantialistic, sacramentalistic, intellectualistic, emotionalistic, voluntaristic, communalistic, dynamistic, and eschatological perspectives has its own validity as well as its problems. If anyone perspective is so predominant as to exclude others as having nothing to do with the Holy Spirit, it will succumb to a narrow-minded view. One should take the positive aspects of each perspective so as to supplement the weak points of other perspectives. In this way one can obtain a healthy and dynamistic idea of the Holy Spirit. With the Scriptures as the standard one should pursue a balanced and holistic understanding of the Holy Spirit, which comprises an intellectualistic element concerning the knowledge of God and judgment of good and evil, an emotionalistic element related to healing and purification of emotions, a voluntaristic element concerned with ethical behaviors, a dynamistic element as regards the power for ministry, a communalistic element with regard to building community, a sacramentalistic element for worship services, an eschatological element concerning hope for the new world, and a substantialistic element as regards the idea of God as the source of all things.

Moltmann's *The Spirit of Life* is one of the most recent theological works that pursues a holistic pneumatology. Moltmann takes notice of how modern society is dehumanized without God, leading to injustice and oppressive social structures and accelerating the pace of ecological destruction. On the other hand, he also witnesses the success of the Pentecostal movement around the world. In this vein Moltmann develops a cosmic and holistic understanding of the Holy Spirit as the Spirit of liberation who grants us justice, peace, life, and hope.[46] According to his holistic pneumatology, the Holy Spirit is at work not only within the church community but also in society, the world, and the ecosystem as a whole. This is one of Moltmann's great contributions to contemporary pneumatology. However, he neither classifies nor analyzes different aspects of holistic pneumatology. Also, while developing a cosmic pneumatology, he makes use of some of Hegelian ideas that he once rejected as abstract speculations in his early writings. Hence, some in the church wonder whether Moltmann has come back to idealism. What is at stake is his reinterpretation of the Jewish concept of *Shekinah* according to Hegel's idealistic scheme.[47]

Unlike Hegel, who understands God as apathetic, Moltmann understands God as the one who participates in the suffering of the world in love. However, Moltmann's idea of the Spirit of *Shekinah* who comes out of God, becomes separate and alienated from God, and finally is united with God is quite similar to Hegel's idea of God who comes out of himself, realizes himself by positing himself against himself, and then comes back to himself. In this sense Moltmann too is exposed to the danger of Hegelian pantheism.[48]

The holistic paradigm that I propose here is that the Holy Spirit

---

[46] Jürgen Moltmann, *The Spirit of Life* (Minneapolis: Fortress, 2001).

[47] Ibid., 49-51, especially 319n.31.

[48] Early in his career Moltmann accused Barth's doctrine of the Trinity as employing the "reflective structure" that he inherited from idealism. One may ask Moltmann if he is not employing the same structure here. Moltmann, *The Trinity and the Kingdom*, 169. Moltmann himself identifies

is the Spirit of life as the source of life. The proposal is made explicit in adopting strong points and criticizing weak points of each of the different perspectives. The Holy Spirit is the Spirit of life. But the Holy Spirit is not the same kind of life as one finds in the world. As the Spirit of God the Holy Spirit is the source of life. As the Spirit of life the Holy Spirit is the Spirit of personal life who has intellectual, emotional, and volitional dimensions. The Holy Spirit is present in our worship service to God the creator as well as in our sacraments, vitalizing them. As the power of life the Holy Spirit saves individuals, the church, and the world. As the Spirit of life the Holy Spirit is the source of life who is present among the network of life and builds community. Also, as the source of life the Holy Spirit is the Spirit of creation who saves and recovers creatures. Furthermore, the Holy Spirit is at work not just in the preservation of creation but also in the renewal of corrupt humanity and the entire creation. In this sense the Holy Spirit is the Spirit of new life who brings the kingdom of God to completion.

---

his position as panentheism, not as pantheism. And his panentheism is a historical panentheism that stresses on the immanence and suffering of God within history. In this sense it is distinguished from the metaphysical panentheism like process philosophy. Moltmann, *The Spirit of Life*, 212.

Chapter 7

God's Peaceful Life:
A Proposal for Holistic Theology

Yo-Han Hyun

The theology of Presbyterian University and Theological Seminary (PUTS) is often described as holistic theology. Ever since it was first proposed by Chungye Jong Sung Rhee, the idea of holistic theology has so far, wittingly or unwittingly, guided the school's theology and theological education. Yi-Tae Kim's "theology standing at the center"[1] and Yong-Gil Maeng's "integrated theology"[2] share the same theological orientation. In the 2002 Chungye Theology Symposium, Myung Yong Kim defined holistic

---

[1] Cf. Yi-Tae Kim, "Jangsindae sinhagui wichiwa geu teukseong" [The Location and Characteristics of the Theology of PUTS], *Church and Theology* 14 (1982).

[2] Cf. Yong-Gil Maeng, "Tonghapsinhak gaeyo" [Integrated Theology: An Outline], *Church and Theology* 18 (1986).

theology as a theology that integrates both ecumenical and evangelical theology, attempts a comprehensive review and evaluation of Protestant, Roman Catholic, and Eastern Orthodox theology, engages in dialogue with other religions and other disciplines, and affirms the supremacy and standard of the revelation in Jesus Christ. Also, Kim refers to several characteristics of holistic theology: namely, trinitarian theology, theology that seeks both personal salvation and God's reign, theology of the whole person that takes into account both human soul and body, theology for the church and the world, cosmic rather than anthropocentric theology, and theology oriented toward the reign of God.[3] Though I do not agree with all the details of this discussion, in the following I will propose a holistic theology oriented toward almost the same direction. Holistic theology refers first of all to a theological method that takes into consideration many different factors in an integrating way. But does holistic theology refer only to a method? If many different factors are considered in an integrating way, then does it not lead simply to a syncretic theology that has nothing original in itself? If holistic theology has something original, then on what basis? If holistic theology claims its own originality, then what is it? In this article I will answer these questions. To be specific, I will discuss holistic thinking that makes possible holistic theology and the ground on which holistic theology can claim its own originality besides its particular method. Finally, I will suggest that "God's peaceful life" could be the content of holistic theology.

---

[3] Cf. Myung Yong Kim , "Tongjeonjeok sinhagiran mueosinga?" [What is holistic theology?], *Academia Christiana Korea Forum* 4 (2002.8.15.).

I
Analytic Thinking and Holistic Thinking

According to the method of analytic science, one attains knowledge by analyzing an object into smaller units and then understanding each of them. But the problem is that what was once regarded as the smallest unit sooner or later turns out not to be. At last, one wonders whether there exists the smallest unit at all. Also, one may ask whether one can rightly understand an object by dissecting it. As an alternative to analytic thinking, therefore, a new scientific study based on integrative thinking emerged.[4] However, integrative thinking that perceives the whole in unity cannot in itself explain everything. We need holistic thinking that assimilates both analytic and integrative thinking.

In the formation of modern sciences the development of a theory runs through the process of detailed analysis of an object, which is then followed by simplification of the data. But some theories, with overconfidence in their analysis, fall into the fallacy of oversimplification that overlooks many other things. When what was overlooked

---

[4] Physicist Fritjof Capra accuses traditional Western science of having a mechanical worldview and analytic method of reducing the world into the smallest components. According to Capra, today's physics, especially the relativity theory and quantum physics, requires a great transformation of the worldview and methodology of traditional Western science. In his book *The Tao of Physics* he also points out that insights of contemporary physics are very similar to those of traditional Eastern mysticism (by which he means experiences and thoughts of Hinduism, Buddhism, and Taoism). According to Capra, the most important characteristic common to the worldviews of Hinduism, Buddhism, and Taoism is "insight into the unity and mutual connection between all things and all events, or experience of all worldly phenomena as a manifestation of wholeness."-

by such an oversimplification comes to the fore, a better theory that can explain it emerges. This is how science develops. The process of scientific development passes through conflict between competing theories. Thomas Kuhn understood it as essential to the process of revolutionary development that brings about a paradigm shift in perceiving objects. The process is revolutionary in nature, probably because one perspective excludes the other perspectives due to excessive self-confidence. Hence, holistic thinking should be open to new data and new thinking while respecting achievements of old sciences.

For instance, one can think of the transformation from geocentric to heliocentric theory. According to the age-old scientific theory, the Earth was thought to be located at the center of the cosmos and all other stars, including the Sun, revolved around it. But as optical technology improved, new data emerged that contradicted the old theory. At first people tried to adhere to the geocentric theory by making small revisions to it. Copernicus's contribution consisted in demonstrating that once we change our thought pattern and think that all planets, including the Earth, are revolving around the Sun, all existing data are explained without complicated amendments. From then on new data that confirmed Copernicus's heliocentric theory continued to appear, and scientists finally accepted it. As a more recent example, one may think of the conflict between two competing theories of light: one that understands light as a particle and the other as a wave. According to today's quantum physics, however, light is both a wave and a particle.

Let's return to theology. In the ancient church there was a debate over the divinity and humanity of Christ. Some people ignored

Christ's divinity and argued for his humanity alone, while others ignored Christ's humanity and argued for his divinity alone. According to the biblical witness and traditional faith, however, the church confirmed holistic Christology that affirms both natures of Christ. Also, the church could not abandon her belief that God is one, even when she affirmed the divinity of the Son and the Holy Spirit as well as the Father. Thus, the church developed the holistic doctrine of the Trinity according to which the Father, the Son, and the Spirit have one divine substance.[5]

In this way, one may say that theology has developed in a holistic direction. But theology sometimes encountered difficulties due to its excessively analytic thinking. For instance, some people argued for either Christ's humanity or divinity alone; and others fell into heresy by denying the doctrine of the Trinity. Even today liberal theology that pursues an anthropocentric theology and minjung theology that argues that, "Jesus is minjung and minjung is Jesus," are prime examples of excessive analytic thinking.

For a right understanding of the biblical revelation handed down to us, holistic thinking is required, because revelation is a mystery that cannot be exhausted by any one-sided and narrow-minded thinking. In general, conflict between different theological positions results from oversimplification and excessive generalization that follows from analytic thinking. Hence, it is very important to think holistically from the start. But holistic thinking does not exclude analytic thinking.

Fritjof Capra, *The Tao of Physics* (Boston: Shambhala, 1999), 130.

[5] Cf. Jong Sung Rhee, *Sinhakseoron* 『신학서론』 (Seoul: The Christian Literature Society of Korea, 1993), 70; Myung Yong Kim, "Rhee Jong Sung-ui tongjeonjeok sinhak" [Jong Sung Rhee's Holistic Theology], *Gidokgyohaksulwon forum* 「기독교학술원 포럼」 [Academia Christiana Korea

True holistic thinking does not conflict with analytic thinking; rather, the former embraces and yet transcends the latter.

II
Holistic Theology as Eastern and Korean Theology

In the 1960s some Korean theologians attempted to develop an indigenized Korean theology. From then on the movement to develop Korean or Eastern theology, as distinct from theology that simply follows in the footsteps of Western theology, continued to exist. If as Koreans and Asians we do theology within the context of Korean history and culture, then Korean theology is inevitable. However, Korean or Eastern theology does not imply that ideas in ancient Korean or Eastern religions are fundamentally identical with those in Western theology. Nor does it refer to a new thought system that derives from combining the two, which is not only artificial and unnatural, but also will finally obscure the clarity of the gospel of Jesus Christ. There is no need to merge ancient Korean or Eastern thought with Western theology; what is needed is to do theology according to Korean or Eastern thought. We need to pay attention to how the Bible and the Christian faith are being perceived by people who think in a Korean or Eastern way—that is, in an integrative manner. In this way, we can discover what has been overlooked by Western theologians, who think analytically in general. In other words, we ought to retrieve the logic or way of thinking that undergirds Eastern religions and Eastern thought, rather than their specific ideas or systems, and bring it to our understanding of the biblical message.

Therefore, the important thing is to develop integrative thinking instead of atomic thinking, and holistic thinking instead of analytic thinking. There are several differences between Eastern and Western thinking, one of which is integrative versus analytic thinking. Throughout history Western people have sought knowledge by starting from the perspective of the individual and then reaching out to the environment as perceived by the individual. They dissected an object into parts, analyzed each of them, and accumulated knowledge. And they believed that it was possible to synthesize those separate parts in a logical way. In the process of seeking a synthesis, a certain part may sometimes illuminate the whole. This way of thinking has significantly contributed to the development of scientific technology and the economy of the West. By contrast, Eastern people were inclined to a way of thinking in which an individual person or entity is perceived within the context of the whole. That is to say, they believed that each individual being is and should be in harmony with the whole world. Western analytic thinking developed into scientific technology, while Eastern integrative thinking developed into ethical knowledge.[6] Then, which of the two is right, Western or Eastern thinking? This is not a good question. They are not in an either-or

---

Forum] 4 (2002.8.15.), 133-135.

[6] Cf. Dennis Lane, "Samwiilcheui jinri, dongseoyang segyegwani mananeun god" [The Truth of the Trinity, Where the Eastern and Western Worldviews Meet], *Bitgwa sogeum* 「빛과 소금」 [The Light and the Salt] (1996.8), 86ff. Jung Young Lee appropriates the Eastern concept of *yeok* (易, change) to his own theology. By his interpretation of the concept he argues for the both-and thought pattern that overcomes the Western exclusive either-or thought pattern. Jung Young

relation. We need to recognize the strong and weak points of each and make use of both of them in a mutually supplementary way. This is the way of holistic thinking. Western theology, which has so far dominated global theology, is based more or less on analytic thinking. Now we need holistic thinking that assimilates both analytic and integrative thinking. In the sense that it differs from the way of thinking characterized by Western theology, holistic thinking may be regarded as Eastern or Korean. But it is not Eastern in the sense that we call holistic thinking Eastern or Korean. Holistic thinking is not only Korean but also can be global and universal; it is analytic as well as integrative, and integrative as well as analytic.

It is interesting to see that one can find a purely Korean word that corresponds to the idea of holistic thinking, or to the concept that refers to the whole consisting of different individual components as well as different individual components comprising the whole. It is 한 (*han*). As an authentic Korean concept *han* has many different meanings: "big," "high," "one as a whole," "the head," "bright," "shining," and so on. The Mongolian word "khan," as is used in "Genghis Khan," has the same etymological origin as *han*. (Mongolian and Korean belong to the same Altaic language family.) In China, "khan" was translated as 忓 (it is pronounced as *han*), but in Korea "khan" was translated as 韓, 漢, 翰 (all are pronounced as han). Those Korean translations mean "big," "high," and "one as a whole," as found in hanbaksan (太白山), hanbaekseong (一民), and hanbaegeom (檀君).[7]

According to Min-Hong Choi, *han* means "big" or "one as a

Lee, *The Theology of Change* (Maryknoll: Orbis, 1979), 40ff, 81ff.

[7] Min-Hong Choi, *Han cheolhak* 『한 철학』 [Philosophy of Han] (Seoul: Seongmunsa, 1990), 14-

whole". It does not allow opposition or division but implies unity or harmony. "Han" does not refer simply to the numeral one, but to the harmony or unity that comprehends and integrates many different things.[8]

Min-Hong Choi explains *han* and individual entities in terms of the relation of the One and the many. "'Han' and individual entities are the One as well as the many, and the many as well as the One."[9]

Also, in Korean traditional thought, *han* does not refer simply to the numeral one, but to a metaphysical reality—namely, the fundamental reality of all things in the cosmos. "Han" is so big and so broad as to transcend all things; it exists by itself and all the time; and there is nothing that is not connected with it. In addition, *han* is not subject to division or change, nor to addition or reduction. To put it another way, *han* is without origin, independent, permanent, universal, and immortal.[10]

When Si-Gyeong Ju, an expert in Hangeul (Korean characters), spoke of "一" (*il*) in his masterpiece *Kugeomunjeoneumak*『國語文典音學』[Korean Grammar and Phonetics], the concept of "一" (*il*) is very close to the concept of *han*. According to Ju, *han* refers to the original unity that unites the entire cosmos; it is a divine being and logic.[11] Min-Hong Choi argues that this *han* philosophy is an authentic philosophy that underlies the founding ideologies of the ancient nation Hwarangdo, Wonhyo's Buddhist thoughts, Twegye and Yul-

---

15.

[8] Ibid., 20-23.

[9] 一卽多, 多卽一. Ibid., 24.

[10] Ibid., 29-30.

gok's Confucian thoughts, Donghak, as well as Won-Buddhism. In short, in Korean traditional thought one can find a way of thinking that comes close to holistic thinking. I believe that if we employ this holistic way of thinking then we can develop holistic theology that is both Korean and global.

III
Is Holistic Theology Syncretic Theology?

So far I have discussed holistic thinking as it concerns the method or attitude of holistic theology before any particular theological statements. The important thing in the development of theology is to pursue holistic theology of greater integrity by preserving the important ideas of traditional theology and also retrieving what has been overlooked by it. For instance, today holistic theology needs to respond to emerging issues, including: the meaning of the body, which has been suppressed as inferior to the soul; a holistic view of humanity as a whole consisting of body and soul; the importance of community; the ecumenical movement; issues related to social structures and justice; the poor; the marginalized; the suppression of women; and the pollution and destruction of creation. Issues that demand theological attention will continue to appear. Therefore, holistic theology will not attain to its fulfillment until the end of the world, though it will make every effort to do so. In this sense holistic theology is always on the way to its completion.

Meanwhile, holistic theology is not a fad theology that discards the old and follows the new theology whenever a new theological insight emerges in a new context. Nor is holistic theology a constructive theology that throws away the old theology and reconstructs a new theological system on the basis of ever-new theological insights. Holistic theology critically accepts the new ideas that the every new theology enables us to recognize, and then critically reflects upon the tradition (for us it is biblical, evangelical Reformed theology) in light of the Word of God in order to make it into a theology that is more faithful to the World of God.

Then, does it mean that holistic theology merges this and that and anything? Is there no conflict or criticism when it accepts different theologies? Does holistic theology not degenerate into a syncretic theology without any originality simply by merging different theologies or negotiating between them? No, holistic theology does not blindly accept other theologies, nor simply merge them. Holistic theology integrates different theologies through critical reflection in light of the Word of God. It is not a compound of different theologies. To use an analogy from ecology, as we learn from the earth's ecosystems, the whole is not equal to, but greater than, the sum of its parts. An ecosystem is not reducible to the arithmetic sum of all its individual living creatures. That is to say, an ecosystem is greater than its constituent parts. In this regard, the concept of emergence is important. When different individual parts are integrated, something new emerges that transcends the arithmetic sum of those individual parts.[12] Holistic the-

---

11 Min-Hong Choi, *Han Cheolhak*, 32.

ology seeks a new emergent integration by critically appropriating many different theologies. In this critical and emergent integration, creative thinking is possible.

If integration in holistic theology does not refer to a simple mixture of different contents but to a dynamic integration that produces emergence, then holistic theology may develop its own original content, in addition to its authentic methodology. The concept of integration that holistic theology seeks comprehends to the whole of all things, and the whole is only one; therefore, it resonates with the concept of *hana* (one). If the concept of *hana* corresponds to that of *han* that I discussed above, then holistic theology may lead us to *hananim* theology.

IV
Hananim Theology

Considering the history of Korean Bible translation and the development of the Korean language, it appears that we had better call God 하느님 (*haneunim*) rather than 하나님 (*hananim*). In the John Ross Version of the Korean Bible, published in 1887, "one" was translated as ᄒᆞ나 (*hăna*) or 한나 (*hanna*), while "heaven" was translated as 하날 ("hanal"). If one attaches an honorific suffix -님 (-*nim*) to the Korean word referring to "one," then the divine name is ᄒᆞ나님 (*hă-*

---

12 Emergence is a concept employed in complexity theory. It refers to the phenomenon in which an attribute or behavior that is not expected from the lower levels voluntarily emerges in the

nanim) or 한나님 (*hannanim*). But if one attaches the honorific suffix "-nim" to the Korean word referring to "heaven," then the divine name is 하날님 (*hanalnim*). In the Ross Version the divine name is *hananim*.[13]

Noh-Sun Kwak understands *hananim* as *hanal* plus *-nim*. In *Magauijyeonhăn bogeumseo eonhăe* 『마가의젼ᄒ 복음서 언ᄒᆡ』 [Korean Annotation of the Gospel according to Mark], published by Appenzeller and Underwood in 1887, the divine name is 상뎨 (上帝, *sangdye*), whose literal meaning is lord of the heavens. Thus, it is connected with heaven, rather than the number one. In *Sinyakjyeonseo* 『신약젼셔』 [The New Testament], which was published in 1900, "one" was translated as ᄒ나 (*hăna*) and "heaven" as 하ᄂᆞᆯ (*hanăl*). Thus, ᄒ나님 (*hănanim*) would refer to the Korean word for one (*hăna*) plus the honorific title (*-nim*), while 하ᄂᆞ님 (*hanănim*) would refer to the Korean word for heaven (*hanăl*) plus the honorific title (*-nim*). This Korean translation used the divine name of 하ᄂᆞ님 (*hanănim*), the combination of *hanăl* (heaven) and *-nim*.[14] Later the Gyeonseong Bible Society Version, *Syeonggyeongjyeonsyeo* 『성경젼셔』 [The Bible], published in 1925, also accepted these translations: "one" as ᄒ나 (*hăna*), "heaven" as 하ᄂᆞᆯ (*hanăl*), and "God" as 하ᄂᆞ님 (*hanănim*).[15] In short, in the Korean Bible the divine name originated from the combination of the Korean word for "heaven" and an honorific suffix. Even the expression 하나님 (*hananim*) in the Ross Version, Noh-Sun Kwak argues, was a combination of 하날 (*hanal*) (heaven) and 님 (-

---

higher level. The terminology was first used by C. D. Broad in the 1920s. Due to the recent development of complexity theory and ecology it is now attracting great attention.

13 Noh-Sun Kwak, "Hangukgyohoewah hananim chingho" [The Korean Church and the Divine Name], *Gidokgyosasang* 「기독교사상」 [Christian Thought] (1971.3), 122.

nim) (honorific suffix), given that the Ross Version was completed with the help of those Koreans from the Northwestern region of the Korean peninsula.[16] But the Ross Version, translated into the Northwestern dialect of the Korean language, was not welcomed by Koreans in the Central and Southern regions. Thus, missionaries decided to use the expression 하ᄂ님 (*hanănim*) but allowed Northwestern Koreans to pronounce it as 하나님 (*hananim*) and the Central and Southern Koreans to pronounce it as 하느님 (*haneunim*). In the Authorized Version of 1906 the divine name was unified as 하느님 (*haneunim*). Due to the objection of Northwestern Koreans, however, the original orthography, 하ᄂ님 (*hanănim*), was recovered.[17] From 1882 to 1936 there were many Korean names for God: 하나님 (*hananim*), 하느님 (*haneunim*), 상뎨 (*sangdye*), and 하ᄂ님 (*hanănim*). But the final decision was 하ᄂ님 (*hanănim*). In this regard Noh-Sun Kwak concludes that what was at stake at that time was not whether the divine name is related to heaven or the number one, but how to pronounce the Korean word for heaven, 하ᄂᆯ (*hanăl*).[18]

The modern Korean orthography was determined in 1933. Then, in the Revised Version of the Bible of 1938, the archaic vowel ㆍ (ă) was eliminated according to the new orthography. In the process 하ᄂᆯ (*hanăl*, heaven) was rewritten as 하날 (*hanal*), ᄒ나 (*hăna*, one) as 하나 (*hana*), and 하ᄂ님 (*hanănim*, God) as 하나님 (*hananim*).[19] From then on 하나님 (*hananim*) could be related to both heaven and

14 Ibid., 122.

15 Ibid., 123.

16 Ibid., 123-124.

17 Hyeong-Gi Ryu, *Seongseosajeon* 『성서사전』 [The Dictionary of the Bible] (Seoul: Methodist Church of Korea Press, 1960), s.v. "hangugeoyeok seonggyeong" [The Korean Versions of the

the number one. In this context the Korean church, in her attempt to make a difference in Korean society in which people in general called God 하느님 (*haneunim*), argued that 하나님 (*hananim*) does not refer to the god of heavens (하느님, *haneunim*) but to the one and only God besides whom there is no other god. In 1939, at last, both the Presbyterian Church of Korea and the Methodist Church of Korea, two representative denominations at the time, insisted that the God of Christianity is not 하느님 (*haneunim*) but 하나님 (*hananim*).[20]

Noh-Sun Kwak criticizes that this was an awkward conclusion based upon an irrational argument.[21] According to Kwak, when the Revised Version was published in 1952, the text was revised according to the new orthography. Every word but 하나님 (*hananim*) turned into the standard Korean as used in Seoul. Since the Northwestern power was too strong within the Korean church, Kwak says, only the one word 하나님 (*hananim*) was left unchanged. But Kwak argues that because the word 하나님 (*hananim*) originally came from the Korean word for "heaven," it should turn into the standard Korean word 하느님 (*haneunim*).[22] After reviewing the history of consolidation of the Korean divine name as 하나님 (*hananim*), Taek-Bu Jeon also points out that it does justice to the history of Korean language to turn 하ᄂ님 (*hanănim*) to 하느님 (*haneunim*) and also that it is grammatically wrong to attach the honorific suffix -님 (-*nim*) to the numerical word.[23] Thus, the history of the Korean language, the history

---

Bible].

[18] Ibid., 124.

[19] Ibid., 124-125.

[20] Josyeonyeosugyojangrohoe jye28hoe hoerok 「조선예수교장로회 제28회 회록」 [The Proceedings of the 28th Assembly of the Presbyterian Church of Korea] (1939). 8

of Korean Bible translation, and the grammatical rule that the honorific suffix cannot be attached to the numerical word all support the divine name 하느님 (*haneunim*). In addition, because Christians also thought of God as the God of the heavens, it is no problem at all to call God 하느님 (*haneunim*). As far as words are concerned, however, the important thing is what people mean by them—namely, their usage and intention. In that sense, the Korean church's decision to use the divine name 하나님 (*hananim*) may mark an important point in the process of indigenization of Christian theology. Thus, the decision should not be regarded simply as resulting from the greater power of people from a specific region. If one takes seriously the power of Northwestern Christians, then not only in the divine name 하나님 (*hananim*) but also in many other aspects Northwestern features should have been retained.[24] In the final analysis, the Korean church's adherence to the word 하나님 (*hananim*), even after her decision to abandon the Northwestern dialectic and use only the standard Korean for Korean Bible translation, suggests that the church made a certain theological decision rather than simply succumbed to the power of a specific region.

한 (*Han*) in the word 하나님 (*hananim*) does not simply refer

---

21 Ibid.

22 Ibid., 127.

23 Cf. Taeg-Bu Jeon, "Hananim mit tyeonjuraneun male gwanhan yeoksajeok sogo" [A Historical Study of the Words 'Hananim' and 'Tyeonju'", Research Institute of Christ and Our Culture (ed.), *Hangeul seongseowa gyeremun hwa* [Korean Bibles and Our Culture] (Seoul: Christian Book Center, 1985), 591-638.

24 The Korea Bible Society published 5,000 copies of the revised Korean Bible, corrected according to the new orthography including abolition of the vowel " ㆍ " and change of diphthongs to monophthongs. But Korean Christians from the Northwestern region argued that if the vowel " ㆍ " were abolished, then the dialect of the Northwestern region would not be correctly translit-

to the number one. Thus, one does not need to adhere to the word 하느님 (*haneunim*). As I discussed above, 한 (*han*) has many different meanings: for instance, "big," "high," "one as a whole," "the head," "bright," "shining," and so on. It sometimes refers even to a metaphysical reality. Hence, 한 (*han*) in 하나님 (*hananim*) includes, but at the same time transcends, the meaning of the number one. In this vein, it is untenable that the honorific suffix -님 (-*nim*) cannot be attached to the numerical word 하나 (*hana*), because 하나 (*hana*) is not simply a numerical word. In fact, there had been an attempt to reinterpret the word 하느님 (*haneunim*), whose original meaning is "the lord of heaven," in monotheistic terms before the Revised Version of Korean Bible was revised again according to the standard Korean language, and even before the controversy over the divine name of 하나님 (*hananim*) first took place. As mentioned above, Si-Gyeong Ju says,

> In the cosmos—which is so broad, so full, and so limitless that it does not have top, bottom, center, or outside—the One exists and fills everything in it. For the One there is neither birth nor death, neither beginning nor end. For the time being a great number of things exist all by the One; and each of them has a limited life as determined by the One. The One is the origin of all things and the lord of all things. Thus, it is called heaven, the lord of heavens (*sangdye*), and the principle.[25]

erated. Thus, the revised version was not accepted and the 5,000 copies were discarded.

Min-Hong Choi interprets the One (一) in this quotation in terms of 한 (*han*), understood as a metaphysical reality rather than simply a number.[26] A similar idea is also found in the thought of Si-Gyeong Ju, who later became a Christian, as well as in Korean traditional thought.[27] We do not need to accept the thought system of Korean indigenous religions, but it suffices to recognize that the Korean word 한 (*han*) may refer to a highest, supreme, and ultimate reality—namely, God, in addition to the number one.

Even if we decide to use 하느님 (*haneunim*) as the name of God, its etymological root is not far from that of 하나님 (*hananim*). According to Ju-Dong Yang, the origin of 하늘 (*hanǎl*, heaven) is 한볼 (볽) (*hanbǎl*, 大光明, 大國原). 한볼 (*hanbǎl*) was transliterated as 한 ㅂ ㅏ ㄹ (*han-b-a-r*), then as 하울 (*hanǎl*), then as 하늘 (*hanǎl*), and then finally as 하늘 (*haneul*).[28] Jeong-Beom Seo once thought of 하늘 (*hanǎl*) as consisting of 한 (*han*, 大, big) and 알 (*al*, 卵, egg). The understanding of heaven as a big egg, Seo argues, derived from the tradition of heaven worship, according to which heaven is regarded as the matrix of life production.[29] This conclusion seems to have resulted from Seo's commitment to Shamanism studies. Later Seo pub-

---

Josyeonyeosugyojangrohoe jye27hoe hoerok 『조선예수교장로회 제27회 회록』 [The Proceedings of the 27th Assembly of the Presbyterian Church of Korea] (1938), 37-38. 7

25 Si-Gyeong Ju, *Kugeomunjeoneumhak* 『國語文典音學』 [Korean Grammar], 1908, Preface.

26 Min-Hong Choi, *Han cheolhak*, 32.

27 The concept of the One (一) as the fundamental reality of all things, as mentioned in *Tan-gun-cheolhak seogui* 『단군철학 석의』, may be identified with the concept of '한 (*han*).' '한 (*han*)' is in circulation and does not stop. It is so big that there is nothing outside of it; it is so small that there is nothing inside it; it has no beginning, so there is nothing before it; it has no end, so there is nothing after it. This big, great '한 (*han*)' is the fundamental reality of all things. Quoted from Min-Hong Choi, *Han cheolhak*, 31. Also, according to *Cheonbugyeon* 『천부경(天符經)』, the fundamental reality of all things in the cosmos is called "the One" (一). The One begins without beginning. Even if it is divided into the three ultimate realities, its essence is not exhausted. Quoted from Min-Hong Choi, *Han cheolhak*, 31.

lished his life-long study of the etymology of Korean words under the title of *Urimalui ppuri* 『우리말의 뿌리』 [The Root of the Korean Words]. In this work Seo argues that 하늘 (*haneul*) is a compound of 하 (ha) and 늘 (*năl*), and that both 하 (*ha*) and 늘 (*năl*) refer to the Sun. 하 (*ha*), as equivalent to 핟 (*had*), 할 (*hal*), 하 (*ha*), refers to the Sun. According to a slightly different explanation, 하늘 (*haneul*) is a compound of 한 (*han*) and 을 (*ăl*), where the former originated from the word 핟 (*had*), whose reference is the Sun, and the latter from a word that refers to day or daytime.[30] What interests us is the fact that the etymological root of the numerical word 하나 (*hana*, one) too is 흔 (*hăd*). Following the Altaic custom that attaches the suffix "-n" to nouns, the last consonant of the word 흔 (*hăd*) was transliterated from ㄷ (d) to ㄴ ("n"). Thus, 흔 (*hăd*) turned into 흔 (*hăn*). When the suffix 아 ("a") was then attached to it, the word 흔나 (*hăna*) was coined.[31] According to Ju-Dong Yang's idea, to which many scholars agree, the world 하늘 (*haneul*) already implied the meaning of 한 (*han*) as one big, bright, great head. Even if we follow Jeong-Beom Seo's opinion, both 한 (*han*) in 하늘 (*haneul*) and 한 (*han*) in the numerical word 하나 (*hana*) originated from the same word 흔 (*hăd*). If 하늘 (*haneul*) contains the meaning of 한 (*han*), then the meanings of 하나님 (*hananim*) and 하느님 (*haneunim*) are not far from each other. For 한 (*han*) in 하늘 (*haneul*) could also mean "one big, high, bright head."

Against this background one can understand what missionary

---

28 Ju-Dong Yang, *Gogayeongu* 『古歌研究』 [A Study of Ancient Lyrics], 4.

29 Jeong-Beom Seo, "Eoneoeseo bon Shamanism" [Shamanism in Language], *Sinhakjinam* 「신학지남」 39 (1972.9), 80.

J. S. Gale wrote in 1890, i.e., before the controversy over the Korean name of God took place. In an article Gale introduced the Korean people's understanding of God and quoted from "Mr. Chu" (probably, Si-Gyeong Ju).[32] Then, he proposed to transliterate 하ᄂᆞ님 (hanănim) as 하나님 (hananim) according to the new orthography. At first his proposal was not accepted by the church. Later, however, an increasing number of people in the church attempted to understand 하ᄂᆞ님 (hanănim) in monotheistic terms. Gale seems to have known that the Chinese equivalent of 하ᄂᆞ님 (hanănim) is 天 (cheon, heaven). Nonetheless, he believed that it is also possible to understand it in the monotheistic sense. Because in the West the word "god" was used to refer to pagan gods as well, it took a long period of confusion and transformation until the word "god" had the monotheistic sense. However, in the case of the Korean language, he believed that the word 하ᄂᆞ님 (hanănim) could be understood as referring to God in the monotheistic sense without much confusion.[33] Gale's opinion was gradually accepted by other missionaries and Korean Christians. At last, the Korean church in general preferred to call God 하나님 (hananim). In other words, early missionaries and early Korean Christians saw that the word 하ᄂᆞ님 (hanănim), which originally meant 하늘님/하느님 (haneulnim/haneunim, the lord of heavens), already contained the meaning of 하나 (hăna, one). In the final analysis, from the Christian perspective they integrated both meanings—the one

---

[30] Jeong-Beom Seo, *Urimalui ppuri* 『The Root of Our Language』, 2nd ed. (Seoul: Koryeowon, 1996), 448, 214, 144-145.

[31] Ibid., 310.

[32] J. S. Gale, "Korean Ideas of God," *The Missionary Review of the World* (September 1900), 573; Seong-Deuk Ok, *Chogi hangeulseonggyeongbeonyeoge natanan juyo nonjaeng yeongu (1877-1939)* 『초기 한글성경번역에 나타난 주요 논쟁 연구 (1877-1939)』 [A Study of the Main Controversies

and only God and the lord of the heavens—in the word 하나님 (hananim).

If 하나님 (hananim) may refer not only to the lord of the heavens (하늘님, haneulnim) but also to the one and only God who is big, bright, great, and the head, then we can understand the meaning of 하나 (hana) in terms of the harmony and unity between the One and the many. In short, the concept of 하나님 (hananim) implies abundant theological content, one of which is the idea of the Trinity. So far traditional Western theology adhered to the belief in the One God, while affirming the divinity of the Father, the Son, and the Spirit. As a result, a complicated doctrine of the Trinity developed in the Western church. Still, the doctrine of the Trinity is very difficult to explain; there will be no end to the related study and debate. But if we turn our eyes to the Korean traditional language and thought system, it is possible to develop hananim theology by retrieving the concept of 한 (han) that comprehends both the One and the many. If we understand God as 한님 (hannim) whom we should worship and love, then hananim theology may be connected with trinitarian theology. The triune God is three, yet in unity as 한님 (hannim). Thus, hananim theology understands the triune God who refers to the Father, the Son, and the Spirit in unity as the source of holistic harmony and peace. In his integrated theology (통합신학, tonghapsinhak), Yong-Gil Maeng also advocated trinitarian theology. He also understood the triune God as the source of peace that integrated theology seeks. The triune God, who exists in the free co-existence, just cooperation, and peaceful participation between the three divine persons, is the motive and driving force of peaceful reunification between South and North Korea.[34] Holistic theology is in itself hananim theology and trinitarian theology.

V

Theology of Peace

According to holistic theology, which is at the same time hananim theology and trinitarian theology, God is the source of creation, harmony, and unity of all things. In this sense, holistic theology is a theology of peace. Holistic theology describes the reign of God, which is the goal of God's creation and redemption, as the world of holistic peace. Holistic theology seeks the peace and reconciliation of the entire cosmos in God. The integration that holistic theology pursues refers to the peace or harmony resulting from the unity of all things. In this vein, holistic theology resonates with the idea of 한 (*han*) or 하나님 (*hananim*) as I discussed above. According to Min-Hong Choi's interpretation, the idea of 한 (*han*) always presupposes the spirit of peace. In the philosophy of 한 (*han*) the standard of the truth is not described as a linear line but as a round circle. The circle suggests harmony, holism, and unity. It also refers to the unity of the three major elements of the world—namely, heaven, earth, and humanity. Thus, Choi argues, the idea of 한 (*han*) implies the idea of peace. Related to this is the fact that from ancient times the Korean people have been a peace-loving nation.[35] In short, holistic theology

---

in the Early Korean Bible Translations (1877-1939)] (PUTS Graduate School, 1992), 39.

[33] J. S. Gale, "Korea's Preparation for the Bible," *The Korean Field* (March, 1912), 86; Seong-

is a theology of the peace of all things. Then what is it meant by "peace"? Does it simply mean a state without war? Or, is the theology of peace a theology that cries out for political participation? No. The two biblical words for peace, *shalom* and *eirene*, do not refer simply to a state without war, but have more positive and comprehensive meanings. One may discern the following three major meanings: 1) welfare, well-being, prosperity; 2) inner peace; and 3) peace in relationships.[36]

1. Welfare and Orderliness of All Things

In the Old Testament *shalom* (שׁלוֹם) has abundant and various meanings that cannot be reduced to what we mean by the English word "peace" today. The basic meaning of *shalom* is completeness or wholeness. The noun *shalom* is derived from the verb *shalem*, which means "make complete, make perfect, complete, and bring to an end."[37] *Shalom* sometimes meant wholeness of life or well-being—especially, in the material sense. People often used the word in greetings. It also meant prosperity and going well (Ps. 73:3), or health and healing (Ps. 38:3; Isa. 57:18-20). It is noteworthy that Hebrew people applied the word not only to individuals but more frequently to their community.[38] In the Old Testament the concept of *shalom* is closed

Deuk Ok, *op. cit.*, 41.

[34] Yong-Gil Maeng, op. cit., 37ff.

[35] Min-Hong Choi, *Han cheolhak*, 27.

[36] The following discussion is an extraction of my earlier writing, "Pyeonghwaui myeot gaji gaenyeumdeulgwa pyeonghwa chuguui useonsunwi: gidokgyo pyeonghwagyoyugui jojiksinhakjeok gicho" [A Few Concepts of Peace and the Priority in Pursuit of Peace: The Systematic

related to that of blessing. Though they are not identical, details of blessing are well summarized in the concept of *shalom*.[39] According to the Old Testament, *shalom* is above all the gift of Yahweh (Lev. 26:6; 22:18; 23:25; 2 Chron. 14:7; 15:15; Job 25:2; 34:29; Ps. 29:11; 85).

Eirene (εἰρήνη), which appears in the New Testament, has a very similar meaning to that of *shalom* in the Old Testament and Rabbinic literature. In other words, it has a different meaning than its original meaning in ancient Greek literature. In the New Testament *eirene* also refers to well-being, prosperity, and salvation. People used the word when greeting or blessing (John 20:19; Rom. 1:7). It also meant health (Mark 5:34; Luke 7:50), safety (Luke 11:21), order (1 Cor. 14:33), and cessation of persecution (Acts 9:31).[40] Also, it was used as an antonym of war (Acts 12:30; 24:3; Mark 10:34). Foerster defines *eirene* as "the normal state of all things." Just like the Rabbinic concept of *shalom*, it does not have simply an ethical meaning, nor does it apply only to the inner world but also to the external world. The healthy and normal state that corresponds to divine will does not apply only to the human soul or humanity but to the entire cosmos.[41] In this sense it is very close to the concept of holistic peace.

Theological Foundation of Christian Peace Education] (February 2003), which I was commissioned to write by the Christian Education Research Institute, PUTS.

[37] F. Brown, S. R. Driver, and C. A. Briggs, *Hebrew and English Lexicon of the Old Testament* (Oxford: Oxford University Press, 1907), 1022.

[38] Werner Foerster & von Rad, "εἰρήνη, εἰρηνεύω, ειρηνικος, ειρηνοποιος, ειρηνοποεω," in Gerhard Kittel (ed.), *Theological Dictionary of the New Testament*, vol. II, trans. G. W. Bromiley (Grand Rapids, Michigan: Eerdmans, 1964), 402.

[39] Claus Westermann, Segen in der Bible und im Handeln der Kirche (Chr. Kaiser, 1968), 27, 33. But Westermann distinguishes between blessing and shalom to some extent. Blessing is

2. Inner Peace

In the Old Testament *shalom* has many different meanings across a broad spectrum. Interestingly, however, there are only a few passages that speak of peace of mind or inner peace.[42] There are some passages concerning peace of mind (Ps. 25:13; 116:7).[43] Also, other passages deal with inner peace, though the word *shalom* is not employed (Prov. 14:30; Ezek. 16:42; Jer. 6:16). "You will keep in perfect peace him whose mind is steadfast, because he trusts in you" (Isa. 26:3). One does not need to understand the meaning of peace in this passage as simply referring to inner peace, but it is certain that the meaning of inner peace is not excluded.

In the New Testament *eirene* also means inner peace. Paul says, "May the God of hope fill you with all joy and peace as you trust in him" (Rom. 15:13). In this passage peace refers explicitly to inner peace. But one may interpret it as referring also to the normal state of all things, or the salvation and order of all humanity, as the word generally means in the New Testament. Of course, the order and welfare of human souls are included in it. Therefore, the New Testament concept of *eirene* is distinct from the Stoic concept of stillness (*galene*).[44] Any way the former is closely related to the inner peace that God gives us (Php. 4:7: John 14:27; 16:33; Col. 3:15; Phm. 1:7, 20). Inner

handed down vertically from generation to generation, while shalom refers to well-being of a group from the horizontal perspective. Ibid., 33.

[40] Foerster & von Rad, "εἰρήνη, εἰρηνεύω, ειρηνικος, ειρηνοποιος, ειρηνοποεω," 411.

[41] Ibid., 412.

[42] Von Rad finds it strange that in the Old Testament there are few passages referring to inner peace of mind. Ibid., 406.

peace does not exhaust the abundant meaning of peace but is an essential aspect to all faith and spirituality and an important part of the holistic concept of peace.

3. Peace in Relationship

For the Hebrew people *shalom* referred to the peace and well-being of the community as well as that of individuals (1 Sam. 17:3; Jer. 29:7; 38:4). In addition, *shalom* was also used to refer to the relationship between nations or states. For instance, in 1 Samuel 7:14 ("there was peace between Israel and the Amorites") and many other passages (1 Kings 4:24; 22:44; 5:25; Judg. 4:17; 1 Kings 5:4; Gen. 34:21; Zech. 6:13) *shalom* refers to peaceful relations between two or more parties. In these biblical passages *shalom* refers first of all to the state without war, but it also implies a relational concept.

The Hebrew people described this alliance with the word "covenant" (ברית, *berith*). In many cases the word *shalom* was used in connection with it. Due to the strong connection between them, *shalom* was often used as an official term. That is, concerning two parties in a covenant relationship, it was said that the relationship of *shalom* was sealed between them, or that the relationship of *shalom* derived from covenant. Ezekiel was especially interested in making *shalom* through covenant. When God makes the covenant of *shalom* with Israel, safety and prosperity will be given to them as a result (Ezek. 34:25; 37:26).[45] Still, it is only in a few passages that *shalom* refers to the right relationship between God and humanity. For in-

---

43 Meanwhile, the Hebrew word *nephesh* in these Psalms cannot be translated simply into "soul,"

stance, in Job 22:21 we read, "Submit to God and be at peace with him; in this way prosperity will come to you." Even when *shalom* refers to the relationship between God and humanity, the main point is that when the community fulfills their responsibilities within the covenant relationship, the result is safety, prosperity, or a state of *shalom* free from war.

In Israel and Judah there was a minority of righteous prophets who proclaimed divine judgment when confronting false prophets and their false message of peace. For them, *shalom* did not refer to an abstract, psychological, otherworldly, or mythological peace. *Shalom* also meant peace in social-political relationships that people should establish in the world by obeying God and cooperating with one another. False prophets ignored the righteousness of God and said to the sinful people, "Peace, peace." But Jeremiah and Ezekiel objected to them and proclaimed that "there is no peace" (Jer. 6:14; 8:11; 12:12; 30:5; Ezek. 13:10, 16).[46] According to them, people could not enjoy prosperity, well-being, or safety because they betrayed God, worshipped idols, and oppressed the poor and marginalized, and even priests and prophets went astray for the sake of their own interests. In other words, there was no peace in the sense of the right relationship between God and the people, and among the people. In Isaiah 32:17 *shalom* is defined as the result of righteousness (צדקה, *tzedekah*). In Zechariah 8:16 ("Speak the truth to each other, and render true and sound [peaceful] judgment in your courts.") *shalom* is mentioned in connection with משפט (*mishpat*), which means justice, judgment, and law. In Isaiah 59:8 justice (משפט, *mishpat*) and peace (*shalom*) are

---

for it has a broad spectrum of meaning. It can also mean life, breath, living creature, desire,

mentioned in parallel. All things considered, *shalom* in most usages is a social concept.[47]

In the ancient Greek language the primary usage of *eirene* does not concern relations between human beings. It more commonly refers to the peaceful attitude of an individual's mind, rather than peaceful relations between human beings. It is rarely used to mean harmony between human beings.[48] However, when *eirene* is used in the New Testament, its meaning is different from that in the ancient Greek language. In the New Testament *eirene* refers to harmony between human beings, in the same tradition with the Old Testament and the rabbinic concept of *shalom*. "When two Israelites were fighting, Moses tried to reconcile them" (Acts 7:26).[49] Just as in rabbinic literature, so in the New Testament does *eirene* also refer to the right relationship between God and humanity. For instance, Ephesians 2:14-17 clearly suggests the relational concept of peace as salvation. When Jesus abolished the law, he abolished both the broken relationship between human beings and the broken relationship between God and humanity. Therefore, the peace of Christ means healing of all these broken relationships. In Romans 5:1 ("Therefore, since we have been justified through faith, we have peace with God through our Lord Jesus Christ.") *eirene* explicitly refers to peaceful relation between God and humanity.[50] Here peace does not mean a mutually equal re-

---

nostril, soul, and so forth. Sometimes it is used simply as a pronoun that refers to a person. Hans Walter Wolff, *Anthropology in the Old Testament* (Minneapolis: Fortress, 1974), 10-25.

[44] Ibid., 417.

[45] Cf. Ibid., 402-403.

[46] Ibid., 404.

[47] W. Caspari, "Verstellung und Wort 'Friede' im AT," *BFTh*, 14, 4 (1910), edited in Foerster & von Rad, "εἰρήνη, εἰρηνεύω, ειρηνικος, ειρηνοποιος, ειρηνοποεω," 406.

lationship between God and humanity but the relationship that God initiates with humanity.[51] For humanity, this peaceful relationship with God means salvation.

In the New Testament *eirene* refers in most cases to a reciprocal relationship between human beings. In Romans 14:17 ("For the reign of God is not a matter of eating and drinking, but of righteousness, peace and joy in the Holy Spirit") peace refers to the peaceful relationship within the community of God's reign. Here Paul's point is that, with regard to eating food, people whose faith is strong should carefully consider other people whose faith is weak. Later in verse 19 Paul mentions "what leads to peace" and "mutual edification" in parallel, which implies that the concept of peace in this passage is relational. Similar cases are found in other passages, including Ephesians 4:3, James 3:18, Hebrews 12:14, and Romans 14:19. In addition, the concept of *eirene* sometimes implies relationship with all creatures as well as with other human beings. In Romans 11:36 ("For from him and through him and to him are all things") Paul makes clear that God is not just the God of the Jewish people but also the source, lord, and destiny of all things, including all of humanity. And in Colossians 1:15-20 the author proclaims that God not only builds the church through Christ's blood on the cross, but also reconciles all things in the cosmos to God's self.

When the Old and New Testaments are considered as a whole, peace in relationship applies not only to the relationship between God and humanity, between neighbors, between men and women, be-

---

[48] Foerster & von Rad, "εἰρήνη, εἰρηνεύω, ειρηνικος, ειρηνοποιος, ειρηνοποεω," 400-401.

tween difference races or nations or states, but also to the relationship with other livings creatures and all of creation. Given the fact that people often seek only inner peace or well-being in their private life, this relational concept of peace is very important. This is essential to the holistic concept of peace.

4. Priority in Pursuing Peace

Thus far I have discussed different meanings of peace: welfare, well-being, safety, prosperity, inner peace, and peaceful relations with God and with others. In sum, the biblical concept of peace is a holistic one that comprehends all of them. It resonates with the concept of 한 (han) as the harmony of all things. However, one should also note that those different meanings of peace are not only interconnected with one another, but also some of them take precedence over others. To be specific, inner peace of mind is more important than peace as well-being and prosperity, and peace in relationships is more important than inner peace. We all wish that the condition of our life might be comfortable, safe, and prospering. But life in the world is not always tranquil; we sometimes encounter affliction and suffering. Sometimes we suffer unfairness. However, the mystery of faith is that even in such times we can enjoy inner peace of mind that transcends our thinking, calculation, and common sense (Php. 4:7).

However, even inner peace of mind is not an absolute value. Jesus Christ, whose inner mind was always peaceful, still wept over the city of Jerusalem for her sin and unwillingness to repent (Luke 19:41f.). Paul was also a great saint who kept peace of mind even in his suffering, but he was anxious and mournful about the salvation of his people (Rom. 9:1-3). Though Jesus often taught not to be anxious, he sometimes said, "Blessed are those who mourn" (Matt. 5:4). For, in the eyes of Jesus, mourning was an appropriate response to the corruption, deterioration, and unrighteousness that he observed among the crowds that followed him. People who feel joyful and comfortable even amid a gloomy reality do not have a right faith. Here peace in relationships—namely, peace based upon right relationships, or just peace—claims priority.

Every genuine peace presupposes justice. Justice implies a right relationship with God, with neighbors, and with God's creation. Thus, it is peace in relationships that takes precedence in our pursuit of peace. What is at stake is that fallen human beings cannot accomplish peace in all relationships by themselves. Jesus Christ is the savior who restores and reconciles those broken, distorted, and antagonistic relationships. As Ephesians 2:14-17 says, Christ is our peace. Karl Barth rightly interpreted this passage when he said that Jesus Christ is the reconciler who fulfills this peace in relationships. God, who reconciled us to himself through Christ, gave us the ministry of reconciliation—that is, to bring peace to relationships with people of other nations, other races, the opposite sex, other classes, and also to the relationship with all creatures (2 Cor. 5:18-19). Just as the life and cross of Jesus Christ show us, so our efforts to fulfill peace in relationships will demand our sacrifice and suffering. Once the right relationship or justice is established, inner peace of mind will follow. Peace of mind in such conditions is always good. But it would be disgusting to God to seek only peace of mind or only personal safety and prosperity amidst broken relationships. For those whom I hurt, those who suffer due to my fault, or the group of people who are suffering due to our wrongdoings, such profound words as "God," "faith," and "justice" would sound meaningless and empty. On the contrary, when we are in a right relationship, our mind is peaceful and all things go well. But such instances are only momentary in our lives, for our lives and our society are still in the shadow of fall and corruption. Meanwhile, we also have eschatological salvation and peace anticipated by Jesus Christ. They are not complete yet, but they ensure that the reign of God and peace will be completed in the future. That is to say, the whole peace in relationships, the whole peace of mind, and the whole peace in all things—including welfare, well-being, and prosperity—belong to the vision of eschatological salvation.

In the Old Testament *shalom* sometimes refers to the final state of eternal peace that will be fulfilled in the eschatological future. Even if one cannot find the exact word *shalom* in the biblical passages about the eschatological future, it is legitimate for us to portray the eschatological state as peace when we consider the multi-dimensional meaning and the far-reaching expectation of *shalom*.[52] For instance, Isaiah 11:6-16 describes the restoration of paradise with the coming of the Messiah as follows: namely, wild beasts and domestic animals, and humanity and animals live together; the exiled Judah returns; and all nations that have been antagonistic toward Israel are transformed to love her. All these events refer to the final state of *shalom*. Peace that will be fulfilled in the eschatological future refers to peace based

---

[49] Ibid., 411.

upon a right relationship with God, with all our neighbors and nations, and with all creatures; it also refers to inner peace of mind as well as the normal state of all things in the sense of welfare, orderliness, and prosperity. All things considered, holistic theology is in total agreement with the Bible in seeking peace in its holistic sense. The holistic concept of peace does not simply mean a state without war, but justice, welfare, and righteousness in all things. It includes both peace in relationship and inner peace of mind; furthermore, it refers to the return of all things to the normal state that God originally willed: the peaceful reign of the triune God.

VI
Theology of Life

Now we live in God's peace. Here the concept of life comes to the fore. Today we find ourselves in a serious crisis, and we need a holistic understanding of life. It is very difficult to define life. Even within the natural sciences there are many definitions of life—for example, physiological, metabolic, genetic, biochemical, and thermodynamic definitions.[53] But none of them can exhaust the phenomenon of life, probably because life itself is a mysterious phenomenon that tran-

---

[50] The insertion of the phrase "προς τον θεον" confirms that this passage refers to the relationship between God and humanity. This interpretation fits well with Romans 5:10, which says that we were God's enemies.

[51] Cf. Ibid., 415-416.

[52] Ibid., 405.

scends our definitions or because our scientific approach is not yet mature enough to reach an intuitive understanding of life. In fact, even if we attain the intuitive definition of life, I am not sure whether it will fully explain the phenomenon of life. According to Hoe-Ik Jang, the difficulty of the scientific definition of life results from the fact that scientists fail to bring partial definitions of life in various disciplines together to make an overall synthesis. Then, he suggests the concept of 온 생명 (on-saengmyeong, global life) as the one life that comprehends all individual living creatures on the globe.[54] This suggestion is very significant. Today the attempt to understand life in terms of the network of living creatures forms an important stream within the life sciences. Many theologians are sympathetic toward it. Still, scientific efforts are not sufficiently holistic yet. Moreover, defining life is not a prerogative of the natural sciences. They may propose descriptive definitions of the phenomenon of life, but they cannot explain what true life is or what life is in relation with God.

Then, what is life in the biblical sense? Today we use the word "bio-" quite often. It originated from the Greek word βίος (*bios*). But in the New Testament βίος (*bios*) is not the primary word for life. It is often argued that βίος (*bios*) refers to physical life, while ζωή (*zōé*) refers to spiritual life. But this is an oversimplified argument.[55] In the Bible βίος (*bios*) refers to life in the world (Luke 8:14; 1 John 2:16),

53 *The New Encyclopedia Britanica*, vol. 22, *Macropaedia* (1985), s.v. "life," 985-986. Fritjof Capra develops the thermodynamic definition of life further in terms of system theory—thus, holistically. He thinks of life as a living system and describes its characteristic features as autopoiesis, dissipative structure, and cognitive process. Here traditional mechanical worldview turns into ecological worldview, and analytic, atomic understanding of life turns into holistic understanding of life. Fritjof Capra, *The Web of Life* (Toronto: Anchor, 1996), 157ff.

54 Hoe-Ik Jang, *Sarmgwa on-saengmyeong* 『삶과 온 생명』 [Life and Global Life] (Seoul: Sol, 1998), 172-174.

lifestyle or behavior (1 Tim. 2:2; 2 Tim. 2:4), and means of life or property (Mark 12:44; Luke 15:12; 8:43; 1 John 3:17), rather than physical life.[56] In the Bible the Hebrew word חיים (*chayyim*, Deut. 28:66; 2 Sam. 15:21; Isa. 38:12; Ezek. 7:13; Ps. 26:9), another Hebrew word נפש (*nephesh*, Gen. 44:30; Deut. 12:23; Lev. 17:11; Gen. 35:18; 1 Kings 17:21; 2 Sam. 1:9; Ps. 35:4), and the latter's Greek translation, ψυχή (*psyche*, Matt. 2:20; 6:25; Mark 3:4; 8:35; Luke 9:24; John 10:11; 12:25; Rom. 11:3; Php. 2:30) are used to refer to physical life. The word ζωή (*zōē*) refers to both spiritual and physical life (Rom. 8:38; 1 Cor. 3:22; Php. 1:20; Luke 16:25; Acts 8:33).[57] In some cases it means physical health (Mark 5:23; John 4:50).[58] However, it is true that in the New Testament the word ζωή (*zōē*) refers in most cases to true life, or spiritual life given through Christ (Matt. :14; John 1:4; 5:24, 26, 29; 6:33, 35, 48, 53, 63; Rom. 5:17, 18; 6:4; 7:10; 2 Cor. 2:16). In particular, ζωή αιώνιος (*zoe aionios*) always refers to eternal life as the true life. In any case the important thing is that whether βίος (*bios*) or נפש (*nephesh*) or ψυχή (*psyche*) or ζωή (*zōē*), life belongs exclusively to God and is under God's sovereign rule. We should note that the Bible does not attempt to define life scientifically but to speak of true life in God. Then, what does the Bible speak about life?

---

[55] George Arthur Buttrick (ed.), *The Interpreter's Dictionary of the Bible* (New York: Abingdon, 1962), s.v. "Life," 172. To distinguish between zoe and bios, the former may be translated into the Korean word '생명 (saengmyeong),' and the latter into the word '삶 (sarm).' In the ancient world, zoe was defined as *vita qua vivimus*, while bios as *vita quam vivimus*. Bertram, "C. ζωή and βίος in the Septuagint," in Gerhart Kittel (ed.), TDNT, vol. II, s.v. "ζαω ζωή (βίοω βίος)," 851.

[56] William F. Arndt & F. Wilber Gingrich, Greek-English Lexicon of the New Testament and

1) According to the Bible, life is understood thoroughly in relation to God who is the creator, ruler, and owner of life. Only God is the creator and ruler of life (Ps. 66:9; 119:116; 139:13; 1 Sam. 2:6).[59] Without a relationship with God, therefore, life has no meaning and no purpose. In Ecclesiastes the preacher laments that under the Sun there is nothing new and everything is meaningless. At last, the preacher concludes his preaching with the following words: "Remember your Creator!" (Eccl. 12:1). Life is meaningful only in true relationship with God the creator. God created the world in accordance with his pleasure and will and gave us life as a gift. Life is something given to us. Creatures can enjoy life only temporarily; it still belongs to God in the fundamental sense. Therefore, no creature is allowed to harm its own life or the life of any other creature (Exod. 20:13; Deut. 5:17). Though animals were given for food, eating blood was strictly prohibited, because blood was believed to contain life in it. For life belongs to God (Gen. 9:4; Lev. 3:17). Since God is the creator, ruler, and owner of life, life-destroying acts such as murder, violence, overhunting, destroying the ecological system, abortion, cloning, and selfish evasion of childbirth are regarded as sinful disobedience to God.

2) Life is more valuable than anything else. For God brought forth life, and God is the owner and ruler of life. The one thing that is more valuable than life is God's mercy (Ps. 63:3). According to the

---

Other Early Christian Literature (Chicago: The University of Chicago Press, 1957), s.v. "βίος."

57 In the Greek world ζωή (zoe) referred to the physical vitality of all living creatures, including humanity, animals, and plants. Bultmann, "A. ζωή in Greek Usage," in Gerhard Kittel (ed.), TDNT, vol. II, s.v. "ζαω ζωή (βίοω βίος)," 832-833.

Bible, life grows and reproduces itself. In the Genesis story of creation, God created living creatures and told them to be fruitful, increase in number, and fill the earth and the water (Gen. 1:20-23, 28). In this way God blessed all living creatures, including humanity. Of course, their life is not eternal. In the world life is weak, passes quickly, and is subject to suffering and death (Isa. 40:6-8). Still, the existence of life is itself God's grace and blessing. In the Bible God's first blessing concerns growing and flourishing of life. Though limited, life is a divine blessing. Thus, it is useless for a human person to gain the whole world if he or she forfeits his or her soul (Matt. 16:26). Life is so valuable that we should respect not just our own life, but also the life of other persons and even of other creatures. Such respect for life is found in Albert Schweitzer's idea of reverence for life.

3) The world of life is a network community in which all living creatures support one another. Every living creature lives in relationship with other living creatures, as well as in relationship with God. Throughout the Old Testament life is described as coexisting with other lives.[60] Each living creature is connected with other living creatures in the form of a food chain or a caring relationship. The Garden of Eden was a life community in which all living creatures were interconnected (Gen. 1:28-30; Ps. 104:27-28). The life community means more than the food chain. The stories of the fall and the flood, where humanity and other living creatures were punished together, suggest solidarity between humanity and other living creatures (Gen.

---

58 Buttrick (ed.), The Interpreter's Dictionary of the Bible, s.v. "Life."

3:17; 6-9).[61] In the Bible the sabbath-command applies to domestic animals as well as to humanity (Exod. 23:12), and even to the earth (Lev. 25:2-5). The Bible also commands prohibition of reckless deforestation (Deut. 20:19) and protection of the mother bird (Deut. 22:6-7). In short, life should not be understood as being comprised of isolated entities; rather, life should be understood holistically in terms of the network of relationships with God and with other living creatures.

That life of any living creature presupposes relationships, which means that these relationship should be just and peaceful. When there is right relationship with God, with neighbors, and with other creatures, all things will enjoy blessing and peace. True life is not separated from justice and good works for others (Deut. 16:20; Amos 5:14; Ezek. 18:6-9, 17). The divine commandments to do what is right are "the decrees that give life" (Ezek. 33:15). Therefore, if God's people turn away from God and commit sins, then not only they but also their land will suffer from many disasters; but if they repent and return to God, then God will forgive their sin and will heal their land (2 Chron. 7:14). The life of humanity and life of the land are connected to each other; and both of them are connected to God. When all these relationships are set right, we call it *shalom* or fullness of life (Ezek. 34:27). Hosea proclaimed the Word of God who wills to restore unrighteous Israel through God's mercy, love, and grace (Hos. 2:21-22):

---

59 Like other Near Eastern people, Israelite people too believed that God is the source of life. But von Rad finds it strange that Israel did not have a deep religious interest in this source of life, but paid more serious attention to the absolute relationship between God and individuals. Von Rad, "B. Life and Death in the OT," in Gerhard Kittel (ed.), TDNT, vol. II, s.v. "ζαω ζωή (βίοω βίος)," 844.

"I will respond to the skies, and they will respond to the earth; and the earth will respond to the grain, the new wine and oil, and they will respond to Jezreel." It is not only God and humanity but also many other creatures that are involved in this mutually corresponding network of life.

These days an organic view of life is prevailing. According to the organic view, living creatures do not exist in isolation but form a system in which they live in mutual dependence and reciprocal communication. This view helps correct the old mechanical worldview. But one should be cautious in adopting the organic view. Organic systems in the natural world often have a hierarchical structure. Think of the food chain in nature or the brain of a higher animal that controls its entire body. The problem is that in such a hierarchical structure some parts may oppress other parts. Therefore, we should seek a non-oppressive life community. According to Isaiah's eschatological vision, wild beasts will live with domestic animals, a little child will lead them, lions will eat straw like oxen, the infant will play near the hole of the cobra without any harm, and nobody will hurt anyone, and the earth will be full of the knowledge of the Lord (Isa. 11:6-9). This is a model of a non-oppressive life community, the world of *shalom*, and the life-filled reign of the big, bright, abundant, and 한 (*han*) God. In the final analysis, the concepts of 한 (*han*), peace, and life are holistically and closely connected with one another.[62]

In our discussion of life, the relationship between God and hu-

---

[60] Cf. Buttrick (ed.), *The Interpreter's Dictionary of the Bible*, s.v. "Life," 125.

[61] Among interpreters there is a debate concerning whether sins that had to be punished by the flood were only of humanity, or of all living creatures. With regard to "all flesh" in Genesis 6:12, Westermann interprets it as referring to humanity alone, while Wenham understands it as re-

manity—especially, the spiritual life of humanity restored through Christ—is very important. Due to excessive focus on it, however, one should not ignore other creatures living in God's world. On the contrary, it is also problematic to consider only the natural environment while disregarding God who is the source of life. Some people understand humanity thoroughly as part of the natural world. This idea may help correct an anthropocentric worldview, but it has the danger of overlooking humanity's special place and duty within the natural world. In the face of human-induced problems, how can we ignore human responsibility? Therefore, we should consider God, humanity, and creation all in combination.[63] God as the creator and ruler of all life made human beings in the image of God and commissioned them to look after and protect other living creatures (Gen. 1:26-28). Then, are the land and all other living creatures in it no more than passive beings that receive human care? God did not create creatures, including humanity, all at once. Before human beings were created, the land, the water, and all other living creatures had already been created. In a sense human life is dependent upon the life of other creatures. When God created the first man, God formed him from the dust of the ground and breathed into his nostrils the breath of life (Gen. 2:7). The breath of God is the source of life; then, what is the dust? Without the divine breath there would be no life; also, without the dust there would be no human beings. That means that the ground and the dust are "the field of life." Because "the field of life" and all other creatures owe their origin and function to the divine breath, they are

---

ferring to all humanity and animals. Gordon J. Wenham, *Word Biblical Commentary*, vol. I, *Genesis 1-15* (Waco: Word Books, 1987), 171.

"the foundations of life" that support human life. Therefore, humans should not treat them disparagingly. In sum, the heavenly God is the creator and ruler of all life, the earth and all its animals are "the foundations of life," and humanity as the species of God is "the one who protects life" by taking care of other living creatures (Gen. 2:15). In this way we can properly grasp humans' responsible place while not falling into anthropocentrism, and we can recognize the importance of a life community while retaining a theo-centric perspective. This idea supplements the earlier view of humanity as a steward of creation by restoring the authentic value of other living creatures. It also overcomes the error of pan-ecologism, which absorbs humanity into the ecological system and thereby overlooks human responsibility.

4) Due to the fall, humanity is corrupt and the entire world is in agony. Created in the image of God, human beings were originally commissioned to take care of and protect the world on God's behalf (Gen. 1:26-28). However, they chose the way of privatizing the knowledge of good and evil, instead of the way oriented toward the tree of life (Gen. 2:9, 16-17; 3:1-7). It is significant that in the ideal world—namely, the Garden of Eden—the tree of the knowledge of good and evil and the tree of life were in conflict. Strangely enough, in our human life, too, the desire for the knowledge of good and evil and the desire for life coexist in a conflicting relationship. People who leave God behind and privatize the knowledge of good and evil tend not to pursue life, but to suppress and harm life. In order to save life we should often overcome the hypocritical, oppressive, and solidified framework of the knowledge of good and evil (and even the law). Hu-

manity abandoned the tree of life but chose the tree of knowledge of good and evil, which shows that human beings disobey God, privatize the knowledge of good and evil, and seek and use such knowledge for selfish purposes. This is the fall at its fundamental level. It destroyed not only the relationship between God and humanity, but also the relationship between human beings and the relationship between humanity and other creatures. In short, it destroys community. Jeremy Rifkin clearly shows us the socio-political implications of the fall. According to Rifkin, humans, especially after modernity, sought to secure their "safety" by enclosing and privatizing lands for commercial benefits and the creation of power. For this purpose they used all kinds of scientific technology and violent wars, which were then supported by the ideology of "autonomy." As a result, the world became devastated and humanity was alienated from the world. Now the objects of human enclosure include sea, sky, and genes. In particular, our world is currently in a serious crisis due to its exploitation by multinational corporations.[64] In the past humans disobeyed God, ate from the tree of knowledge of good and evil, and thus privatized the knowledge of good and evil. Do they attempt once again today to disobey God and to privatize the tree of life (which has been prohibited from the fall) by means of biotechnology?

5) Jesus Christ is the savior not only of humanity but also of the entire world. Humanity and the world, though fallen, still have hope. In Jesus Christ God gives us true life through grace. This New Testa-

---

62 In his proposal of "ethic of survival" Yong-Gil Maeng asks for the three modes of existence: free coexistence, just cooperation, and peaceful participation. In this way, he connects concepts of

ment understanding of life is clearly distinct from the Old Testament view of life. Ever since humanity sinned and was subject to the fall, we have been alive but not in a genuine sense (cf. Rev. 3:1). In the beginning life was not something human beings obtained by their own power, but it was given to them by grace; likewise, restoration of the lost true life is not possible by human power. True life is given to us as a gift in the grace of the redemptive death and resurrection of Jesus Christ the redeemer (Rom. 6:23; 1 Pet. 3:7). When we repent and believe in Jesus Christ, our distorted relationships are set right so that we are justified and receive the righteous and peaceful life. This is embodied within us by the Holy Spirit, or the Spirit of Christ who is given to us. In Christ, and in the Holy Spirit, we receive true life, or new life. This is what is meant by regeneration (John 3:3-5; 1 Pet. 1:3). Now Christ is the life itself for us (1 John 5:20). People with Christ have life, but people without Christ do not have life (1 John 5:12). Of course, wholeness of life still remains in the future of our hope (Rev. 2:7, 10; 20:4f). However, in the Holy Spirit we can fore-taste the reign of God and eternal life that have already come to the earth in Jesus Christ. The Holy Spirit ensures their complete realization (2 Cor. 2:4-5). Paul and John offer us deep insights into the present reality of eternal life.[65] Eternal life is given to us now as a gift that we can experience on earth (John 5:24; Eph. 2:1; Col. 2:13). "Now this is eternal life: that they may know you, the only true God, and Jesus Christ, whom you have sent" (John 17:3). Here "knowing" does not refer simply to obtaining information but to personal and rela-

---

peace and life with that of community. Yong-Gil Maeng, *Gidokgyowa juchesasang* 『기독교와 주체사상』 [Christianity and the Juche Idea] (Seoul: Christian Book Center, 1990), 205-206.

tional knowledge.[66] The important feature of Christ's life was his personal fellowship with God. This marks one of the important characteristics of Christian spirituality.

It is true that in the New Testament the history of new life is usually mentioned in relation to the salvation of individual human beings in Christ and in the Holy Spirit. But one should also note that in the New Testament the history of new life is not confined to humanity alone. Yes, through the Holy Spirit, not only our souls but also our bodies are enabled to participate in resurrection of life, and so too do all other creatures wish to be liberated from their bondage to decay and to be brought into the glorious freedom of the children of God (Rom. 8:21). The blood (that is, life) of Jesus Christ on the cross reconciles to God not only human beings but also the church and all things (Col. 1:15-20). Also, according to the eschatological vision of the new heaven and new earth in the Book of Revelation, the life of God renews not only individual humans and all nations (Rev. 22:1-5) but also all things (Rev. 21:5).

Life exists in dynamic relationships and has an orientation. To use physical terminology as an analogy, life is not scalar, but vector. Life is oriented toward God and neighbors. Paul speaks of the death and resurrection of Jesus Christ as follows: "The death he died, he died to sin once for all; but the life he lives, he lives to God" (Rom. 6:10). Life is not only given a certain duration, but is also oriented toward God. Christ died to sin (for us and with God), and Christ

---

63 To use traditional Eastern terminology, it is a view of life that takes into account all the three elements of heaven, earth, and humanity.

64 Cf. Jeremy Rifkin, *Biosphere Politics* (New York: HarperSanFrancisco, 1992). As an alternative

lives to God (for us and with us).[67] According to the parable of the rich fool (Luke 12:16f), the ground of a certain rich man produced such a good crop that he plans to tear down existing barns and build bigger ones. But God says to the rich man, "This very night your life will be demanded from you. Then who will get what you have prepared for yourself?" Jesus concludes the parable with the following words: "This is how it will be with anyone who stores up things for himself but is not rich toward God" (Luke 12:21).[68] In short, the life of the rich man has a certain orientation—namely, toward wealth. This orientation is what makes his life dynamic. This relationship and orientation are essential to life. Thus, life that has distorted or lost its orientation cannot be a true life.

In trying to address the ecological crisis, many contemporary theologians have made theological reflections on life. This has led to the development of ecological theology and the theology of life. The ecumenical movement also refined its vision by incorporating the idea of "integrity of creation" into the ideas of justice and peace: thus, the Justice, Peace, and the Integrity of Creation (JPIC). Here the important issue is to develop a theology of life. Meanwhile, some theologians are inclined to a new theology of creation, a new doctrine of God, or a new doctrine of life. Others who are not satisfied with the Bible or Christian theology turn their attention even to Eastern

to it Rifkin suggests awakening the biosphere consciousness.

65 R. Bultmann, "E. The Concept of Life in the NT," in Gerhard Kittel (ed.), TDNT, vol. II, s.v. "ζαω ζωή (βίοω βίος)," 865ff.

66 Here "knowing" means more than intellectual function, but includes relationship and koinonia. George R. Beasely-Murray, *Word Biblical Commentary*, vol. 36, "John" (Waco: Word Books, 1987), 297.

67 "τῇ ἁμαρτίᾳ ἀπέθανεν ... ζῇ τῷ θεῷ." Here the words for God and sin are expressed in the

thought.[69] It is important to review and critically examine the earlier doctrines of God, creation, and life within the context of today's serious ecological crisis. In fact, Christian theologians have long misunderstood the divine command to "subdue the earth" (Gen. 1:28) as divine permission to misuse creation. For that reason Christianity has been accused of having promoted the ecological crisis. But new theological reflections have corrected some misunderstandings. Be that as it may, theological reflections on life cannot remain within the so-called "pan-ecological" perspective that focuses exclusively on ecological preservation. Reformation of our worldview does not directly bring about renewal of our life world. It is intertwined with many complicated political, economic, and social issues. No one would deny that in the past human ignorance and a false worldview—namely, an anthropocentric and mechanical worldview—were primary reasons for ecological destruction. But these days such scientific, philosophical, or theological understandings of life may not have much bearing on the ecological crisis. Today there are few who do not know that the ecological crisis is very serious and almost irrecoverable. In particular, all our leaders and policy makers are well aware of it. Then, why do they not take appropriate measures? This has more to do with our greed, self-interest, anti-ecological lifestyle, and economic structure of production and consumption, than with our worldview.

---

dative case. Grammarians call it "the dative of benefit or harm." The dative case then has the meaning of "for" or "against," or sometimes the meaning of possession or belonging. Friedrich Blass and Albert Dehbrunner, *Grammatik des neutestamentlichen Griechisch*, bearbeitet von Friedrich Rehkopf, 16. Auflage (Goettingen: Vandenhoeck&Ruprecht, 1984), 152. I attempted to understand the whole discussion in terms of the concept of "orientation."

68 "θησαυρίζων αὐτῷ καὶ μὴ εἰς Θεὸν πλουτῶν." Here the dative case of αὐτῷ may be understood as the dative of benefit, and εἰς Θεὸν as referring to orientation. Ibid., 169.

Today's ecological crisis is intertwined not only with our worldview but also with our personal greed and laziness, as well as with structural problems in politics, the economy, and society.[70] Therefore, theology of life is inseparable from theology of peace, which seeks the world of divine *shalom* in which all things enjoy justice and blessing. Therefore, in practice we are required to sacrifice some of the economic comfort and convenience we enjoy and change our selfish lifestyle. Here again we recognize the value of the traditional understanding of faith as fighting against greed, laziness, and other sins.[71] Therefore, a new theology of life should be a holistic theology that pursues both justice and peace at the same time and that seeks to save both individual souls and communal life.

In this light the attempt to make a theology of life into creation theology without Christ looks problematic. It is not desirable to separate creation from salvation or to absorb the former into the latter;

---

[69] For instance, one can think of Jeong-Bae Lee's Korean life theology. Drawing from the Donghak ideas of 至氣 (jigi, ultimate spirit) and 侍天主 (sicheonju, worship of the heavenly lord), as well as Yeong-Mo Yu's '얼 (Eol)' Christology, he develops a Korean life theology from the pneumatological perspective. Jeong-Bae Lee, *Hankukjeok saengmyeong sinhak* 『한국적 생명신학』 [Korean Life Theology] (Seoul: Doseochulpan Gamsin, 1996). I find this work inclined to syncretism that makes obscure Christian identity. It is natural to make pneumatology the main motive in theology of life, but one should not lose sight of the close connection between Jesus Christ and the Holy Spirit as testified by the Scriptures.

[70] For instance, the Kyoto Protocol was prepared to regulate emissions of greenhouse gases, which are often regarded as the primary cause of global warming. But the United States, the country that emits the greatest amount of greenhouse gases in the world, refused to ratify it. In this regard the global society expressed regret. Also, within the ecumenical movement Western advanced countries and those in the so-called second and third world have different positions concerning this issue. In the Seoul JPIC Convention in 1990, the countries of the second and third world affirmed the fundamental idea of the integrity of creation but objected to the position of Western advanced countries. According to their argument, the current destruction of the created world has resulted from the West's indiscriminant industrialization, exploitation of the natural resources of the second and third world, and disposal of industrial wastes to the Two-Third Worlds. Thus, it is unfair to make countries in the second and third world, which have now embarked on economic development to overcome poverty and pay the cost preserving the environment. Cf. Ju-Seop Geum, "WCC saengmyeongui sinhage daehan hangukjeok eungdapgwa

nor is it desirable to pursue ecological theology as a doctrine of creation without the redeemer.[72] For due to human greed, ignorance, and exploitation, the creation of God is groaning, and the restoration and fulfillment of creation are not simply an issue in the doctrine of creation but also an important soteriological issue. Jesus Christ is the savior not only of humanity but also of the entire cosmos and all things in it (Rom. 8:19-23). Thus, we seek not only the preservation and restoration of our environment but also of God's new creation—namely, the salvation of the entire world. Given the current situation, however, ecological destruction seems irrecoverable by human effort alone. We recognize that divine grace is necessary not only for the salvation of individuals but also for the salvation of the natural world. Today some people attempt to understand life without reference to God. They fail to see the fundamental relationship between life and God, who is the creator and source of life. Meanwhile, others take God into their understanding of life but ignore Christ. Therefore, they cannot have hope for salvation of the cosmos, including the natural world. Therefore, our understanding of life should focus on God as the creator, ruler, and sustainer of life and presuppose Jesus Christ as the savior who will bring humanity and the world to true life. Also, while recognizing that true life is a vector oriented toward God, neigh-

---

jeonmang" [Korean Response to the WCC's Theology of Life and the Propect] (PUTS Graduate School, Th.M. thesis, 1999), 60-61.

[71] In this regard we are reminded especially of the spirituality of Francis of Assisi. He turned his back upon greed and arrogance and entered into deep prayer and meditation, through which he enjoyed fellowship with God. Also, he left behind his rich father's house and lived in poor conditions. And he took care of the poor and the sick. He made songs like "Canticle of Brother Son," in which he called the Sun his brother, the moon his sister, the wind his brother, and water his sister. He also had fellowship with animals.

bors, and other creatures, we should make an effort to save humanity and the world in the Holy Spirit.

Conclusion

As I discussed above, holistic theology is an academic method that seeks balanced thinking as distinct from narrow thinking. Also, holistic theology does not refer simply to a methodological mixture but has the potential to develop a creative theology in the process of synthesis. In this vein I proposed the idea of "God's peaceful life" in order to elaborate holistic theology. Here I suggested two themes: peace and life. I did not mean to reduce all theological contents to these two concepts but simply to show a model of holistic theology responding to today's situation. Now I conclude this writing by reviewing some significant aspects of the theology of "God's peaceful life."

1) Theology of "God's peaceful life" can serve the biblical message. According to the biblical faith, the Father, the Son, and the Holy Spirit have the same divinity but are one. The concept of 하나님 (hananim), derived from the concept of 한 (han), is very useful in explaining the triune God. Also, according to the concept of 한 (han), the One comprehends the many; the spirit of peace implied in this concept resonates with the biblical witness to the gospel of peace and the biblical pursuit of peace. God the creator is the source of life given to us.

2) Theology of "God's peaceful life" can develop holistic theology by realizing holistic harmony within itself. Those concepts of 한 (*han*), peace, and life all pursue holistic harmony and should be understood holistically. Some people who define peace only as a state without war understand theology of peace simply as a theology of social participation. Others focus too much on inner peace. Still others think only of personal blessings such as welfare, well-being, and prosperity. But I pursue a holistic understanding of peace. Some people who understand life only in terms of the individual's spiritual life disregard other people, other living creatures, and the entire created world. Others who are possessed by pan-ecologism overlook the issue of the individual's spiritual life. But I pursue a holistic understanding of life.

3) Theology of "God's peaceful life" is a Korean theology appropriate to Korean thought and culture. From ancient times the Korean people have loved peace and pursued peace and life. 한 (*han*) and 하나님 (*hananim*) are purely Korean concepts with which Koreans feel familiar, but at the same time they can be used as universal concepts that are globally applicable.

4) Theology of "God's peaceful life" is appropriate to the historical context of the Korean people. Due to the strategic location of the Korean Peninsula, the Korean people have experienced numerous invasions and have suffered greatly. Nonetheless, they continued to love peace. Given that the currently divided Korea is witnessing an increas-

ing threat of war, we should believe in and hope for the God of peace and make every effort to establish the whole peace of God. Today we are also faced with ecological destruction, pollution of our air, water, and soil, frequent occurrence of terrible disasters resulting from our insensitivity to safety, human cloning, increasing violence and suicide, abortion, and evasion of childbirth. In this situation we are commissioned to restore the just and peaceful life.

5) Theology of "God's peaceful life" has a depth, while it is not speculative but applicable to people's concrete life. For instance, one of the chronic diseases afflicting the Korean church is blessing-centered faith that focuses on material blessing in the world. Another problem of the Korean church is individualistic faith that seeks only individual salvation or inner peace of mind, while neglecting divine mission toward human society and the entire creation. To pray for God's blessing is in itself not evil at all. However, what is problematic is the selfish attitude that breaks justice, ignores love, and seeks only one's own prosperity and well-being. Indeed, personal salvation and peace of mind are essential to faith. But peace and life as pursued in holistic theology—or, peace and life grounded upon the 한 (han) God—do not exclude, but rather include, the welfare and well-being of individuals. Furthermore, they lead us not only to inner peace of mind but also to peace and life in our relationships with God, with society, and with the entire cosmos. In other words, they encourage us to pursue the whole salvation. This is what we expect from life for the reign of God.

Chapter 8

A Pilgrim Seeking the Eternal Truth: The Life and Theology of Chungye Jong Sung Rhee

Do-Hoon Kim

In Commemoration of Chungye Jong Sung Rhee's Pilgrimage

Several years have passed since Chungye Jong Sung Rhee passed away. I recall the trajectory of his life and ask myself who he was, what he did, and what he would do if he had survived. While arranging his writings, pictures, and stories in a sequential manner, I could feel his enthusiasm, pain, struggle, love, and dream. His innocent smile at the big picture I look at now makes me miss him.

Chungye called himself "a pilgrim seeking the eternal truth." This description befits him well. I was once surprised to find among a pile of his works a passage that encapsulates his life. While I was pondering over it, it seemed that he was talking to me:

> Mr. Kim! (When I was his student, he called me Mr. Kim.)
> A pilgrim seeking the eternal truth ... The "truth" is ... And "seeking" means ... Do you understand what I mean by the "pilgrim"? ... ???????

> Even if the sky were a scroll of paper and the sea were ink, one could not write it all down ...

> While looking at heaven through a slender bamboo tube, do not say that you know heaven;

> While drilling a hole into the earth, do not say that you know the depth of the earth...[1]

> The entire world is encased in a grain of rice,
> The mountains and rivers are boiling in a small pot.[2]

No one would say that it is an easy task to describe a certain person's whole life. It is incomparably more difficult than editing a two-hour video down to three minutes by cutting and pasting.

When I examine the pieces of his long life and then paste to-

---

[1] From the writings of Zhuang Zhou.

[2] The clause that as a sojourner seeking the eternal truth Chungye Jong Sung Rhee made the guide for his own thinking.

gether some of them, I ask myself whether some of the missing pieces might not be among the more important ones, and whether I am not drawing a distorted picture. I did my best, but I feel something lacking.

Would he be angry with my poor writing? No, he would show me a big smile, just as he used to do.

I
Between Egyptian and Hebrew Culture: Chungye's Childhood and Exodus

On April 8, 1922 Chungye was born the second of two sons and four daughters of Kyu-Bong Rhee and Seong-Ryeon Kim at an annex of a Buddhist temple in Geosan, Mungyeong-gun, Gyeongbuk Province. Just before his birth his family moved from Binggye-dong, Chunsan-myeon, Uiseong-gun to Mungyeong, because his father needed to help his grandfather who was the head priest of the Buddhist temple, Geumryongsa. In the early morning of the day when Chungye was born, his grandfather gave him the name "종성 (鐘聲)" (Jong Sung, bell sound). By this name his grandfather wished that in the future he might become the bell sound that reverberates through all the rivers and mountains in Korea. Until he was three years old, he stayed in the Buddhist temple and grew up listening to the bell sound and Buddhist scripture reading in the temple. In 1924 his family returned to Binggye-dong, Chunsan-myeon, Uiseong-gun, which became his hometown. He learned handwriting and Chinese characters from his grandfather. In his youth his religious background was Buddhism and Confucianism. But might it be according to divine providence? A Christian church, Binggye Church, was established in his hometown, which was then filled with the spirit of Confucianism. On Sundays his older sister carried him on her back and went to the church. Since he was three years old he listened to hymns and sermons, which were gradually changing his destiny. In his youth he attended Sunday school and participated in Bible study. He listened to sermons, sang hymns, and actively participated in church-related activities, including the Christmas festival. At that time he had no idea where these activities might lead him, or how they might change his destiny. Later he confessed: "At Sunday school I could not understand what the pastor or assistant pastor preached. But the hymns that I sang together with the adults gradually settled down in my soul. When I was suckling at my mother's breast, the Buddhist scripture reading of temple priest had occupied my deepest soul. Now the lyric and melody of Christian hymns, little by little, took its place."[3] One may be reminded of Moses who learned Hebrew culture within Egyptian culture.

In 1929 Chungye entered Binggye Academy, an elementary school run by Binggye Church. In the school he encountered several good teachers, as people generally wish to have in their youth. From a young teacher named Mr. Kim he learned an important lesson:

---

[3] "Hymns That Accompanied My Faith Life," in *Chungye Jong Sung Rhee Jeojakjeonjip* 『춘계 이종성 저작 전집』 [Complete Works of Chungye Jong Sung Rhee, hereafter CW], vol. 38 (Seoul: Academia Christiana of Korea, 2001), 136-137.

"Never give up." Chungye states that this became the motto of his life. There was another teacher, Mr. L, from whom he learned the idea of motherland. In his later writings we detect how much he loved his motherland. Even when he was living in Japan, he never forgot that he belonged to Joseon. When the Korean War broke out, he was staying in Japan. At that time he expressed his concern about his motherland. This he was taught by Mr. L.

Chungye then moved from Binggye Academy to Chunsan Elementary School, where he completed fourth grade. In order to enter middle school, however, he had to complete fifth and sixth grade as well. But his family was too poor to support him. A policeman, named Jong-Sik Lee, who was well aware of the poor condition of Chungye's family, decided to support him so that he could attend Uiseong Elementary School. Chungye was a very good student in many respects—not only with regard to his studies but also with rhetoric, singing, and athletics. He graduated first on the list from Uiseong Elementary School. Then he applied for Daegu Education School, but his application was rejected because of the fact that his parents could not afford his tuition.

In despair Chunggye came back to his home and helped on his father's farm, but this could not satisfy him. He then contacted his sister in Japan and decided to continue to study in Japan. However, it was not easy to obtain a visa. He applied three times, but each time in vain. His applications were rejected, owing to the groundless interference of the police. There was nothing that he could do but be frustrated. So he left home without the permission of his parents and departed for Seoul. He hoped to find work and succeeded, but it did

not last and he returned to Daegu once again. Some time later he decided to venture something else: traveling from Pusan to Japan in a
ferryboat with a forged visa. At last he succeeded in reaching Japan
with his forged visa. That was on July 15, 1938.

II
Entering the Unknown Territory:
Beginning of Study in Japan

Without any awareness of what would happen to him or who
and what was awaiting him, Chungye arrived in an unknown terri-
tory, Kyoto, Japan. He lived in his older sister's house in Kyoto and
entered the evening school of the famous IpMyunggwan (立命館)
Middle School as a freshman. At one time he was arrested because his
secret passage was discovered. After protesting for five hours he was
released. After that incident he was able to continue his studies. Japan
was like the Canaanite land for him. In the wilderness of Japan he
was tired and worn out. In the daytime he worked in a secondhand
store, and in the evening he went to school. To add to his troubles,
Japanese people despised and humiliated Koreans. He could hardly
bear the ostracism by Japanese students.

In 1940 Chungye decided to move to Tokyo, for in Kyoto the
business of his brother-in-law did not go well, and the discrimination
against Koreans was too extreme. So he left Kyoto. As an emergency
measure he found a job in a small paper-box manufacturing company.

At that time attending school was inconceivable for him. But in the company he could not find hope, so he quit one year later and moved to another company. He could not abandon his studies. For the next two years he collected some money. Bringing it to Reverend Yeong-Chul Park, who was running a dormitory called "Sungdeokryo," he asked him for help. With the help of Reverend Park he was able to take evening classes at Seongrip Commercial School (成立商業學校) as a senior student. From then on he needed to earn money to pay his school expenses. To do this he delivered milk and worked in a steel workshop. He thought that he had passed through the Red Sea, but a tough wilderness was awaiting him.

In March 1945 Chungye graduated from Seongrip Commercial School. Then he applied for the department of literature in Waseda University. However, his application was not accepted because he came from Joseon. At first he wished to major in politics in order to contribute to the Korean independence movement, but he found it impossible from the beginning. So he changed his mind to delve into the nature of human life through literature. Indeed, his writings reveal the depth of his thoughts. He thought over humanity deeply. With his experience of war he began to reflect on human nature and misery. Even after the war, whenever he encountered death, he asked himself about the meaning of human life. To quote his own words, human life is sometimes like "an elastic cord easily cut off by a knife," sometimes like "an insect put to death under the rolling wheels of a wagon," sometimes like "a flying fish which jumps out of an infinite sea, flies temporarily in the air, and then returns to the sea again," or "an animal which comes from an unknown world, appears temporarily in the temporal line called history, and then returns to the unknown world."[4] All things considered, it does not sound strange that Chungye wished to find an answer to the question of human life in literature. In addition, he enjoyed literature. His journals written in 1950 show how well versed he was in literature. He read extensively the literature of England, Russia, Japan, and China. At one time when he was deeply impressed by Eo-Dang Im's writings, he wished to write novels, and indeed, drafted a novel entitled "Another Pastor," which deals with conflict in faith.[5]

However, he had to abandon studying literature. For he failed to receive the recommendation letter from the Scholarship Committee for the Joseon People, which was required for a Korean to enter a university in Japan. Koreans were forced to study one of the natural sciences, rather than literature or philosophy, so that they might make contributions to the war. Hence, Chungye decided to major in engineering and entered Cheongsan Academy, a Christian school focusing on industrial education. His specific major was aviation. He wanted to become a pilot who would destroy the Japanese Palace. At that time Koreans lived a miserable life while suffering from discrimination. It is quite understandable that in this context Chungye had such a radical thought.

---

[4] "Humanity is Humanity," in *CW*, vol. 38, 306.

[5] During the first two years in middle school in Japan Chungye read the complete works of world literature. And in the fourth and fifth grades he read Rousseau's *The Social Contract*, Smith's *The Wealth of Nations*, Pascal's *Pensees*, Darwin's *The Origin of Species*, and Kant's *Critique of Pure Reason*. Even after he entered theological school, he enjoyed reading books.

III

Confessing God in the Wilderness: Baptism from the Bell Sound of a Buddhist Temple to the Bell Sound of a Christian Church

As I mentioned earlier, when Chungye was born he was destined to become the bell sound of a Buddhist temple. He was born in a Buddhist temple, and his name, "Jong Sung," means "bell sound"—namely, the bell sound of a Buddhist temple that reverberates through all the rivers and mountains in Korea. Whether the paradox of destiny or the destiny of paradox, however, he grew up listening to the bell sound of Binggye Church. The sound wave that resounded through the ice valley ("Binggye") penetrated his heart little by little. After his move to Japan, however, the bell sound of the church did not remain within his heart. In Japan he attended Sungdeok Church. He was baptized in December 1944 by Rev. Chonjeonsarang (村田四郎), who was the president of Japan Theological Seminary. "My faith sprouted and grew while I was listening to the bell sound of Binggye Church in 1922. And it was confirmed twenty years later when I was baptized by a Japanese pastor."[6]

I would like to mention a few more memories of Chungye's concerning the bell sound. The first one is when he was serving Hagwan Church as a minister. I quote his own words:

---

[6] Quoted from Jong Sung Rhee's *Memoirs*.

There was a bell in the church garden. The Japanese government took away every bell from the region's Buddhist temples and other buildings in order to make cannon balls out of them. But the war ceased abruptly, and some of the bells were left in warehouses. One of the church elders brought one of them to the church in order to use it as a church bell. I proposed that the congregation build a bell-house so that we might ring the bell every Sunday. But when we hung the bell in the bellhouse, we found that it was broken. I wished I might get some benefits from the bell sound, for this is the meaning of my name. I was very disappointed. To make things worse, people from Cho-chongnyon, the pro-Pyongyang federation of Korean residents in Japan, laughed at us. They said, "Heaven, heaven? No, hell, hell!" The congregation members who heard of this mockery proposed to buy a good bell so that it may cry out "Heaven, heaven!" The church bought a good one in Daepan and proclaimed "Heaven, heaven" to all people in that region every Sunday.[7]

The bell sound, as Chungye's name implies, had a great significance on his life. The bell was not simply an object of his memory but a metaphor for his life. In his subconscious it guided his life, even without his awareness. It may be compared to God's burning bush that led Moses to Israel. Like the burning bush, the bell sound burnt

---

[7] Quoted from Jong Sung Rhee's *Memoirs*.

up in a flame within his heart in every painful moment. This is his confession:

> I realized that the mystery of human existence, the world of values, the problems that even our best efforts cannot solve, beauty, emotion, conscience, eternity, and the like are inexhaustible by human reason. Wandering among these unsolvable problems, I was led by resurging doubts to an irrevocable predicament. At that time I heard a calm bell sound resounding from a distance, as well as Jesus saying, "Come to me, all you who are weary and burdened, and I will give you rest." I felt as if the incalculable power of Jesus' saying were bringing me close to him. I could not help but succumb to and obey it. Thus, I became a Christian.[8]

The bell sound he had heard in his youth resounded again a long time later when he felt lonely with the recognition of the transience of life. After he spent many years in a foreign country he climbed again the hill in his hometown, and there he found nothing. His sisters, old friends, and the old tree upon which a swing had been hung were no longer there. Loneliness came to him. He realized once again that life is transient. With a gloomy mind and a heavy step he came down the hill and thought:

---

[8] "Why Am I a Christian?," in *CW*, vol. 38, 181.

Is it not because of the transience of human life that people are seeking something immutable? This is why so many saints and wise persons lived as pilgrims seeking something eternal, while turning their eyes away from the transient life. As a pilgrim like them I should steadily walk along the same way! Yes, I would like to walk along this way unto my death. When my mind was full of these ideas, I heard a bell sound informing of the Wednesday worship service.[9]

IV
On a Pilgrimage to the Eternal Truth:[10]
Beginning to Study Theology

1. Suffering: Flames of Fire within a Bush that Does Not Burn Up

Chungye's life in Japan was not an easygoing one. He had to endure discrimination. He also had so much difficulty in finding a job that he had to stop studying. As time passed, he began to hate the Japanese people and lost hope. The Greater East Asia War was increasingly violent, and numerous people died. He realized the meaninglessness of human life. As is always the case with people in extreme situations, he made himself isolated from others and immersed in

---

9 "Tano Festival," in *CW*, vol. 38, 418.
10 "My Theology Has Formed in This Way," in *CW*, vol. 38, 80.

tragic films, carrying deep despair like a weight on his back. When disappointment and anxiety drove him even to think of taking his own life, the hymns and biblical passages he sang and memorized in his youth began to move in his mind. He walked to the church, which he had not attended for a short period. The church provided him with great comfort, joy, and the will to live.

Does God call God's people through their suffering? On the evening of March 9, 1945, B29 bombers from the United States bombed Tokyo and reduced one-third of the city to ashes. The next afternoon Chungye summoned the courage to visit the bombed area. Houses were broken into pieces. Heaps of half-burnt corpse were found here and there. Some people were digging up the heaps in order to find the dead body of their relative. One hour later he was coming back home with his mind full of thoughts. The street car was passing by a stone dealer's shop. Through the car window he saw stone statues in the image of human beings. With the shock of witnessing death still fresh in his mind, the statues looked to him like the corpses he had seen just an hour before. It was not easy to overcome the shock. He asked himself again and again about human nature, the purpose of human life, and the difference between human beings and stone statues. He became skeptical about his current major. "What am I studying now? Am I not learning a skill that helps kill human beings? Is this the right way? Is there not a better way?" He immersed himself in a deeper thought.

In May of the same year he experienced another calling from God. Once hearing a fighter plane flying loudly, Chungye and people in the same dormitory (Sungdeokryo) went out to watch the plane.

Right at that time he heard a large object falling abruptly from the air. When he regained consciousness, he found a broken piece of a cannon ball at his feet. He picked it up and spent quite a long time pondering it. "Why did this piece not strike me? If I had been standing a few steps ahead, then I would have died. I had no idea of it in advance. Then, why did it miss me? Is it then not me, but someone else who determines my life and death?" Many thoughts, questions, and ideas ran through his mind.

From then on he could not concentrate on his studies in the industrial school. His mind began to be possessed by the biblical passages and the lyrics of hymns that he learned and memorized in his youth. Also, he was reminded of his sister who went to church even under severe persecution. He was obsessed by the idea that he should walk in a different way. At that time Yeong-Hui Lee, who was working as a minister in Sungdeok Church after graduating from the department of theology in Cheongsan Academy, gave him advice: "Study that which can save human beings." A ray of light illuminated his perplexed mind, which was at a crossroads. Rev. Lee's valuable advice changed Chungye's destiny. At last, in May 1945 he quit Cheongsan Academy and began to study theology, which he regarded as a science that saves humanity, in Tokyo Theological Seminary (Japan Christian Theology School).

2. Learning from Calvin and Barth: Basic Theological Training in Tokyo Theological Seminary

Chungye's education in Tokyo Theological Seminary consisted

of preparatory and regular courses. The former were courses for basic theological training, and the latter were course for advanced theological study. In seminary Chungye was frequently exposed to German theology. Of many theological disciplines he was particularly attracted to systematic theology. The seminary had many excellent professors in this area. From them he learned the Reformation theology of Martin Luther and John Calvin, liberal theology from Schleiermacher to Harnack, and the neo-orthodox theology of Barth, Brunner, and Niebuhr. The overall atmosphere of the seminary was critical of liberal theology, while favorably disposed toward neo-orthodox theology. In this context Chungye read and was affected by Barth's writings. According to his own statement, he thought highly of Barth "for restoring the idea of the transcendent and absolute God which had long been suppressed by the liberal idea of the immanent God, understanding the Bible as the Word of the living God, emphasizing preaching as the Word of God, and advocating a Christocentric trinitarian theology."[11] At that time, Kozoh Kitamori was a professor in Tokyo Theological Seminary. He was famous for his idea of "the theology of the pain of God." But Chungye did not place high value on his theology. According to his judgment, the theology of the pain of God beautifies the Japanese people by taking only their own pain into theological consideration, while overlooking the pain of neighboring nations suffering from the Japanese imperialism.

While studying theology Chungye came into contact with existentialism, particularly through Dostoevsky and Kierkegaard. He in-

---

[11] "My Theology Has Formed in This Way," 83-84.

dulged in their writings. In the works of Dostoevsky he could read the joys and sorrows of the Korean people living in Japan. Also, he was deeply impressed by the thoughts of Kierkegaard. Probably his own suffering and painful search for God in Japan overlapped with the language of Kierkegaard. He once said, "By a paradoxical leap the soul in loneliness, anxiety, and despair ascends to the world of faith and experiences salvation. I found that this process resembles the journey of my soul."[12]

At the end of his five-year-long theological study Chungye had to write a thesis for graduation. The most important thing was to decide the topic of the thesis. For two reasons he decided to study Calvin's understanding of justification and sanctification. First, in his view, "Calvin's theology is most biblical, evangelical, and academic, and pietistic." Second, "he thought that in order to work in a Korea dominated by the Presbyterian Church, he had better study Calvin's theology."[13] With completion of the graduation thesis he finished the first step of his theological training in the wilderness.

Meanwhile, there are a few more things to be noted. Despite the difficult situation of his theological study Chungye planted three posts for evangelism in Yokohama, Gawasaki, and Denechofu. Every Sunday afternoon he opened Sunday school for poor Korean children. Also, Chungye's theological orientation that had formed in Tokyo Theological Seminary continued to affect his later theological judgments and activities. He was exposed to both liberal and neo-orthodox theology, but he preferred the latter. Moreover, he studied Calvin for

---

12 "My Theology Has Formed in This Way," 83.
13 "My Theology Has Formed in This Way," 84.

his graduation thesis, for which he read carefully Calvin's *Institutes of the Christian Religion* three times. Thanks to this study, when the Korean church was in conflict between conservative and new theology, he took the conservative side.

3. The First Field: Pastoral Ministry in Hagwan Church

In March 1951, the day after graduating from Tokyo Theological Seminary, Chungye moved to Hagwan (Simonoseki) for his first pastoral ministry. When he left Tokyo, where he had lived for 13 years, for a strange city, he felt many emotions, probably like Abram leaving Haran. Recalling his past, Chungye writes:

> I put into six boxes books and notebooks that I had bought for the past six years and made two bundles of coverlets and clothes. I brought them to Tokyo Station in order to send them to Hagwan. Since I was a third grader in the middle school until I studied in Tokyo Theological School, there had been many difficulties in my life. I also had many dreams. I suffered a lot. Sometimes I starved. I was once involved in a scuffle with a Japanese man. With the passion of youth I wished to build a magnificent house of life. Around the end of the war I happened to walk through a dark tunnel. I had almost died three times from bombing. For six years in theological school I mortified my youth and made every effort to follow only the footsteps of the Lord. I prayed and wept a lot. I was so immersed in study-

ing that I had never fallen in love. Lamentation and tears followed me because after Korean independence some of my compatriots lived a dissolute life and were arrested again. I was so shocked by the confrontation and conflict among a small number of pastors, ministers, and elders that I once thought of leaving the school. But I was convinced that I was called for them. So I endured all of them in theological school for six years. After completing all the requirements, I left for the place of my first appointment, Hagwan Church.

His ministry in Hagwan did not go well. It was filled with agony and hardship. On the first day he was involved in trouble. It was not simply a problem within the church. People from Chochongnyon, the pro-Pyongyang federation of Korean residents in Japan, interfered with him. Also, he was faced with his own problem. He found his preaching problematic. In his view, few people from the congregation were moved by his preaching. To make things even worse, he tried to think of his sermon topics one month after he had given the sermons, but nothing came to his mind. For the following one year he had difficulty preparing sermons. Then he realized that both theology and pastoral work should start from and be centered upon the Bible. On March 1, 1952, Chungye and his friend, Won-Chi Kim, were installed in Tokyo Church as pastors of the Presbyterian Church of Korea in Japan.

V

Continuing Pilgrimage to the Eternal Truth: First U.S. Visit

1. Learning American Conservative Orthodox Theology: Fuller Theological Seminary (1952.9.~1954.6)

When Chungye completed his pastoral work in Hagwan, he found himself standing at the crossroad of three different ways: staying in Japan as a pastor, returning to Korea to work for the Korean church, and departing for another theological journey. For over a year he thought over and prayed for this issue. After several times of hesitation he finally decided to walk along a new way—namely, studying in the United States. On August 17, 1952, he went on board a ship "Wilson," bound for the United States. His first destination was Fuller Theological Seminary. Originally he was supposed to study at Princeton Theological Seminary, but the pre-arranged scholarship from the Missionary Society of the Presbyterian Church in the United States was cancelled. Thus, he chose Fuller as his second best option.

In the first semester at Fuller Theological Seminary Chungye felt embarrassed by the theological atmosphere that was quite different than what he had experienced in Japan. But he had no other choice. He worked hard. He learned theologies of Alexander, Hodge, and Warfied, Baptist theology, millenarianism, fundamentalist Orthodox theology, strict biblicism, and parachurch movements. In short, what he learned was American fundamentalist and conservative theologies. They broadened Chungye's theological horizon and formed another pillar of his theological thought. Many years later his learning at Fuller helped him play the role of a guiding post amidst the theological chaos of the Korean church. To quote his own words,

> Due to my learning of conservative American Orthodoxy at Fuller Theological Seminary, I believe, I could find an opportunity to work in the Korean Presbyterian church as a theologian. At that time the Korean church was suffering from a great theological confusion regarding conservatism, Orthodoxy, Calvinism, and fundamentalism. Repeated divisions of the church produced many denominations. But what I had learned at Fuller helped me discern them.[14]

Though his study at Fuller broadened the horizon of his theological thinking and gave him a great help for his later activity in Korea, Chungye did not uncritically appropriate it. He pointed out several negative aspects of the theology that he learned at Fuller. First, the theology of Fuller Theological Seminary was a reproduction of American fundamentalism that had made negative impacts on American theology and the church in general. Second, its theological attitude was very legalistic and exclusive. Third, there was a conflict between professors who argued for the organic inspiration of the Bible and those who argued for the literal inspiration of the Bible. Fourth,

---

[14] "My Study Abroad (2)," in *CW*, vol. 38, 122.

it unconditionally objected to the theology of Barth and Brunner. Fifth, it justified its own divisive tendency in the name of the protection of the gospel.

2. Conception of Holistic Theology: Louisville Theological Seminary (1954~1955)

After finishing his study at Fuller Theological Seminary, Chungye moved to Louisville Theological Seminary in 1954. His final goal was Princeton Theological Seminary, but he decided to go through Louisville for several reasons. First, he wished to know the theology of the Southern Presbyterian Church before studying the theology of the Northern Presbyterian Church. At that time J. K. Foreman was a professor of systematic theology at Louisville Theological Seminary. As a son of the Korean Missionary Foreman, his theology represented the theology of the Southern Presbyterian Church. Second, he wished to learn more deeply about the theology of Calvin from Professor Rule, an expert in Calvin who came from the Presbyterian Church of Scotland. Third, he wished to experience the peaceful atmosphere of Louisville Theological Seminary. At that time American Protestantism was in a divisive conflict due to the emphasis on fundamentalism and evangelism. But Louisville Theological Seminary pursued an open conservative theology, and the president of the seminary was a leading figure in the movement of reunion between the Southern and Northern Presbyterian Church. In his view, his study at Louisville would help him contribute to the reunion of the Korean Presbyterian church and even of the entire Korean church.

In Japan Chungye studied primarily modern theology and Calvin's theology. In order to look over the whole Christian theology he needed to study medieval theology and the theology of St. Augustine. Thus, he decided to write his master's thesis on medieval scholasticism, while postponing study of Augustine's theology for his doctoral studies. After consulting with Professors Foreman and Rule, he decided to compare the doctrines of atonement in Anselm's and Abelard's theology. The title of his thesis was "When Divine Honor and Divine Love Meet." This study proved very helpful when he later wrote his Christology.

While studying at Louisville Theological Seminary Chungye accomplished three important achievements. First, he had the opportunity to compare the theologies of the Southern and Northern Presbyterian Church. Second, he studied medieval theology, especially the theology of St. Anselm. Third, holistic theology, as a unique theological method of his own, was conceived in his mind. He says, "while studying in this school, the idea of holistic theology that would characterize my own theology was first conceived. I was convinced that the redemptive work of God is not selective but totalistic. Thus, my thesis title was "When Divine Honor and Divine Love Meet." By this title I meant that the cross of Jesus is a holistic work of divine righteousness and love."[15] Although he spent a short time at Louisville, it was an important period for him because he conceived of holistic theology during the period.

---

15 "My Study Abroad (3)," 124.

3. Laying the Foundation for the Theology of the Presbyterian Church of Korea (PCK, Tonghap): Princeton Theological Seminary (1955~1956)

After completing the master's program at Louisville Theological Seminary, Chungye entered Princeton Theological Seminary where he had long been wishing to study. Since his goal was to receive a doctoral degree, he first enrolled as a graduate student in the preparatory course for the doctoral program. There he was exposed to diverse theologies. He concentrated on the lectures of Hendry, Kerr, and Hoffmann. He also attended some lectures in the area of biblical studies, as well as Lehmann's lecture on ethics. He learned to understand Barth's theology from a different perspective and recognized the weak points of John Gresham Machen's theology. However, professors of systematic theology at Princeton overall failed to satisfy Chungye, who already possessed considerable theological knowledge. But he did not abandon the goal of completing his doctoral program at Princeton. Thus he took the preparatory examination. Professor Homrighausen informed him that he passed the first examination. But his joy did not endure long. The news that his father was critically ill brought him back to Korea. The greatest benefit he earned at Princeton is that he recognized the problems of the theology of Machen through those professors at Princeton who engaged in face-to-face debate with Machen. This experience gave him some help when he later sided with the theological direction of the "Tonghap" side of the Korean Presbyterian Church (Presbyterian Church of Korea, PCK). He said, "When there was a theological debate with the 'Hapdong' side of the

Presbyterian Church [the General Assembly of Presbyterian Church in Korea, GAPCK], what I had learned at Princeton Theological Seminary helped me point out the problems of the theology of Machen and thus to establish the theology of the 'Tonghap' side."[16]

VI

From Theory to Life Situation (*Sitz im Leben*): Pastoral Ministry and Theological Education in Korea (1957~1966.2)

1. Life Situation of Pastoral Ministry: Youngnak Church (1957.3~1959.2)

When Chungye returned to Korea due to the news that his father was critically ill, the situation in Korea was different than what it was when he had left. His father had already passed away. The overall condition of the country after the Korean War was still horrible. People's lives looked shockingly miserable. "Everybody was worn out from war, poverty, chaotic social conditions, political struggle, injustice, and unrighteousness. Hope was invisible. It seemed that my hometown and my motherland had disappeared from the Earth."[17] To make things worse, he had difficulty finding a job. Nobody helped

---

16 "My Study Abroad (4)," 126.
17 "My Theology Has Formed in This Way," 95.

him. Also, he had no financial support. To quote his own words, "I decided to continue my studies in the United States and began to prepare for that. I felt disappointed by my personal circumstances: namely, cold treatment from my motherland and continuing pilgrimage toward the truth."[18]

One day in early February 1957 Chungye was asked by Rev. Kyung-Chik Han to preach at the Wednesday evening service of Youngnak Church. He prepared a sermon and went to the church. There were lots of people. Because he had never preached in front of such a great number of people, he was seized with fear—that is, "pulpit-phobia." When he came back home after preaching, many ideas came to him. The next day he was surprised when Rev. Han's called him, asking him to become an associate pastor at Youngnak Church. He was surprised because he thought that his preaching was not good.

In late February he was appointed as an associate pastor at Youngnak Church. He began a new phase of his pilgrimage in pastoral ministry. In this situation he focused on three points. First, he devoted himself to dogmatic and theological sermons, whereby he wished to supplement Rev. Han's evangelical and pastoral sermons. Second, he tried to intensify the education program in the Sunday school. He trained teachers with biblical and theological knowledge. Third, he made efforts to look after his parish members. At the same time he did not cease his theological work. He gave lectures in seminary, translated the Westminster Confession and Calvin's *Institutes of the Christian Religion*, and published his first article, "Siganihae" [Understanding

---

[18] "My Theology Has Formed in This Way," 95.

of Time].

For Chungye the pastoral ministry at Youngnak Church for the following two years was a special experience. He said, "I learned the reality of the Korean church. I learned pastoral skills. I learned church politics. I came to know many people. I came to know different local colors. I came to know the currents of the Korean church. At Youngnak Church I came to know the path I ought to walk in the future. There were three options: pastor, preacher, and theologian. While working at Youngnak Church for two years, I discovered that I was destined to walk along the way of a theologian."[19]

2. Life Situation of School: Yonsei University (1959.3~1966.2)

In March 1959 Chungye left Youngnak Church and became an assistant professor of systematic theology at Yonsei University. At that time Korean politics was in a state of confusion. As the chief of the office of student affairs he experienced students' demonstrations and political activities. At that time the Korean church was divided into two: the ecumenical side and the NAE (National Association of Evangelicals) side. Despite many misunderstandings he became a theological representative of the ecumenical movement. While teaching as a professor at Yonsei University he felt the need to obtain a doctoral degree. Therefore, he asked for a leave of absence for two years and returned to the United States. At last he earned his doctoral degree at

---

[19] "My Theology Has Formed in This Way," 97.

San Francisco Theological Seminary, where he studied Augustine. After completing the doctoral program he returned to Yonsei University as a professor and school chaplain. He also worked actively in school administration and in the ecumenical movement. As he confessed, the two practical fields of church and school helped him to move from theoretical discourse to real life situations (Sitz im Leben). From then on his theology became "faith confession arising out of life realities."[20]

3. Exploring Augustine's Doctrine of the Trinity: Second U.S. Visit (1961~1963.8)

As mentioned above, Chungye had to abruptly stop his studies at Princeton and return to Korea. While working in Korea he decided to complete his doctoral program in the United States. He had already studied medieval theology, Reformation theology, and modern theology. Therefore, he decided to study ancient theology and went to San Francisco Theological Seminary. After consulting with Martin A. Schmidt he decided to write his doctoral dissertation on Augustine's doctrine of the Trinity. Since at that time the United States had few resources regarding Augustine's theology, he visited Bonn University in Germany to collect resources. After returning to the United States, he was permitted by Professor Schmidt to write his dissertation on Plotinus' influence on Augustine's idea of the Trinity. Then he began "the life of a monk," which lasted for two years. During this period

---

[20] "My Theology Has Formed in This Way," 102.

he wrote his dissertation in his personal study. Finally, he passed the doctoral dissertation on August 18, 1963. In Korea he came back to his former position and continued his "pilgrimage to the eternal truth."

VII

Unfamiliar Pilgrimage along the Road of Gwangnaru: From Appointment to Retirement in Presbyterian University and Theological Seminary (PUTS, 1966~1987)

1. Appointment in PUTS, and His Dream

In 1966 Chungye confronted another turning point in his life. He had to decide whether he would continue to walk along the bumpy yet visible and familiar road with milestones, or pioneer a new road in the invisible forest of Acha Mountain with jagged stone edges and thorns. Several church leaders who worried about the theology of PUTS insisted that he should walk along the road of Gwangnaru. They were people whom he had respected for a long time. Among them were his mentor and teacher Rev. Kyung-Chik Han, Rev. Ho-Jun You, Rev. Sin-Myung Gang, Rev. Pil-Sun Jeon, and Rev. Gwang-Guk Ahn. But Chungye refused several times. In the eyes of the church leaders, however, there was no one better equipped than Chungye to overcome the crisis of PUTS and promote it to a higher rank. As many times as they repeated their request, Chungye's thoughts and prayers only deepened. The more time he spent praying, the more inclined his heart, in contrast with his reason, was toward PUTS. Rev. Gwang-Guk Anh, who continued to ask for Chungye's help, was already preparing for Chungye's position and related legislations at the school. At last, Chungye made up his mind to grant their request. On March 3, 1966 he was appointed as a professor and academic dean of PUTS.

It did not take a long time before as PUTS' academic dean Chungye discovered that the faculty was weak, the financial condition was poor, there was neither a professional administrative ability nor a blueprint for the future of the school but only factionalism and in-fighting. But he had already become a part of it. He had already entered into the thick forest with no road in it. He began to display his administrative ability in a decisive manner. In Chungye's judgment, it was most important for the school community to share the same vision. At the end of the year he announced his dream for PUTS. He described the future of the school as follows: first, a flower garden of the gospel of Christ, or a beautiful garden of the gospel where Christ's flowers blossom; second, a supply base for the proclamation of the gospel, or a supply center that trains all the workers the church needs and sends them to the front of the gospel; third, a sanctuary of theological studies, or a center of contemporary theology; fourth, finally but not the least, a mission center of Asia, or a center of missionary movement that may contribute to the church movement not only in Asia but also globally.[21] These goals could not be accomplished within a brief period of time but needed sufficient time and sufficient financial investment. When he was inaugurated as PUTS' tenth dean, he reminded the community members of his vision that he had kept in mind since he was first appointed at the school.

2. For the Development of PUTS

First of all, Chungye made efforts to expand financial resources and improve the faculty in both quantity and quality. When he was first appointed, there were few professors who had doctoral degree. He offered the existing professors the opportunity to continue to study. Also, he picked up new talented persons, helped them to study in many different countries, and hired them as professors when they came back after completing their studies. In this way he planned the faculty to teach a broad spectrum of Christian theology. In the past they taught only American theology. Chungye wished to teach a globally approved and most Orthodox theology.

Furthermore, Chungye created the department of church music and made an agreement with San Francisco Theological Seminary to newly establish the Doctor of Ministry program for continuing education of pastors who had graduated from PUTS. Also, he strengthened cooperation with other institutions. With the aid of the Theological Education Fund (TEF, an affiliated organization of the WCC), he played the leading role in organizing the Korea Association of Accredited Theological Schools (KAATS) and was appointed its first director. Through this organization he supported foreign schol-

[21] "My Theology Has Formed in This Way," 103.

arship and contributed to the improvement of relationships among accredited theological schools in Korea, including PUTS. Also, he created the North East Asia Association of Theological Schools (NEAATS) in order to encourage fellowship and solidarity between theological schools in Korea, China, and Japan, and published *The Journal of Theology*. Since then he served as a staff of East Asian Christian Conference (EACC, currently Council of Churches in Asia [CCA]), the chairperson of the board of trustees of the Korea Institute of Theological Education, the chairperson of the board of trustees of Jeongsin Academy, and a member of the advisory committee of the Ministry of Education. Through all these activities Chungye contributed to PUTS' rising status.

In Chungye's plan there was not only PUTS but also the Presbyterian Church of Korea (PCK) as a whole. Thus, he encouraged leaders of the denomination to have interest in global church organizations. He was interested primarily in the World Council of Churches (WCC) and secondarily in the World Alliance of Reformed Churches (WARC). For he believed that "through close relationship with these institutions the PCK may outgrow the past fantasy of Orthodoxy and become a church in the world addressing and serving the world."[22] In short, Chungye's influence was not confined only to PUTS but reached the entire denomination.

---

[22] "Theologian Who Has a Dream," in *CW*, vol. 37, 26-28.

3. Departing from the Road of Gwangnaru: Retirement (1987)

In 1987, twenty two years after his first appointment at PUTS, Chungye retired. He was a visionary. He was enthusiastic about and faithful to his mission. He devoted himself to "raising ministers equipped with both piety and scholarship, developing biblical and evangelical theology, and teaching theology that serves the church."[23] How much of his first dream had been accomplished? In a speech that he gave when he left the school Chungye stated that he had kept about 70 percent of his promises. Even after retirement he was always happy to see PUTS rapidly growing. It is no exaggeration to say that in the 21st century PUTS and the PCK keep developing on the basis of his love, sacrifice, devotion, and efforts.

VIII
Chungye's Other Activities on the Way of Pilgrimage

In addition to theological writings, Chungye was very active in many other areas. First, he organized the Korea Association of Accredited Theological Schools (KAATS) and the North East Asia Association of Theological Schools (NEAATS), and he played an

---

[23] "The Final Speech as the Dean of PUTS," in *CW*, vol. 37, 47.

important role in both institutions. Also, he served on staff of the East Asian Christian Conference (EACC), as the chairperson of the board of trustees of the Korea Institute of Theological Education, as the chairperson of the board of trustees of Jeongsin Academy, and as a member of the advisory committee of the Ministry of Education. In addition, he established United Graduate School of Theology within Yonsei University. Yonsei College of Theology, Presbyterian University and Theological Seminary (PUTS), Methodist Theological Seminary, and Korea Theological University (currently, Hansin University) agreed to participate in the united school, and Van Hierob, the dean of Yonsei College of Theology, was appointed its first director. The United Graduate School of Theology was the first cross-denominational education project in the Korean church, which made a significant contribution to the development of the Korean ecumenical movement. In 1984, moreover, he served the Korean church as the 70th president of the Presbyterian Church of Korea (PCK).

Another project Chungye focused on was to establish the Academia Christiana of Korea (ACK). At that time many church leaders agreed upon the need for a Christian academic institution committed to promoting Christian culture in Korea. But they were hesitating to embark on the project because they were well aware that it would require considerable financial support, strong leadership, and many committed persons. Chungye believed that he was asked by the Korean church to establish such an academic institution. In 1988, at last, he ventured on the project. It was not an arbitrary decision. He was encouraged by James McCord, the director of the Center for Theological Inquiry (CTI) at Princeton Theological Seminary. In 1990 he organized a special committee for the project. The committee discussed how to activate the project. To be specific, "it decided to focus on discerning not only theological issues but general issues in which Christianity may contribute to global history and culture, exploring how to address and solve the problems in them, and proposing theological and evangelical solutions that may prevent global history and culture from falling into an anti-theistic and destructive way."[24] Also, the Academia Christiana of Korea newly established the Award for Outstanding Scholars and held academic symposia on many different topics.

Furthermore, Chungye participated as a speaker in many international conferences. He was the main speaker in the Asia-South Pacific Congress on Evangelism in 1968, supervised by Rev. Billy Graham. This motivated the foundation of the Asia United Theological University. He also participated in the World Conference of Reformed Christians (1975, South Africa), the World Conference of Reformed Theologians (1966), the World Alliance of Reformed Churches (1975, St. Andrews), and the World Conference of Reformed Theologians (1974, Lausanne, Switzerland). Through all these meetings he enjoyed fellowship with many scholars from all round the world. These international conferences helped him to broaden his theological horizon and later develop his holistic theology. Finally, he never ceased teaching and preaching until the last moment of his life.

---

[24] Jong Sung Rhee's *Memoirs*.

IX

Theologia Viatorum Seeking the Eternal Truth

1. Theologians Who Taught the Way of Pilgrimage toward the Eternal Truth

Every theologian has his/her own teacher and prefers some theologians to others. Who influenced Chungye's theology? Whom did he think of as his companion on the pilgrimage toward the eternal truth? Chungye mentions three theologians who made him a theologian. They are Augustine, Calvin, and Barth. Of course, there are also many others who have affected his theological pilgrimage. Nonetheless, Chungye was most decisively influenced by these three theologians. According to him, they are the three most important figures in the history of theology, since they brought about a shift in theological paradigms in their own time. Thus, he liked them and spent much time and energy studying them. He said, "Today's biblical, evangelical, grace-centered Christian theology has resulted from the revolutionary theological movements of these three figures. This is the reason why I like these three theologians and read their works more often than other theologians. My bookshelves are full of their books."[25]

To be specific, Chungye liked Augustine's experience of conversion and his theology of grace. And he liked Calvin for the following reasons: Calvin had unyielding conviction and thrust; he was a re-

---

[25] "Theologians Who Made Me a Theologian," in *CW*, vol. 38, 40-41.

former who did not negotiate with unrighteousness; he was a biblicist ahead of his time; he had a holistic vision of education—namely, piety and science (*pietas et scientia*); and he had such a humble mind as to reject an inscription on his gravestone. Chungye was proud of Calvin's life and theology.[26] The third figure that Chungye liked next to Augustine and Calvin was Barth. He spoke highly of Barth's view of the Bible, doctrine of the threefold Word of God, emphasis on the absoluteness of God, his draft of the Barmen Declaration, and his masterpiece, *Church Dogmatics*. Chungye described these three theologians' influence upon his theology with the following words: "I learned the example of life from Augustine, the direction and goal of life from Calvin, and the nature, method, and technique of theology from Barth. I find myself very fortunate to know these great forerunners."[27]

2. Fruits of Ceaseless Pursuit of the Eternal Truth: *Outline of Systematic Theology*

1) Intention: In Order to Explain the Mystery of God

Chungye Jong Sung Rhee was a prolific writer. The twelve volumes of his *Outline of Systematic Theology* [*Jojiksinhakdaegye* 『조직신학대계』] were a collection of his technical theological writings. In addition to them he wrote a great number of articles, essays, sermons, and columns addressing various contexts of Korea and the global world. He wrote all of them while acting as a theologian, educator,

---

[26] "Theologians Who Made Me a Theologian," 44.
[27] "Theologians Who Made Me a Theologian," 46.

and partner in many theological education centers, as president of a denomination, as a participant in debates over many issues, as an administrator of theological education centers, as a preacher, and as a theological explorer. In his writings he integrated all that he learned: for instance, German theology, Japanese theology, American fundamentalist theology, Orthodox theology, ecumenical theology, and neo-Orthodox theology. These writings were also fruits of his efforts to reflect upon the past and envision the future of the Korean church. But he became such a prolific writer primarily because he wished to explain the mystery of God that surprised and astonished him. This was the rationale for his life and the way in which he responded to God's calling. He said:

> The task of a theologian is to explain the mysterious and holy God who transcends human knowledge and human reason, with the help of the Bible and the Holy Spirit and by means of the language and logic that are intelligible to humans. ... It seems that I wrote too much. One of my American friends, who was told that I completed twelve volumes of *Outline of Systematic Theology*, said for a joke that the second Barth came from Korea. But with the twelve volumes I could not exhaust God's mysterious essence, providence, and works. Thus, I cannot stop theological writing. For I was called to do the work. This is my mission as an author of theology. Even if I were to write until the moment of death, I would not be able to describe even one millionth, or one billionth of divine mystery. I

just do my best with the help of the Holy Spirit.[28]

2) Principle of System

When studying at Cambridge in 1975 Chungye first conceived the idea of writing *Outline of Christian Theology*. Debating with professors at Cambridge he began to develop his own theological system. He elaborated his authentic theological method by challenging Barth's theological method, which had thus far influenced him to a considerable extent. He completed his book on theological anthropology in 1979 according to his theological method. At last he completed the twelve volumes of *Outline of Systematic Theology* in 1993. What interests us is that in Chungye's theological system the prolegomena is followed by anthropology. This makes his theological system unique and distinct from the standard system of Western theology. Why did he plan in that sequence? To quote his own words:

> When treating Christian theology as a whole Western theologians in general begin with the doctrine of God and conclude with eschatology. I was trained in that tradition. But I always felt difficulty with such a sequence. I was intrigued by the question: "Who is the person that has interest in God, asks questions about God, discusses God?" So, I decided to depart from the Western tradition and tried my own way of doing theology. That is, I decided to discuss anthropology prior to the doctrine of God. And in-

---

[28] "The Mission of Author," in *CW*, vol. 37, 332.

stead of concluding with eschatology I put eschatology at the entrance of holistic theology. According to this fundamental principle I wrote *Outline of Systematic Theology*.[29]

By "the entrance of holistic theology" he implied that he would complete his theological system by writing *Holistic Theology* for the rest of his life. But we now have only an outline of his *Holistic Theology*, whose full picture has not yet come to the world. In this sense his outline of systematic theology may be called "an incomplete completion."

3. For the Establishment of the Theology of PUTS and the PCK

1) Biblical Evangelicalism

In 1971 Chungye was inaugurated as the tenth dean of PUTS. In his inaugural speech he announced that his first task as a dean would be to make the Assembly of the PCK accept sound ecumenical conservative theology.[30] He saw debates over theological issues dividing the Korean church, debates in which he himself was personally involved.

From the time he began to work in Korea, Chungye was often accused of following Barthian theology rather than evangelical or Or-

---

[29] Jong Sung Rhee's *Memoirs*.

[30] Cf. Yoon-Bae Choi's excellent introduction to the theology of Chungye Jong Sung Rhee's theology: Yoon-Bae Choi, "Daehanyeosugyojangrohoechonghoe 100nyeon: jojiksinhagui eojewa oneulgwa naeil" [The One Hundred Years of the Presbyterian Church of Korea: Yesterday, Today, and Tomorrow of Systematic Theology], *The Korea Presbyterian Journal of Theology* 44/2 (2012), 53-55.

thodox theology. Again, he was accused of trying to make PUTS follow the neo-orthodox theological tradition. This became a controversial issue even in the Assembly. With this regard he had to respond to questions of the Assembly. In fact, it is not right to define his theology as neo-orthodox. As mentioned above, his theology has three pillars— Augustine, Calvin, and Barth—and Barth is only part of his entire theological system. At that time Chungye described his own theology as "biblical evangelicalism," "open conservatism," and "biblical, evangelical, ecumenism-oriented theology." He believed that the theology of both PUTS and the PCK should pursue this direction. In response to the questions of the Assembly he claimed that there is no problem in his theology:

> Neo-orthodoxy, following the ideas of the Reformers, tries to defend the traditional doctrines of Christianity while giving heed to the contemporary atmosphere. Therefore, I stated that among the three positions mentioned above [conservatism, neo-orthodoxy, liberalism] neo-orthodox theology seems to be the best at responding to the challenge of modern ideas. I am convinced that there is nothing wrong with this statement in light of biblical teaching, theological thoughts of the Reformers, or the traditional theology of the Presbyterian Church.[31]

It is certain that Chungye favored neo-orthodoxy, but he never

---

31 *Daehanyeosugyojangrohoe 64hoe chonghoerok* [Proceedings of the 64th Assembly of the Presbyterian Church of Korea], 103.

defined his theology as neo-orthodox.

The next day after he sent his response to the Assembly (1979. 4.9) Chungye reviewed "the theology of pilgrimage (*theologia viatorum*)" and asserted that one should not blindly follow any theological system or school.[32] In the same year (1979.9.10.) the Assembly asked him, "Does it mean that you would like to make neo-orthodoxy the theological direction of PUTS?" Chungye answered this question by saying "PUTS' theological direction is the biblical, evangelical theology based on the Westminster Confession affirmed by the PCK and the ecumenical movement."[33] His appeal to the biblical, evangelical, and ecumenical theology was not a temporary expedient. From the beginning he had this idea. He came to this conviction during his theological education. Four years before he was questioned by the Assembly he made clear this point:[34]

> Our school (PUTS) does not teach the so-called Orthodox theology that is narrow, exclusive, blind, self-righteous, high-browed, and with no window toward the world. Rather, we teach the most evangelical, biblical, and living theology: namely, one that inherits the biblical and evangelical theology of the great Reformer John Calvin and the father of the evangelical theology St. Augustine, one that keeps step with the theology of the World Reformed

---

[32] "Theologica Viatorum," in *CWs*, vol. 22, 168.

[33] *Proceedings of the 64ᵗʰ Assembly of the Presbyterian Church of Korea*, 108.

[34] "New Workers for the New Era," in *CW*, vo. 37, 85. In his earlier essay written on July 18, 1972 he already said that "the theology of mission this school pursues should be thoroughly evangelical and biblical." See "Theological Education in the 21ˢᵗ Century," in *CW*, vol. 37, 158.

Church, which has made significant contributions to the development of global theology and played the leading role in the ecumenical movement, and one that provides today's Koreans with motivations for life, guidelines for truth and salvation, and grounds of hope.

On March 29, 1968, when Chungye was dean of PUTS, the board of trustees unanimously declared that PUTS' vision of education is "conservative faith based upon ecumenical spirit." Conservative faith and ecumenical spirit are in fact compatible with biblical evangelicalism. Chungye did not abandon conservatism or ecumenicalism. He did not need to. He was regretful about the division of the Korean Presbyterian Church in 1959. Whatever the reason for the division, the division demanded that the PCK (Presbyterian Church of Korea, Tonhap) establish her own theological identity. After the division of the Korean Presbyterian Church "the GAPCK (General Assembly of Presbyterian Church in Korea, Hapdong) took conservative Orthodox theology, and the PROK (Presbyterian Church in the Republic of Korea) took neo-orthodox theology (at that time new or progressive theological method was called neo-orthodoxy). Then what does the PCK (Tonghap) have? People criticize that the PCK has nothing and is still wavering between the two." Chungye was well aware of this criticism. But he resolutely affirmed that the PCK's theological position has always been clear and distinct. According to him, the PCK's theology "seeks to work in cooperation with other denominations while retaining the characteristics of the Presbyterian tradition. It is the matrix and driving force of the ecumenical spirit in Korea."[35] In

1960 the PCK decided to withdraw from the WCC, which was confirmed again in the 1962 Assembly. Even after that, Chungye rightly argued that the PCK Assembly had never abandoned the ecumenical spirit.[36] In the 1962 Assembly the PCK confirmed its withdrawal from the WCC and then declared the principle of unification. "We reject the stubborn attitude of self-righteous and narrow faith; instead, we seek a way of unification with separate brothers in accordance with our purpose to remain in solidarity with the World Reformed churches that accept the Apostle's Creed and the Westminster Confession, to have fellowship with other Christians who believe in the triune God, and to accomplish in cooperation with them our common mission in today's world."[37] By appealing to this principle Chungye argued that the PCK had never abandoned the ecumenical spirit. In short, Chungye's early theological work focused on "contributing directly or indirectly to the orientation of the PCK's theological position toward the biblical evangelicalism based upon the Bible, Augustine, Calvin, and Barth."[38] In my view, Chungye's efforts did not prove fruitless. For today's PUTS and PCK stand in the same theological position that he developed.

2) Korean Theology

Amidst the above-mentioned theological controversy Chungye published "The Theology that We Pursue." The point of this article

---

[35] "The School's Reaffirmed Vision of Education," in *CW*, vol. 37, 22.

[36] "The School's Reaffirmed Vision of Education," 22.

[37] "The School's Reaffirmed Vision of Education," 21.

[38] "My Theology Has Formed in This Way," 112.

was biblical evangelicalism. He defined biblical evangelicalism as follows: "While taking into full account different theologies that past theologians developed, we make efforts to develop a theology that is appropriate to our context today and at the same time is universal in nature. This I call biblical and evangelical theology."[39] To summarize, biblical evangelicalism seeks to develop a theology that not only takes seriously the past tradition but also is appropriate to the current Korean situation without losing its universal nature.

Noteworthy is the contextual nature of biblical evangelicalism. Chungye referred to "our context" as one of several concerns of biblical evangelicalism. By this phrase he hinted at the possible development of his own theology into a Korean theology. He thought of the establishment of a Korean theology as one of his theological tasks. To our surprise, his writings show his enthusiasm for the establishment of a Korean theology and his affirmative attitude toward indigenized theologies. Later when he spoke of the PCK's theological principle and identity, he added "Korean" to the three existing principles of "biblical," "evangelical," and "ecumenical."[40] In other words, Chungye believed that the PCK's theology should be a Korean theology. According to him, theology should not simply cling to and reiterate the past tradition. God wills to give the truth of the immutable Word of God every time anew to specific time, space, and people. Thus, theology attempts to make the truth present according to the divine will.[41]

Chungye, therefore, described biblical evangelicalism as one type

---

[39] "The Theology That We Pursue," in *CW*, vol. 22, 179.

[40] "The Korean Presbyterian Church and Theology," in *CW*, vol., 22, 158-159.

[41] "To Become the Window of Asian Theology," in *CW*, vol, 37, 44.

of Korean theology. According to his analysis, there are three types of Korean theology: theology of "seong" (誠, sincerity), minjung theology, and biblical evangelicalism.[42] Then, what is the task of biblical evangelicalism as a Korean theology? Chungye answers this question as follows: (1) The Korean church should pursue biblical and evangelical theology; (2) a Korean understanding of the Bible should be established, i.e., the biblical message within the Korean context should be explored; (3) the contact point between the gospel and the mind of the Korean people should be investigated. For the gospel is not given to abstract humanity but to a concrete and existential human being; (4) a deeper understanding of the Holy Spirit needed; (5) we should establish our theological identity and compare it with that of Western theology.[43] According to Chungye's judgment, Korean theology had thus far been deformed. He meant not only so-called Orthodox theology, which had repeated divisions within itself, but also one-sided minjung theology, which too narrowly understood the essence of the gospel.[44] In this vein Chungye advised as follows: "Do not follow certain Korean mystics who fall into shamanism; do not follow certain indigenous theologians who fall into syncretism; do not follow certain conservative theologians who just memorize foreign theology; do not follow certain authoritarians who have fundamentalist mentality; instead, we should seek to indigenize the eternal truth of the gospel on the soil of the Korean people so that all Koreans may find a new way of life in the gospel."[45]

---

[42] "The Korean Church Seen From Within," in *CW*, vol. 21, 242-245.

[43] "The Task of Korean Theology," in *CW*, vol. 22, 206-209.

[44] "The Theology of the Korean Church in her Second Century," in *CW*, vol.22, 226.

4. At the End of the Pilgrimage toward the Eternal Truth: Toward the Holistic Theology

In his later years he planned to develop a holistic theology that would complete his *Outline of Systematic Theology*.[46] I quote his own words:

> As my lifelong task I am currently planning to further develop holistic theology. Holistic theology has the following foci. First, it does not regard each theological discipline as isolated from others, but seeks to find what is common in all theological disciplines. Second, all the disciplines of theology are penetrated by the doctrine of the Trinity. Third, the universe does not refer to the solar system alone, but includes nebulae. It assumes that life may exist in nebulae, too. Fourth, it regards all the other religions and sciences as preparation for the gospel (*preparatio evangelica*). Hence, it acknowledges all religions, if with Jesus Christ at the center.[47]

This is what he wrote at the end of his memoirs. To our regret, he could not have his wish. He handed down the unfinished task to

---

45 "The Theological Task of Korean Church," in *CW*, vol.22, 143.

46 Regarding the holistic nature of Chungye's theology, see the other chapters of this book—especially, Myung Yong Kim's contributions.

47 Jong Sung Rhee's *Memoirs*.

his successors. In fact, Chungye had hardly used the phrase "holistic theology" in his writings of the early and middle phase.

X
Completing the Pilgrimage:
His Last Dream Left to Us (2011.10.2.)

Chungye summarized his own life as follows:

In July 1963 I came back to Korea after completing the doctoral program. Since then and until recently I have done my best as a theologian, theological educator, administrator of theological education, partner in many international theological institutions, president of a denomination (PCK), dean of a seminary (PUTS), champion in theological debates within the denomination, speaker in many national and international conferences, organizer and director of the theological education center, pioneer of many important theological ideas, preacher in numerous churches, and writer who published over thirty books. I sacrificed my personal life and family for the Korean Presbyterian Church and the churches in Korea and abroad.[48]

---

[48] *CW*, 6.

Indeed, Chungye accomplished many things and left behind a rich theological legacy, while keeping his dream in his heart until the last moment of his life.

On the hill at the back of my hometown there was an old pine tree. It was about 150 years old. The pine tree, slanted 60 degrees, was very good for children to climb and play. Every year at the Tano festival women of the village hung a swing on the tree and got on the swing all day long. In my youth I often sat down beneath the tree and dreamed of my future. I decided to live as energetically as the pine tree. 'Just like a pine needle, which never frowns even in the face of storms, heavy rain, cold winter, and the freezing north wind, I would never retreat or fall.' That old pine tree was the best friend of old people who took a nap under its shadow. Its branches blocked the sun's rays to make a cool shadow, and sometimes made a shelter from an abrupt shower. With the dark cloud gone and the sun appearing again, the pine needles full of drops of water shone like precious stones. Keeping time with the cool wind they played a natural music. This pine tree was my friend when I grew up cherishing my dream. But now I find myself running toward the end of my life just like the old pine tree. However, just as even in its old years the pine tree remained spirited and dignified in front of miscellaneous small trees, I will do my best to do the same.[49]

As a poet Chungye left a poem containing his last dream.

Where Can I Go?

Jong Sung Rhee (2006.12)

Every night / without notice / without reason / a calm voice
calls upon my name, saying / it's time to leave

Tonight as usual the voice / calls upon my name, saying
"since the destination is remote, / it is better to leave early.
After laying down the heavy burden, / come quickly."

No, I can't leave / for there's something to be done.
The old man living in front of my house
and the old woman at the back of my house
call me / and say "Let's go anywhere."

When I woke up in the morning / and looked around,
Here is garbage, / there is waste, / in many layers.
How can I leave them behind?

No I can't. / I would not leave.
If I depart from this land / where can I go?
Instead, I would make this place / heaven.

---

49 "Yearning of an Old Pine Tree," in *CW*, vol. 37, 347-8.

He left us with the task (or dream) of clearing the waste. After having invited us to the pilgrimage to the eternal truth, he passed away—peacefully, with smile in his mouth. But his bell sound never disappeared but continues to resound. He is still alive and resounding in our heart. With his sound in our heart, we hope to live as faithful servants of the Lord.

I secretly hid
the yearning of the autumn under fallen leaves,
but by all means
it pushed out to become dew.